The Uncanny Gaze

D1488636

. . . .

Women and Film History International

Series Editors
Kay Armatage, Jane M. Gaines, and Christine Gledhill

A new generation of motion picture historians is
rediscovering the vital and diverse contributions of
women to world film history whether as producers,
actors or spectators. Taking advantage of new print
material and moving picture archival discoveries as well
as the benefits of digital access and storage, this series
investigates the significance of gender in the cinema.

*A list of books in the series appears
at the end of this book.*

The Uncanny Gaze

The Drama of Early German Cinema

Heide Schlüpmann

Translated by Inga Pollmann

Foreword by Miriam Hansen

University of Illinois Press
Urbana and Chicago

The publication of this book was made possible,
in part, by a translation subsidy from the
Society of Cinema and Media Studies.

Library of Congress Cataloging-in-Publication Data
Schlüpmann, Heide.
[Unheimlichkeit des Blicks. English]
The uncanny gaze : the drama of early German cinema / Heide Schlüpmann ;
translated by Inga Pollmann ; foreword by Miriam Hansen.
p.   c. — (Women and film history international)
Includes filmography.
Includes bibliographical references and index.
ISBN 978-0-252-03283-7 (cloth : alk. paper)
ISBN 978-0-252-07671-8 (pbk. : alk. paper)
1. Motion pictures—Germany—History. I. Title.
PN1993.5.G3S3513   2009
792.0943'09041—dc22   2009024499

Contents

Translator's Acknowledgments

This translation would not have been possible without the engagement and persistence of a number of people who have shared the belief that Heide Schlüpmann's book will provide Anglo-American film scholarship with crucial theoretical and historical material concerning not only early German cinema but film theory and history more generally. Jane Gaines got the ball rolling and brought me into the project. The Society for Cinema and Media Studies supported the translation financially, and Natasa Durovicova went way beyond her role as treasurer and spent many hours revising drafts. I want to thank Miriam Hansen for always being willing and able to help with translation questions or to facilitate communication between the various parties involved. Heide Schlüpmann likewise helped clarify the text whenever that was necessary. Joan Catapano from the University of Illinois Press saw the project through to the end, and I want to thank the two anonymous readers of the translation for their thorough comments. Most of my thanks, however, go to Rob Mitchell, the native speaker at my side who spent countless summer days in Berlin and then some, correcting Germanicisms and discussing Critical Theory.

Foreword

Miriam Hansen

Heide Schlüpmann's book *The Uncanny Gaze: The Drama of Early German Cinema* was originally published in German in 1990. After almost two decades it is worth reminding the reader of what was then an eye-opening discovery for both film scholars and festival-goers—that German cinema had a significant history preceding the so-called Expressionist films of the 1920s as canonized by, respectively, Lotte Eisner in *The Haunted Screen* and Siegfried Kracauer in *From Caligari to Hitler;* that, rather than just a matter of individual precursors, this other German cinema had a shape of its own, with distinct stylistic and thematic preoccupations and particular configurations of genre, authorship, and film culture.

If this discovery is now commonplace, and if films of that period have become more accessible and more of them have been recovered from nitrate decay, it is partly thanks to Schlüpmann's work. In 1990 the Pordenone festival of silent film, in collaboration with Schlüpmann, presented the retrospective Prima di Caligari (Before Caligari), which revealed a hitherto unknown chapter in German film history (in keeping with the previous year's groundbreaking presentation of prerevolutionary Russian film). Since then, restoration projects at the Netherlands Film Museum and other archives have yielded additional treasures, and a selection of early German films was circulated in the United States by the Goethe Institute. The latest fruit of Schlüpmann's work has been the marvelous retrospective of Asta Nielsen films, beginning with screenings and an international conference in Frankfurt am Main, which has since traveled to Bologna, Berlin, and Vienna.

The Uncanny Gaze maps a central and hotly contested terrain of German cinema preceding World War I, the *Kinodrama* (narrative fiction film). On the basis of close to a hundred films listed in the filmography, ranging from 1908 to 1914, as well as detailed analysis of about forty, Schlüpmann structures her account according to genre formations such as comedy, melodrama, "social drama," crime films, and "sensational drama." The book's subtitle, *The Drama of Early German Cinema*, refers as well to her own historiographic—descriptive, critical, and theorizing—narrative. This drama deals with the articulation and acknowledgment of female subjectivity and its simultaneous containment and suppression. It proceeds from the *Veröffentlichung* (rendering public) of women's *Schaulust* (pleasure in looking)—its becoming *unheimlich* (uncanny, un-home-ly) in both a psychosexual and a literal sense—with the emergence of cinema as a technologically based form of modern mass culture whose market substantially depended on the female consumer. Schlüpmann traces the fate of female scopic and epistemephilic pleasure at multiple levels: in the films' narrational perspective and stories, which revolve around everyday experience, intimacy, and gender inequality, and in their harking back to an earlier "cinema of attractions"; in conditions of production that favored a complicity between culturally marginal, bohemian male directors (such as Joseph Delmont, Charles Decroix, Harry Piel, Franz Hofer, Urban Gad) and female performers and the interests of women in the audience; and in the systematic containment of the female gaze, along with the tradition of showmanship and display on which it thrived, on the part of bourgeois *Kinoreform* (cinema reform).

In the confluence of these factors, early German cinema began to constitute an alternative, specifically modern public sphere—alternative to that of bourgeois culture but also distinct from the partial publics of the traditional labor movement and culture of associations. Schlüpmann delineates the contours of this alternative public by situating cinema in the sociopolitical and cultural force field of Wilhelminian society. This force field is significantly marked by the relative weakness of the German bourgeoisie (compared to its French and English counterparts) vis-à-vis a bureaucratized monarchy, its insistence on distinction vis-à-vis a new bourgeoisie of industrial power and the compensatory inward turn to individual culture and education—*Bildung*. The fixation on a concept of culture that excludes technology and economy, Schlüpmann argues, made cinema reform in Germany more vehemently and influentially hostile than anywhere else in the West. It also prevented the bourgeois women's movement from engaging with the cinema and, conversely, muted the political concern with sexual and gender relations on the part of the few women who did write on cinema, notably, sociologist Emilie Altenloh and reformer Malwine Rennert.[1]

The Uncanny Gaze was written at a time when the paradigm of psychoanalytic-semiotic film theory was on the wane; when, nonetheless, feminist film theorists sought to import some of its insights into what became known as the new film history, inspired by the study of early cinema. Central to psychoanalytic-semiotic film theory had been the category of the gaze, in particular, its function in the constitution of the subject. The critique of classical Hollywood cinema had as its object the dominance of the male gaze and the ways in which its organization in relation to the spectator reproduced social hierarchies of gender. Schlüpmann, similar to other feminist film scholars of her generation (among others, Gertrud Koch, Laura Mulvey, Mary Ann Doane, myself), shifted the focus of concern to the problematic of the female gaze. This shift entailed both a historicization of the category of the gaze—for instance, by taking into account the empirical predominance of women in cinema audiences through the end of the 1920s—and, in Schlüpmann's case, a philosophical reflection on "women's love of cinema" in the context of an aesthetic theory of cinema.[2] It also entailed turning the conception of cinema as an "apparatus" into a more complex understanding of cinema as public sphere, lived social space, and locus of aesthetic experience. Consequently, in Schlüpmann's subsequent work on "cinema theory" the category of the gaze is replaced with a wider understanding of aesthetics as theory of sense perception that includes affect, intimate sensations, memories, and fantasies.[3]

Even in the earlier book, though, Schlüpmann assumes a wider concept of the female gaze than psychoanalytical, apparatus-based feminist film theory. She loosens the concept from its a priori narcissistic and masochistic inscription and seeks to evoke a more nuanced range in the modalities of the female gaze and its interplay between film, performer, and spectator. Proceeding from beautifully written ekphrastic accounts of the films, she sketches out an iridescent multiplicity of looking relations: the desiring and the commanding gaze; the gaze productive of visual attractions (as in *The Fan Painter* [*Die Fächermalerin*]); the curious, exploring, reflective, and exposing gaze (as in the crime films and female detective serials such as *Miss Nobody*); or the erotically perverse, terrifying, uncanny gaze (as in the Ellen Gray detective film *The Wanted Poster* [*Der Steckbrief*] or the sensational drama *The Black Viper* [*Die schwarze Natter*]). In Asta Nielsen's self-staging defiant and violent act at the end of *The Sins of the Fathers* [*Die Sünden der Väter*], the female gaze is powerfully asserted in its absence against its systematic negation on the part of traditional art and the social organization of looking. As her life is once more destroyed by the young male painter (this time the model's increasingly happy expression undermines the naturalist-pessimistic conception of his painting), Nielsen ends up slashing the portrait of herself as Woman without Hope, whom she had to become for the sake of art and the artist's career.

If *The Uncanny Gaze* engages with debates in film theory and film history of the time it was written, it is also dated by the juncture of two other contexts that, at first glance, may appear unrelated if not incommensurate. The chronologically prior of the two is the context of Critical Theory (in American usage, the Frankfurt School), which in addition to the members of the Frankfurt Institute for Social Research included writers such as Georg Lukács, Ernst Bloch, Walter Benjamin, and Siegfried Kracauer. Unlike orthodox Marxist theory, Horkheimer and Adorno's *Dialectic of Enlightenment* (1947) had posed the question of sexual and gender relations as a central contradiction in its critique of bourgeois society. And their indictment of the culture industry, as Schlüpmann writes retrospectively in her most recent book, "opened up perspectives toward the break with male-dominated cinema and the emancipation of the female spectator as a corporeal, sensorial being."[4] Moreover, as the reader of *The Uncanny Gaze* will note, Schlüpmann's recourse to psychoanalytic categories is at least as refracted through the historical-philosophical lens of *Dialectic of Enlightenment* as it is indebted to Freud and his contemporaries.

It seems unlikely that the influence of Critical Theory would have contributed to the second context that informed *The Uncanny Gaze:* a women's cinema movement that began in the early 1970s and persists, in changed configurations, to this day—with women's film festivals, archival projects, fund-raising for new productions, and the journal *Frauen und Film*. Yet Critical Theory did provide an impulse not only in individual biographies like Schlüpmann's and Koch's but also through the mediation of a book that played a key role in the emergence of the women's and other alternative movements at the time: Oskar Negt and Alexander Kluge's *Öffentlichkeit und Erfahrung* (1972; *Public Sphere and Experience,* 1993). Central in this regard were Negt and Kluge's theory of publicness based on the recognition and (self-)organization of experience on the part of all constituents, their critique of the bourgeois public sphere and idea of a proletarian public sphere, as well as related analyses of counter, alternative, and partial publics. Moreover, unlike their Frankfurt

School mentors and contemporaries, in particular, Jürgen Habermas, the authors did not exclude technologically mediated and market-based formations from qualifying as public—the very public sphere in which Kluge's practice as a filmmaker (and, subsequently, videomaker for commercial TV) sought to intervene. Negt and Kluge's methodological premise that even if no positive traces of a counterpublic were to exist they could still be inferred by the force of their negation seems to resonate in Schlüpmann's book, in particular, her reading of the cinema reform movement—and efforts to culturally legitimize cinema through recourse to theater, literary authorship, and science—as antagonistically indicative of another repressed cinema, one in which women were productive as performers, writers, and spectators.

The most important precursor whom Schlüpmann revises and develops for her own purposes is Siegfried Kracauer, with his *Theory of Film* (1960) and writings of the 1920s probably more than the *Caligari* book. Like Kracauer, she emphasizes film's aesthetic affinity with material life and contingency— with the ephemeral world of things, the anarchic traffic between animate and inanimate, and incidental configurations that elude symbolic meaning and intention. Similarly, she valorizes the documentary, kinesthetic quality of scenes that display locations of everyday modernity such as urban streets, squares, cafés, means of transportation, and industrial structures but also the "moving stillness" of nature scenes and landscapes that evoke the sublime. Like Kracauer, she allocates particular significance to room for improvisation, in her case with a view to the performance and self-staging of the actress. Finally, harking back to Nietzsche, she conceives of the spectator as a corporeal being—the human being "with skin and hair," as Kracauer put it—whom the cinema enables to experience the subject's bond with and contingency upon/ within the material world.

However, Schlüpmann significantly transforms Kracauer's materialist aesthetics of film and spectatorship. In her account the experiencing subject, like the depicted world, is not just one of "skin and hair" but one of sexuality and gender. And she may be indebted to Kracauer's discovery of the cinema as an alternative public sphere defined less by class than by an emerging mass culture of (largely female) consumption and a mass subjectivity thriving on decentered perception and fantasy. But her analysis of the growing ambivalence of female subjectification in the course of the cinema's institutional consolidation clearly differs from his condescending, self-disavowing gendering of that public in the notorious essay "The Little Shopgirls Go to the Movies" (1927).

Perhaps Kracauer's strongest legacy in Schlüpmann's book is the critical stance on narrative and a preference for the undercurrent that Tom Gunning has termed the "cinema of attractions." Already in Kracauer's reviews of the 1920s there is a preference for genres with roots in popular entertainment forms, physical arts, and the culture of display in the context of which films were initially shown and produced—genres such as the circus film, sensational drama, the crime film, any film that features camera tricks and other visual attractions; Schlüpmann expands this preference to include female performers in strong if marginal roles as artistes. The critical attitude toward narrative is not against narrative per se—women's stories must be told, attractions can only survive in what Gunning calls a cinema of "narrative integration"—but against closed narratives based on bourgeois drama with its ideologies of fate and individual interiority and, in Schlüpmann's case, against a naturalization of narrative perspective as male. In both Kracauer's and Schlüpmann's retrospective assessments the narrational and film-aesthetic principles developed on that basis were too much part of the arsenal of bourgeois cinema reform and gentrification to pass for politically neutral. Instead, both endorse forms of narrative that are porous enough to admit moments of display, improvisation, incidental details, and indeterminacy—fissures that allow the viewer a similar degree of autonomy (of affect, memory, imagination) in his or her response.

When Schlüpmann, like Kracauer, insists on the tension between narrative and its other (material qualities that elude thorough motivation and closure), she obviously goes beyond the model of an allegedly objective, disinterested historiography to develop something like a normative aesthetics of cinema. Her account of the drama of early German cinema is nonetheless not a narrative of decline, not least because of her concomitant commitment to discover, rescue, and reactualize these films' appeal through projects of restoration and live-music performance, as in retrospectives of Germaine Dulac and Asta Nielsen that she cocurated.[5] Judging from the success of these projects with younger generations, they in turn are productive in inspiring new modes and styles of film practice.

There is another reason why a non-narrative-centered aesthetics of film is not merely a matter of the cinema's past but also a question of its future. Video and digital technologies have not only put into question both photographically based film and the institution of cinema—a challenge that Schlüpmann takes up in her subsequent work.[6] They have also loosened the classical dominance of narrative vis-à-vis the elements of cinematic discourse, setting free intensities of composition, movement, editing, and sound-image relations. Watching a film on video or DVD, we are no longer subject to the compulsive temporality of classical narrative or, at a more fundamental level, that of projection—the creation of the illusion of movement in the *défilement* of a strip of individually still, discrete, and differential frames at a certain speed. The non- to antinarrative impulses of 1920s writers on film (e.g., Jean Epstein, Germaine Dulac, Louis Aragon, Béla Balázs, Kracauer), like the avant-gardist *dérive*, or "cinema hopping," of the Surrealists, have to some extent been normalized by the vernacular practices of contemporary film consumption and modes of film practice catering to them. Whether or not it is useful to speak of a new "cinema of attractions" emerging from the hybridization of film with digital visual media, including videogames, remains to be seen.

This development has also changed our access to film history. As Laura Mulvey writes, "If watching films digitally has contributed to a sense of narrative disintegration, digital editing systems have enabled film to be quoted and referred to with unprecedented ease."[7] What is lost here is a good part of the cinema illusion as well as the cultural configuration of cinema as a public sphere and site of aesthetic experience. At the same time, as Jean-Luc Godard has powerfully demonstrated with his *Histoire(s) du cinéma* (1998), we may gain new approaches to film history, including different insights into the relationship between film and history.

What are the implications of these shifts for the historical mapping of early German cinema? With Schlüpmann's book the drama of the uncanny female gaze, the at once aesthetic and political stakes of these beautiful, poignant, and surprisingly modern films, can no longer be ignored, let alone erased. The book makes a compelling case for restoration projects that seek to retrieve more of those films—and more films by women directors and performers as well as early cinema in general. What emerges in hindsight is the possibility that new historiographic and aesthetic practices on the basis of Schlüpmann's work will develop different perspectives that have the power to change the outcome of the drama of German cinema in the present. To end with Kracauer: "Germs of new beginnings may develop within a thoroughly alienated environment."[8]

Author's Acknowledgments

I want to thank a number of people and institutions who assisted in the realization of this book.

This book has its foundation in the invaluable work of the film archives; without the concrete support that I received from their employees, my film analyses would not have been possible. Among these archives are the Bundesarchiv-Filmarchiv, Stiftung deutsche Kinemathek, Deutsches Institut für Filmkunde, Deutsches Filmmuseum, Staatliches Filmarchiv der DDR, and the Nederlands Filmmuseum. Friedrich P. Kahlenberg engaged the first draft with motivating and expert attention. This work received further critical reading and inspiration from Norbert Altenhofer, Annette Brauerhoch, Jutta Brückner, Ute Gerhard, Miriam Hansen, Claudia Honegger, Anton Kaes, Ulrich Keller, Renate Lippert, and Hartmut Winkler. The lavish images of the book were made possible by the Bundesarchiv, Stiftung deutsche Kinemathek, Deutsches Filmmuseum, Deutsches Institut für Filmkunde, and the Nederlands Filmmuseum. With respect to these, I especially want to thank Peter Bucher, Walter Seidler, Jürgen Berger, Eberhard Spieß, Erich de Kuyper, and also (and not least) the photographers, as well as Benno Witzenrath and Thomas Hübscher, who quite patiently helped me to select the images. Frank van der Maden made it possible for me to view a copy of *Padre,* which was at that time difficult to obtain. Finally, I want to emphasize that this publication would not have been possible in this form without a subsidy from the Deutsches Filmmuseum.

The Uncanny Gaze

Introduction

On the Secret Complicity between Cinematography and Women's Emancipation in Wilhelminian Society

> Only man, not woman, looks at himself.
> —Jean Paul

As in other countries, cinematography in Germany had its origins in show business as well as in technical-scientific innovation.[1] The cinematograph emerged from photography studios and optical workshops and was promoted for industrial and military uses before making its way to the public through variety theaters and fairs. The invention of the so-called tachyscope [*Schnell-seher*, literally, "fast-seer"] by Ottomar Anschütz, the son of a photography studio owner, was supported in 1896 by the Prussian ministries for culture and war, and the Siemens Company had already in 1892 begun to market it. The brothers Skladanowsky—who, as is widely known, organized the first film presentation of their own films in the Wintergarten in Berlin in 1895—were the sons of a showman and a projectionist of so-called dissolving views [*Nebel-bilder*]. Oskar Messter's father, Eduard Messter, in turn, owned a garage and a lens-grinding shop, where he produced medical instruments, electrical-medical gadgets and microscopes, as well as optical-mechanical devices for showmen. After Oskar Messter took over his father's business in 1892 he became primarily interested in cinematographic techniques and built his first film projector in 1896. At the same time he not only shot films but also brought them on the market along with his projectors.[2] Back then, the Skladanowskys and Messter were shooting typical vaudeville acts such as comical scenes, short trick films, street scenes, natural scenes, and actualities. The two producers were soon joined by other companies: these were in part German branches of foreign companies such as the Deutsche Bioskop (1897) and the Deutsche Mutoskop- und Biograph-Gesellschaft (1898) and in part actual start-up companies like the Duskes Company (1906), the Internationale Kinematographen GmbH (1903), and the Internationale Kinematographen- und Lichteffekt GmbH

(1905). The two latter companies are of interest retrospectively because of their sensationalist productions, for example, reenacted "real" events such as *The Murder at the Spandau Schiffahrtskanal* [*Der Raubmord vom Spandauer Schiffahrtskanal*].[3] As a whole, though, German film production during the first years remained relatively small, especially in comparison with countries like England, France, Italy, and the United States as well as Scandinavia.

Until World War I, cinema in Germany functioned, for the most part, as a marketplace for international film business.[4] In contrast to film production, though, the development of movie theaters kept up with that of other countries: from 1900 on traveling cinemas and vaudeville theaters were replaced as places of projection by stationary cinemas. By 1904 the nickelodeons [*Ladenkinos*] constituted serious competition for traveling cinemas. With the establishment of approximately forty-two new movie theaters, 1906 represents the first high-water mark of movie theater development, and by 1910, the era of high-investment, large movie theaters began so-called picture palaces [*Lichtspielpaläste*] that were located in city centers and bourgeois neighborhoods. This shift went hand in hand with a change in film production, which was now experiencing a decisive upswing.[5] Paul Davidson is representative of this period: in 1906 he founded the General Cinematographic Theater Company [Allgemeine kinematographische Theatergesellschaft] and built the first of his Union Theaters in 1909–10 in Berlin. On this basis he also built one of the most important prewar production companies in Germany, the Projektions AG Union [PAGU]; Asta Nielsen became their first star.[6]

Insofar as one can tell from the films that have been preserved, German film production developed a very specific profile between 1909 and 1914 by introducing short feature films. These differ from the famous German silent films of the 1920s in that they present a transition from the cinema of attractions—a cinema of vaudeville exhibition that played with new technological possibilities—to narrative film.[7] The particular aesthetics as well as the social significance of this cinema can be inferred today from two types of sources: on the one hand, from the films that have been preserved from this period and, on the other hand, from texts that document the battle against cinema, that is, the reform debates and the first outlines of a film aesthetic. These two types of "production," the economic-technological and the cultural-journalistic, remained separate for the most part. This is different from the United States, where a broad spectrum of reform movements was already decidedly engaged in film production around that time—an engagement that the liberal press supported as well.[8]

The feature film had its beginnings in Germany as the so-called film drama [*Kinodrama*]. While German film reflected the variety of cinema genres that were developing internationally around this time, it consisted primarily of social dramas, melodramas, detective films, and sensational films. In addition, there were comedies, which were, for the most part, distinguished from "film drama" in the language of the period. As far as we can tell from the preserved films, the staged action was set mainly in bourgeois and urban milieus; the life of workers as well as life in the countryside were neglected. On the one hand, through their mixture of documentary and staged fiction, these films captured public life: streets, city squares, cafés, places of entertainment, transportation devices, industrial sites—the face of a changing urban environment but also the contrasting serenity of landscapes. On the other hand, these films already thematized, on the way to narrative fiction, the nonpublic, especially the private and intimate realms of life. The stories presented the mostly "authentic" reality of the inside of a factory, a bank, or a manufacturing company or else they re-created in the film studio the rooms and apartments of the *Gründerzeit*—the salon, the terrace of a grand bourgeois villa, or a petit bourgeois kitchen and living space.[9] Sometimes the stories dealt with the financial worries of a single woman, sometimes with the problems of a bourgeois social climber, but on the whole they almost always dealt with the private life between marriage and prostitution. In addition to the private sphere, the other area hidden from public view with which the films were preoccupied was the world of crime and of outlaws, outsiders of the bourgeois society, circus performers, and the bohemian.

The writings of the reformers were concerned with the unnatural, uncultured, amoral, and un-German nature of cinema. They condemned the representation of sexuality and crime as well as the stimulation of the senses and the agitation of the "nerves"; they turned against the presence of women on the screen and naturally called for the protection of children. Their writings expressed fears of moral and social revolt and anarchy. While at times the reformers also conjured up the specter of a film production controlled by the Social Democrats, it was the destabilization of traditional cultural and moral values of which they were most afraid, since that ultimately threatened their own identity.

A closer look at these two aspects of Wilhelminian cinema (i.e., film production, on the one hand, and the reform movement, on the other) reveals that the debate revolved less around class oppositions than around contradictions within the bourgeoisie itself. As it underwent a transformation into a bourgeois institution, early German film production achieved its unique character by developing its own "bourgeois" form *against* the strong opposition of the cultural bourgeoisie [*Kulturbürgertum*], a cinematic form that finds a certain degree of support among members of the urban intelligentsia. Mainstream film criticism, in contrast, sought to draw the contours of a restorative, state-supportive, institutional cinema—an effort that indeed influenced film production by means of censorship but that could not otherwise find its footing. Only the foundation of the Universum Film AG "UFA" in 1917, initiated by the Supreme Army Command under General Ludendorff, created the economic and institutional conditions for a film production supportive of the state [*staatstragend*]. The National Socialists were later able to fall back on these structures as well.[10] It was Goebbels who realized the reformers' demand for an institutional as well as an aesthetic reorganization of cinema under the oversight of the state.

It was not just in Germany that cinema's transition to a bourgeois mass-cultural institution coincided with the working out of contradictions within the bourgeoisie. In similar fashion the American movie reform movement was not exclusively or primarily trying to protect a middle-class ideology and way of life against the new promiscuous pleasures of immigrant masses. Rather, the "progressives" tried to cope with a contradiction produced by capitalism, namely the erasure of class differences and the erosion of the bourgeois family that capitalism conjured up when it established cinema as a new economic branch—in short, a threat to the old-style democratic order with the male citizen in a dominant position.

> Not only did modern industrialism unleash conflict and exploitation, but the breakdown in class divisions within amusements and the great increase in consumption of goods and services that followed seemed to threaten the old democratic culture. In response, the progressives tried to unify all groups around vice and civic reform in order to restore the good family as the controlling force over society. More than searching for order, these people tried to re-create the sexual order of the past and make it relevant to the modern era.[11]

The restoration of Victorian values meant the restitution of the family as the disciplining factor for society as a whole: "rescuing the family" became film's central task.[12]

While "rescuing the family" can be said to be the motto of the German reform movement, it was not the slogan of prewar film production. The dichotomous situation between cinema and reformers mirrored the particular societal and political situation of the German bourgeoisie. The situation of the bourgeoisie was schizophrenic: an enormous economic upswing opposed political powerlessness, and bourgeois-industrial power opposed a feudal-agrarian government.[13] It was Bismarck who deprived the bourgeoisie of its political power, but the bourgeoisie itself accepted this disempowerment: the federal alliance with the nobility guaranteed security against the workers' movement. After the failure of the 1848 revolution, the bourgeois public had given up on its attempt to eliminate the contradiction between its economic power and its political powerlessness. Instead, the effort went toward covering up this contrast. The educated bourgeoisie, the so-called *Bildungsbürgertum,* which had once been the vanguard of bourgeois emancipation, took on the position of the state and identified itself with a culture that excluded economy and technology—and this at a time when the entire power of the bourgeoisie rested on industrialization.

Such exclusion of economy and technology from "culture," however, was not a product of the contemporary situation but rather a fairly traditional position. The German terminology of education [*Bildung*] and culture [*Kultur*] was developed in the eighteenth century in contrast to practical knowledge and civilization at a time when scholars within the emergent bourgeoisie played a key role in the "transformation of an essentially feudal state into a heavily bureaucratic monarchy."[14] Education was the citizens' means of gaining access to administrative positions formerly reserved for nobility. This social ascent was accompanied by political theories that formed around the terms *legality* and *legitimacy.* The doctrine of legality made the position of the "scholar" indispensable within the governmental system and, at the same time, strengthened the constitutional liberty of all citizens. The doctrine of legitimacy, in contrast, helped to commit the state to "culture." Consequently, this doctrine served to secure the position of a cultural elite, the "mandarins," who did not have to prove their "usefulness."[15] In the eighteenth century such cultural freedom still retained possibilities for political opposition. Over the course of the nineteenth century this was to change:

> The mandarins' ties to the rest of the middle class were loosened, and their obligation to the status quo increased. A moment arrived at which their leadership was threatened more from below than from above, and from that point on they gave an ever greater emphasis to the defensive and vaguely conservative side of their philosophy. By around 1890, at any rate, many German academics had come to assume the stance of Platonic philosopher-statesmen preparing to meet the onslaught of the mechanics.[16]

The unusually abrupt industrialization in Germany contributed to an intensification of the opposition between culture and civilization and as a consequence supported the closing off of the cultural realm from the "materialist" realm of economy and technology.

But even as culture cut itself off from the utilitarian sphere, it was simultaneously, and more or less covertly, made to function toward preserving the state. Culture thus underwent a transformation from a realm guaranteed by the state to a free social space [*Freiraum*] that could only survive if culture in turn guaranteed the existence of the feudal state against any opposition from the people.[17] This utilitarianism that stood behind the "bearers of culture" not only carried forth the mass education movement [*Volksbildungsbewegung*] in the second half of the nineteenth century but enabled as well an affiliation with cinema without challenging the traditional idea of culture. From the beginning the reformers could make good use of a technical medium as a means to educate the people and to "spread culture": after all, it supported their position. What they opposed, however, was cinema as an independent institution, as an autonomous culture based on technology, commerce, and "the people" and therefore outside of the control of the "educated."

Cinema erased the barriers between economy and technology, on the one hand, and culture, on the other hand. Over the course of its transition from a technical innovation—a mere medium for science and research—to a kind of entertainment, film slowly made its way into the bourgeois refuge of culture. Initially, the cinematograph remained within the confines of vaudeville and fairgrounds, that is, within the marginalized "low" culture (which was itself, at the same time, the subject of increasing control, as exemplified by the movement against "filth and trash" [*Schmutz und Schund*]). Radical irritation occurred only when sites were established for the sole purpose of projecting films and when film sought to grasp forms of the bourgeois art of acting. From 1907 on this irritation led to the formation of specific initiatives in the fight against cinema.

Given the economic importance of cinema, such a fight was doomed to fail from the start. Thus, during the prewar years the reformers' path led from a rejection of cinema to the first outlines of a film aesthetic that adapted film to bourgeois culture. Just before the war broke out it became clear that the same cinema that could undermine the position of the cultural bourgeoisie could also be used to restore it, if one knew how to make cinema help preserve the status quo. Judges were the first to proclaim openly such utilitarian thinking: for them, it was a matter of supporting a film economy that ultimately was also important for the state. The control of undesirable cultural side effects they left to teachers and scholars, who, for their part, concerned themselves with cinema's capacity to restore order in the face of a crisis of the bourgeois public sphere. This capacity consisted in translating the private forms of production that occur within the family into public forms of mass culture consumption, that is, in an ideological "rescue of the family" as a disciplinary instrument.

Bereft of his political public sphere, the Wilhelminian citizen as private man—and therefore businessman—was confined to the private sphere of the family as the only basis for a literary public sphere. The family itself was made to feel insecure not simply because of the political powerlessness of its head but also because of economic development, which increased employment for women. The crisis of the public sphere therefore went beyond parliamentary institutions to include all cultural realms. What became manifest in the crisis of culture, however, was not only political resignation but also—as the various women's movements pointed out at the time—that the bourgeois public sphere depended on restituting a feudal-patriarchal role for the citizen at home. There were, for example, attempts in the work of Georg Simmel to discuss anew the relationship between the sexes. These attempts, though, aimed at raising the familial order of the sexes to a form of generalized cultural division of labor rather than abandoning the feudal residue in the bourgeoisie.

Simmel's reflections can serve here as indices of the structural changes that occurred as modernity moved toward mass culture. Instead of developing a public sphere that would include women and the working masses, bourgeois culture "expanded"—this is the program of the mass education movement—so that the familial order was elevated to a public form of culture, which in turn submitted to the reigning power.[18] The attempt of cinema reformers to reestablish the model of the family against the background of a mass cultural public sphere therefore meant more than an ideological confirmation of a bourgeois way of life; it meant the subjugation of mass culture to the current power relations without the necessity for this power to make an appearance itself.

In the Germany of Wilhelm II, cinema and film production were nonetheless to a great extent able to develop independently from the cultural bourgeoisie. They relied on all those bourgeois powers that found themselves excluded from "culture": technology, business, the world of performers and showmen, and actors as forces of production. Similarly, the audience consisted of women of all backgrounds, "simple people," workers, and white-collar employees. Cinema stressed not only the formative element of culture in the "material" forces of economy and technology but also the "interest" inherent in aesthetic pleasure. In cinema both dime novel romanticism—a "cultural asset" fallen to the level of mass commodity—and the iconography of kitsch were exhibited for all rather than forbidden from above; in cinema the internationalism of modernity triumphed over the nationalism of the prevailing culture; physical performance, the art of the body, triumphed over sensitivity and inwardness. Finally, cinema accommodated women as social and cultural beings beyond their familial ties. In cinema they did not fulfill a "culture-reproducing" function, as Simmel would have wanted it; they were not nurses at the bedside of male culture but rather participants, beneficiaries of a new culture that was developing on the basis of technology. For this reason it was not only conservatives who met cinema with resistance and a lack of understanding.

Cinema gathered together bourgeois powers that had not yet come into their own over the course of the history of the bourgeois public sphere and gave them for the first time an entrepreneurial basis. Cinema was attacked insofar as it constituted competition for the theater, but its threat was more than economic.[19] It was a candidate for the inheritance of the bourgeois public sphere, a sphere that the bourgeois liberals had wanted to secure for theater:

> When the bourgeois citizen retreated from politics and/or was driven out of it, theater became "overbalanced" vis-à-vis other realms of life. This was true especially of the liberal bourgeoisie. . . . Its theater-mania and need for entertainment and for representation grew to the same extent that it lost possibilities for political representation. In traditional realms of the public sphere such as parliament, university, and the press the liberal bourgeoisie lost influence vis-à-vis the prevailing political and social conservatism. Theater became, as has been so frequently the case over the course of its history, albeit under different circumstances, the liberal bourgeoisie's refuge for self-representation and self-development. It emerged as the site of a functioning public sphere.[20]

Cinema thus called into question theater's claim to be "the site of a functioning public sphere." Cinema was able to accomplish this not just because it attracted the masses but also because it really was able to lay claim to theater's pretension to constitute an early form of political emancipation. Cinema tested the possibility of emancipating bourgeois culture from its immanent restoration of feudal-patriarchal structures.

Looking back at the history of cinema, its adoption of theatrical forms appears simply as an adaptation to bourgeois norms. Had this been perceived in this way from the outset, the reformers would not have turned so fiercely against "film drama." The phenomenon of "bourgeoisification," that is, of acquiring middle-class norms, is a contradiction in itself. Rather than establishing early cinema as a preliminary form of later cinema, recent scholarly work has discovered a paradigmatically different aesthetic of nonnarrative, nonvoyeuristic film, a "cinema of attractions."[21] At the same time, initial attempts at narrative fiction film within this kind of cinema attracted attention. In particular, the relationships between the beginnings of narrative cinema and changes in audience structures have been subjects of discussion.[22] The preserved films of early German cinema also indicate a transition from a "cinema of attractions" to narrative film. A few films that have been preserved from around 1909 were the first to tell little stories. These films reflect an ambivalent attitude toward the women in the audience. On the one hand, with respect to their content, these films deal with the reality and the real problems of women; on the other hand, the stories repress forms of exhibition whose appeal to the eye, to curiosity, is not appropriate for women.

As early as 1908 the professional magazine *Der Kinematograph* pointed toward shifts in what was understood to constitute the pornographic in cinema. The magazine ascribed these changes to the influence of the morality movement [*Sittlichkeitsbewegung*], which, as the writings of the reformers showed, did not oppose private "gentlemen's nights" [*Herrenabende*] even while opposing any public presentation that contained even the slightest hint of eroticism. In issue 87 (August 26, 1908) under the heading "Berlin Small Talk," one reads the following:

> In many movie theaters there used to be a "separate screening" at least once a week, though it was of course usually unable to make good on its promise. . . . At most, love played a harmless role in these separate pictures [*Separatbildern*]. Far less harmless pictures were shown every year—and last year too—in a cinematograph booth at a fair in a Berlin suburb. Over the summer, though, this movie theater had to make place for another one, which stays within the prescribed boundaries. Finally, then, the cinematograph in and around Berlin has become morally pure.

The "danger" posed by the cinematograph around this time was not just that female audiences would gain insight into the erotic pleasure of men but also that it enabled women's self-perception. The prejudice of a gender-specific self-reflexivity as formulated by Jean Paul—"only man, not woman, looks at himself"—was shaken.[23]

The development of film into feature film did not proceed along the lines of a continuous adaptation to bourgeois norms. Rather, prompted by the introduction of stories from a female world, an engagement with masculine norms, with female reality, and with sexual difference developed independently in the cinema. As a consequence of this confrontation film drama developed an aesthetic of its own. We need to rid ourselves of the prejudice that makes film drama only an early, incomplete version of later feature film and acknowledge film drama's singularity and difference. Film drama was not developed "from above" but is rather a consequence of film production resisting its exclusion from culture. By producing "dramatic" films, film producers forced their way into the bourgeois world, shocking its representatives.

This shock was not just a result of the transgressive act of basing "the art of drama" on a medium defined by technical reproduction and associated with showmen. Above all, the still-unfulfilled claim inherent in the concept of a bourgeois public sphere, including the role this sphere assigned to women, made itself felt in this transgression. Many aspects of the reform debates were reminiscent of the debates about the role of theater in the eighteenth century. When in the eighteenth century theater came into being as the first bourgeois public sphere that competed with the representative public sphere of the nobility, it was not unequivocally supported by citizens. At a minimum, the precarious social standing of the actor and especially the actress in bourgeois society expressed this ambivalence:

> The fact that it became possible in Germany in the eighteenth century to present women *and* men in person, in the way women *and* men really behaved, broke the mold of what had been self-evident until then. It is precisely for this reason that [such presentations] were able to help citizens to understand themselves as human beings. Yet the unrestricted representation of sexual differences—and the possibility of putting it all onstage—already seemed in itself scandalous to bourgeois citizens. The degree of unrestricted and liberal representation (or representative liberation!) that citizens gained through actors made them sufficiently uneasy that they were not able to give up their ambivalence toward actors—an ambivalence that was especially obvious in the citizens' attitude toward actresses.[24]

On the one hand, since Rousseau the attitude toward actresses has been connected to the definition of woman as "true nature" [*wahre Natur*] and domestic being. As someone who is preoccupied with beautiful illusions and who appears in public, the actress fundamentally contradicts this concept. On the other hand, the attitude toward actresses was also determined by contradictions arising between bourgeois society and theater. If the bourgeois self was to be addressed, sexual differences and questions relating to the private sphere had to be addressed as well; these issues, however, should not be handed over without restrictions to the cultural public, especially not if the latter included women. Consequently, their discussion was handed over to the private discourse of scholars and scientists.[25]

The public sphere of the theater had the potential to call into question the separation between public sphere and domestic intimacy and privacy, a separation that was cementing the power relations between the sexes. The domestication of this potential was initiated around the actress as a person as well as a figure onstage, that is, with the role of women in drama. By the end of the nineteenth century, as a result of economic transformations, a cultural revision of the separation of public sphere and family had become due, yet at the same time this was rejected. These economic transformations, however, became manifest in the cinema: cinema realized the unused potential of the theater as a chance for its own cultural education of the public—the potential for a self-address that did not come to a halt at the boundaries of the private sphere, the difference between the sexes, or the role of women. The film drama concerns itself with a topic that the *Gründerzeit* theater—as a "bulwark against bad reality"—long believed itself to have mastered: the past.[26]

Before the emergence of the film drama, several tendencies in early cinema are discernible that participate in the formation of film drama: documentation of public events; male self-representation in the medium of technical reproduction; film as mirror; and, in the case of film actresses, a confrontation with a femininity that does not fit into the familial order. While technicians and showmen created public excitement with their films, they did not yet reach a broader cultural public. This step was only taken as actors and actresses entered the film business. Even though they always remained close socially to show business, film actors and actresses nevertheless introduced a different cultural self-understanding and most of all the ability to represent culturally those who—like technicians and showmen—had been excluded from culture. Film, however, forced actors and actresses to accomplish such representation through the means of those excluded from culture rather than by means of the familiar art of acting. Beyond requiring simply an adjustment, this also set free possibilities that the theater had not been able to offer. These possibilities that the theater had denied were different for actresses than for actors. The film actor, for his part, found himself reduced to exhibition, to his body, but therein lay a chance to address the problems that the body poses, to present physical appearance itself as a role, and to play out the difference between the sexes. This is what happened in early comedies. The equality in exhibiting the body in front of the camera is likewise the actress's basis for emancipation, albeit in a different way. On the theater stage her social role always had to be coordinated with a semblance of "nature" [*Schein von Natur*]. The reproductive power of the medium of film freed her from this pressure because now it produced this appearance itself. The film actress was able to focus her abilities on the representation of social conditions, especially since working with film challenged her, in terms of both imagination and performance skills, to satisfy the needs of an audience on which the film industry could count: women.[27]

While the bourgeois theater visitor rejected the cinema, his wife was already spending her spare time there.[28] Generally, cinema constituted the only pleasure women could enjoy on their own, away from home. At the same time, it meant more than mere entertainment; women brought to the cinema a demand that had remained unanswered in theater, namely, to "see themselves": their desires and possibilities but also their everyday experience, their milieu. This was something a director could stage and produce and a cameraman film. But if cinema wanted to come up with something new and contemporary, something different from what theater offered, it needed the actress, who expressed a woman's look at the world, her hopes and battles.

The reformers spoke of "film drama" as soon as distinct acting entered the film screen. Initially, however, this term simply represented an accusation leveled against the film form, which itself reflected cinema's adoption of theater as a form of public sphere. Economic interests played a role in this takeover as well. From 1911 to 1914 "drama" became the most frequently used term with which the film trade advertised movies.[29] With the production of these dramas an alternative cultural public sphere developed that responded to the interests of technicians, showmen, actors and actresses, and, most decisively, the female audience. And while genres like the detective film [*Kriminalfilm*] were ruled by the pleasure taken in documentary outdoor shots and technical innovations, films made expressly for women placed dramatic performance at the center.

Cinema's pursuit of drama, however, developed along two paths, paralleling the conflicting implications that arose when female audiences were taken into account: on the one hand, the path of film melodrama [*Kino-Melodrama*] and, on the other hand, that of social drama [*soziales Drama*]. Melodrama respected the boundaries between low and high art by going back to a form of folk theater long subject to bourgeois control in Germany. As a result, though melodrama too was attacked in the course of the antismut campaigns, the form as such engendered little protest; on the contrary, it was eventually supported. This makes sense, since in its form melodrama simply translated into a mass medium theater's tendency to make woman appear as a male projection. Melodrama translated this tendency not only *into* another medium but also *for* another audience. Filmic reproduction conveyed a male projection to a specifically female audience that could appropriate this projection in its technically objectified form as its own.

Rather than opening the eyes of women, melodrama produced the perfect illusion of looking at oneself on the screen. The social drama, in contrast, was not just one-sidedly produced for a female audience; rather, in social drama this audience became the force driving the development of a specific aesthetic of film drama. Women's interests were noticed and taken up by the actress; in turn, she conveyed these interests in her performance alongside moments of a cinema of attractions—and thus also presented women's interests to a male audience. Social drama was the aesthetic core of film drama insofar as all genre forms had in common an emphasis on sexual differences and changing gender roles in modernity. Thus, social drama plays a decisive role for an approach to early cinema that is interested in the significance of the cinema for a female audience and for emancipatory developments in the relationship between the sexes. Another reason for this central position of social drama is the difficulty of identifying it as a definite genre. Not only did social drama share elements with melodrama, but it also emanated into other genres like the detective film and the sensational film [*Sensationsfilm*] to the degree that those represented female positions.

Social drama is not to be confused with what in the United States has been termed the *social problem film*. Social drama does not encompass the latter's breadth of social problems, from those related to labor unions and sexual politics up to those related to the women's movement, and it cannot even be characterized solely in terms of its social content. Rather, in its mixture of attractions designed for the curious eye and episodes from the private sphere and woman's life, it is related to the Danish "moral drama" [*Sittendrama*].[30] This, at any rate, is the development Emilie Altenloh traced in *Zur Soziologie des Kino*—the only source I know that points out the contemporary importance of "social drama."[31] Altenloh came up with a characterization of German film production along the lines of the Danish tradition. Realistic and close to everyday life, these dramas deal with social problems; that is, "for the most part, these dramas show a woman struggling with the conflict between her natural, female-sensual instincts and the social conditions that oppose these instincts."[32]

I follow Altenloh's definition of social drama insofar as it emphasizes the close relationship of social drama to everyday life and its concern with "women's fight" against social conditions. At the same time, though, these definitions are not sufficient, and especially not if one wants to distinguish social drama from melodrama. In social drama moments of classical stage drama also resurface, but they do so under the sign of the interests of female audiences in self-representation and, more generally, in the representation of gender differences and of the private and intimate. This interest leads to the appropriation of drama by film, but it also renders powerless the classical form of drama that had provided the basis for all events and had rendered them in present tense. In social drama classical drama presents itself for the first time stripped of power and reveals its mythical content.[33]

The visualization of female and private life in cinema received its constitutive, "actualizing" moments not from the language of drama but from the medium of technical reproduction and from show business [*Schaustellung*]. The camera conveyed to women a gaze into "their world"—not only the traditional world of domesticity but also the modern public world that they were about to enter as well as the secret world of love affairs and prostitution. Both cinematic mise-en-scène and the manipulation of film material through tinting or tricks such as superimposition, fade-ins, and so on followed the principles of show business and exhibition; that is, they appealed to the sensual interests of the audience. In depicting devastating fires, the magical appearance of an angel, or even thrilling acrobatic numbers and magic tricks, an interesting object or environment, or an emotionally powerful scene, films spoke to female as much as to male scopophilia. The case was different, though, when it came to the presentation of women and men as erotic objects.

Sexual difference in the audience was primarily reflected in the performance of the actress: she maintained an erotic attraction, especially for the male gaze. For the female audience, though, she also presented herself in her social role. The self-representation of the actress gave the social drama its specific shape, a self-representation that could unfold to an even greater extent, since no literary models limited her performance. The actress had always been a "modern" woman, as Ursula Geitner has shown. She appropriated for herself, like a man, a public, self-determining existence and engaged in an experimental relationship to the world:

> Actresses distance themselves from their natural determination—the deter-
> mining condition into which they are born, so to speak—by conquering new
> terrains and combining knowledge, experiences, and expectations to form
> new roles. In so doing, they are comparable to those male individuals who
> have learned to use without reflection [*selbstverständlich*] the advantages of
> a modern society that is no longer hierarchically organized.[34]

Onstage, actresses had to hide their intrinsic modernity beneath the presentation of images of women constructed by men. Film, in contrast, gave them a chance for self-representation in the sense of an emancipation from these images: no dramatist, no director determined their performance before the camera.[35] The actresses had no other imperative than to discern and take up the new needs of female audiences. Their self-representation interpreted and satisfied this need as one emerging from "the entry of woman into modernity."

An actress's exhibition of her modernity does not mean simply an embodiment of modern female characters. Rather, it means primarily that she presents femininity as nonunitary [*nicht Identisches*]—that is, as not identical with her image—and as something that is possible in many roles. The actress was finally able to be mobile in her skills of transformation, just like an actor, rather than being rendered immobile in the beautiful semblance of expressive nature. Finally, she was able to act against the prejudice that as a woman she was affiliated with sentiment rather than action and that sentiment has to be real rather than acted; she was able to act against the prejudice that woman cannot actually present herself openly and in public without prostituting herself.[36] In addition to the "mandate" of the audience, she was also supported in her performance by the new medium itself: its mobility met her skills of self-transformation, and the inherent separation of image and real body in the new medium—rather than a naive belief in cinematic illusion [*Illusionskino*]—supported the fictionality of her physical performance. Someone like Georg Lukács realized early on that film aesthetics were based on the "absence" of the actress; in contrast, the reformers took exception to the exhibition of female bodies in film. Beyond a theoretical discussion about cinematic realism, film from the beginning gave to the actress something of the autonomy of art, the security to perform an emotion for the eye of the camera rather than for the man in the audience who would like to take her emotion as real.

But the ability of the actress as modern woman to serve as a "role model" was only one side of her performance and a result of the self-reflexivity inherent in her skills of performance. The other side was a result of the reflection of social experiences; self-presentation [*Selbstdarstellung*] turned into representation [*Darstellung*] of an existence that was forced upon the actress—an existence that was neither modern nor autonomous but rather archaic and dependent. In Wilhelminian Germany the social situation of the majority of actresses was grim.[37] Despotic contracts, low pay, and pressure on actresses to provide their own costumes (which was not the case for their male colleagues) kept this profession on the borders of prostitution. The hope that one would find a lover may be one of those ideas that has always drawn women to the theater and that was inherent in the concept of an independent life, but in reality it was often not choice but material misery that led women there. After all, the male theater audience, and critics as well, liked to see actresses as sexually available. The case of Paul Lindau and Elsa von Schabelsky caught the attention of the public. When a successful actress refused to remain his lover, Paul Lindau—who later became the author of the "first German art film," *The Other* [*Der Andere*]—could depend upon all theater managers and most of his colleagues in film and theater criticism to penalize her. She was no longer able to get theater work in Berlin.[38]

By making visible her social situation along with the presentation of her body, the film actress opposed the one-sided image of her in the male spectator's imagination (i.e., the image of erotic availability), and she allowed the female spectator insight into "life." In 1911 *Der Kinematograph* published in issue 259 an article called "The Movie Girl" ["Das Kinogirl"], which proposed the thesis that film dramas could prevent many real-life dramas:

> How a young girl ends up in theater is obvious to anyone interested in either the theater or the girl. However, hardly anyone thinks much about how a young girl is able to assert herself onstage. But our audience should know how many sad real-life dramas the photoplay *prevents* because it *shows* dramas

taken from the life of the audience. If this were known, the old accusation that cinema cuts off theater from its living foundation would long since have been silenced, since cinema offers a lifeline for those who would otherwise perish in theater.

The article goes on to describe the everyday experience of an actress on the verge of slipping into prostitution. Cinema, which needed actresses (a "mass squadron of extras"), also became their savior:

> I am sure [the author writes at the end of the article] that there are people who mourn the blessings of the cinematograph.[39] Those nice and pretty movie girls who peer at us from the films: where can one find them? One cannot send flowers via the theater box attendant, one cannot mail invitations for a small dinner, one cannot go behind the screen to wait for the movie girl whom one admires, one cannot get to know her. In a word: the film world is too impersonal. . . . There are, it is certain, people who hate the cinematograph simply because it is so extremely moralistic and impersonal.

This (anonymous) text turns the author's argument into an unmistakable polemic against the moral double standard of cinema's enemies. This is all the more interesting because the text finds its weapon in the domain of women's emancipation. In social drama, in contrast to melodrama, the presentation of erotic appeal was not impeded by internal censorship, cloaked morality, or pedagogic intention. Instead, erotic presentation was connected to the exhibition of what one could call the nonmodern—and even archaic or asocial—position of women in society.

Aspects of modernity and a reflective, even aggressive eroticism implicit in the self-presentation of the actress in front of the camera are to be found in different forms of film drama; both detective film and sensational film impel the mediation of these two. The task of exposing social reality, however, was reserved solely for social drama, and it was this task that gave it its name. To visualize how the actress—a modern woman—was imprisoned in patriarchal structures it was necessary to be aware of that reality that was lying beyond the "reality" of the presence of the actress in front of the camera. For this reason, in addition to the staged scenes, the documentation of reality takes up considerable space in social drama. In order to present this reality in its social power structure, however, documentation was not sufficient. In stage drama, in contrast, the actress had always had a frame that represented this structure. Consequently, social drama took up elements of theater drama but from the standpoint of the actress and with an interest in visualizing the repression of both the female sex and its representation.

Social dramas took up the form of stage drama, which had entered a crisis, at the point when Naturalism, in vain, had sought to save stage drama. The Naturalist stage drama was characterized by its attempt to rescue the ability of drama to present actions [*dramatische Handlungsfähigkeit*] by transposing action into the milieu of the lower classes. As a consequence of this rescue attempt, dramatic action presented itself as distanced, embedded in an "alien" milieu, but this milieu in turn referred back to the author to whom it presented itself. The autonomy of drama, its "presence," became untenable—for example, in the work of Gerhard Hauptmann—precisely because it was recreated by introducing proletarians who were able to act despite the experience of the powerlessness of the bourgeois individual. The mythical narrator, who had been left behind by drama earlier, became visible again:

> The background to the actions of people, the atmosphere in which they move, these are visible only to the author who stands before them or who visits them as a stranger: the epic narrator. This positioning of the drama relative to the narrator, which is a prerequisite for the Naturalist drama, is mirrored within it by the relative position that the characters assume vis-à-vis their milieu, which seems alien to them.[40]

The development of film drama presented the reversal, so to speak, of the process of the decomposition of drama that occurred in Naturalism: the narrator joined the technical reproduction of external reality, and drama reconstituted itself in the tension between the two. However, the author of the film distinguished himself from that which was "alien" [*dem Fremden*] in the film—that which was alien was presented by the actor rather than created by the author as a person. Moreover, this "alien" element was frequently represented by a woman. The reconstitution of drama met with resistance; an identification of the narrator in the film with the author and his eventual return to a place "behind the stage" could only occur at the cost of the repeated denial of sexual difference. Such a denial was the signature of later narrative cinema, which, through its self-containment, its distance from the audience, and the repression of the different perspectives of all who participated in the production of the film, produced the fiction of the personal unity of the film author.

The lack of a traditional author in early film drama is the foundational point of its distinction from stage drama. There is an additional difference between film drama and Naturalistic stage drama: instead of the milieu of the lower classes, it is the bourgeois milieu that stands in the foreground. As the world of acting subjects, this milieu was just as alien to woman as the proletarian milieu was to the poet. The actress in early social drama was a female narrator to whom the technologically reproduced bourgeois world became a "milieu" in the sense of Naturalistic drama. The attempt to repeat drama in film had its primary and particular meaning as a representation of woman's attempt to enter the bourgeois world as a subject. Yet this meant that as social drama moved toward stage drama it at the same time negated the fulfillment of drama as form. For if stage drama were to reestablish itself in film, the male inscription of the acting subject would return as well, and woman's subjectivity would again be lost. It was a matter of what was most important to early film: (re)presentation of the rise of women or the salvation of drama. Social dramas did not restore the form but rather submitted the latter to the primacy of the content.

Asta Nielsen is generally known as an autonomous actress of early cinema who also controlled the design of her films. Her sovereignty, her exorbitant unfolding of acting skills with respect to film, was only possible, though, because of the general structure of film drama and especially social drama. The Danish actress was familiar with the latter before she began to work for the German PAGU. What has been praised as Nielsen's invention of an original film language was also evident—at least as a tendency—in many other actresses of this period. In their performances exhibition was simultaneously self-communication, so that it is possible to speak of a female narrative perspective in the stories of early cinema.[41] This narrative perspective is missing in melodrama, which communicated the image of woman according to prescriptions of drama, such that an independent dynamic of performance was impossible.

The boundaries of social drama were to be found in its taboo of the male body. If the actor, like the actress, had presented his body to the interested gaze of the other sex, not only would female subjectivity have competed with the subjectivity of men, but, in addition, patriarchal power as such would have been sublated [aufgehoben] within the "dramatic" performance, and social drama would have come to an end.

Early cinema did not sublate social drama in this way. Instead, there was, on the one hand, an emphasis on the subjectivity of women in the cinema and on modernity as something that made possible manipulation, role-play, and the gaze; these were emphasized in detective films and sensational drama. On the other hand, there was a reestablishment of the power of the author, a process in which the introduction of well-known actors (a development that occurred later than the introduction of unknown actresses and actors) played an important part. Yet authorship not only entered cinema from the outside. The internal conflict between female and male actors, between female and male audiences, led, in the context of the extant external conditions, to a latent restitution of a dominant male narrative perspective that supported the position of the actor as well as the male audience. Indications of such a development can already be found in dramas from 1913–14.

Cinema lacked the support of those critical forces in the Wilhelminian era, especially those of emancipatory movements such as the women's movement and the sexual reform movement, that would have been necessary for it to force through its emancipatory aesthetic as the beginning of an alternative public sphere. As a result, not only were the oppositional possibilities of cinema barely noticed, but they were also blocked by a restorative discourse on the aesthetic and social importance of cinema, the latter of which had consequences for film production and film theory far beyond this early period.

The following discussion of films from 1895 to 1914 is speculative in several respects. First, it treats the comparatively small number of films that have been preserved and viewed as though these are representative. Second, it assumes that films are more than objects of art and that their aesthetics can therefore be grasped adequately only within the framework of cinema understood as an institution. This is even more so the case insofar as part of the aesthetic quality of early films is that they did not lay claim to being a finished work, nor did they attempt to anticipate their reception in the way that classical film later did. Rather, they anticipated finding an audience with certain experiences and desires, an audience that would do its part to give significance to the film.

Consequently, the usual means of critical film analysis do not or only partially apply to the understanding of the social and aesthetic quality of the films in question here. The filmstrip itself, viewed forward and backward on the editing table in the archive, is not sufficient as a basis for this investigation; such an investigation also requires a supplemental mediation of audience experiences from this time. Yet such a supplement is missing, by and large.

Emilie Altenloh's qualitative survey of moviegoers in Mannheim is a unique windfall. However, the many texts of the movie reform movement document the resistance to cinema as a place for specific experiences, satisfaction of certain needs, and stimulation of fantasies. In these writings one can detect, as in a film negative, the aesthetic-social qualities of early cinema that cannot be understood from the preserved films alone. Therefore, the second part of this book, which discusses film criticism from the beginnings of film theory, not only is a necessary addition to my film analyses but also contains, so to speak, their preconditions.[42]

In 1912 Peter Altenberg laconically pointed out the discrepancy between public discourse on cinema and cinematic experience itself; clearly, female company was a significant part of the latter:

> My tender fifteen-year-old female friend and I, a fifty-two year old, gave ourselves over to tears during "Under the Stars," a scenic sketch in which a poor French barge-puller draws his dead bride upriver, heavily and slowly, and through blooming fields! Those whose "dry spirit" we are supposed to enjoy with a "dry heart" will be sorry! We don't have to, and we don't want to!
>
> A famous writer said to me: "We understand one another [*Wir sind jetzt unter uns*]—what do you find so special about film screenings?!?"
>
> "No," I said, "you don't understand me, you stand under me [*wir sind nicht unter uns, sondern Sie sind unter mir*]!"[43]

Commitment to one's girlfriend implies commitment to cinema as well, and this separates Altenberg as a writer from his colleague.

Such rare solidarity with "female" movie experience does not replace the self-expression of the latter, for women writing at that time were less arrogant in their response to the demands of the community of "experts and artists," a community of which they were fighting to be part. But even though there were a few women among the first film critics, cinema is almost completely ignored by the contemporary publications of the women's movement.

Finally, one can only speculate about the forms that films took on in the minds of a receptive audience; speculation is therefore unavoidable in this project of understanding the aesthetic and social significance of the films under discussion here. But there are various means at one's disposal for reconstruction: to begin with, knowledge about the social situation of women in the period before World War I; knowledge about the changes in sexual and gender roles that developed around this time; and, bound up with the latter, knowledge about the seismic shifts in cultural relationships between the sexes. In addition, there is the feminist critique of dominant cinema, which sharpens the senses for certain moments of a cinema that is different. Finally, and above all, there is one's personal reception of these films, which might take place in completely different conditions but which is still connected to the experiences of an early cinema audience because of the coherence of social traditions [*gesellschaftlicher Tradierungszusammenhang*]. Objectivity of analysis, the presentation of historic facts, and the explicit mediation of current scientific discourses are not the primary concerns of this work. Rather, it not only seeks to make lost film present "in the mind of the female spectator," but it also seeks to make a lost cinema present in the mind of the reader.

Chapter One

The Heart of Reason

The Beginnings
of Narrative Cinema

Staging the Male Self

The few films that have been preserved convey, until ca. 1907, predominantly a male world: the documentary shorts revolve around technical events (*Alarm at the Fire Department* [*Alarm bei der Feuerwehr*], *Arrival of a Train in Berlin-Schönholz* [*Einfahrt des Eisenbahnzuges in Berlin-Schönholz*], *Chemnitz Fire Department* [*Chemnitzer Feuerwehr*], *The Transport of a Saxonian Machine Factory Locomotive through the Streets of Chemnitz on June 28, 1898* [*Lokomotivtransport der sächsischen Maschinenfabrik durch die Straßen von Chemnitz am 28.6.1898*]) and the deployment of sentries and public appearances by sovereigns (*The Deployment of the Sentry* [*Die Wache zieht auf*], *King Albert of Saxony Passes the Interim Bridge on His Way to the Wettin Federation Shooting in Döbeln* [*König Albert von Sachsen passiert die Interimsbrücke zum Wettin-Bundesschießen in Döbeln*], *The Reception of King Albert of Saxony in Chemnitz* [*König Albert von Sachsen wird in Chemnitz empfangen*]);[1] in addition to these films there are those that feature street scenes (*Unter den Linden, Berlin Alexanderplatz*).[2] Among the "numbers" of the brothers Skladanowsky's film presentation at the Wintergarten, artistic performers dominated; ring fights and boxing kangaroos constituted the main attractions, while female performers appeared only in the context of a family (i.e., in the "Acrobatic Potpourri" of the gymnastic family Grunato) and not least also in the figure of Mlle Ancion, who performed the then-popular "Serpentine Dance." The Serpentine dancer also figured in the first filmstrips of the Skladanowskys and of Messter, but, in contrast to the tinted American recordings of Annabelle's Butterfly and Serpentine dances from 1895, these do not seem to have been preserved.[3]

The range of film subjects was modest. Like Skladanowsky, Messter, in 1897, simply recorded vaudeville acts by famous performers. And Messter presented, just like Skladanowsky, a Serpentine dancer in one of his films. But then he also made filmstrips whose content was taken from the funny pages, for example, a man in white pants standing in front of a park bench, while the pants show the dark stripes of the freshly painted bench.[4]

The funny shorts feature male protagonists: the cyclist who crashes in Skladanowsky's *A Gay Party in Front of the Tivoli in Stockholm* [*Eine lustige Gesellschaft vor dem Tivoli in Stockholm,* 1896] or "Farmer Klaus" in *How Farmer Klaus Was Healed of His Disease* [*Wie Bauer Klaus von seiner Krankheit geheilt wurde,* 1906]. The humor has a sadistic touch; in the latter film a scene that constitutes the climax of a cruel cure depicts the farmer's wife as she approaches the bed of the tortured husband with an oversized syringe.

The first narrative films were based on sensational news stories. *The Murder at the Spandau Schiffahrtskanal* [*Der Raubmord vom Spandauer Schiffahrtskanal,* 1904] was well known in literature. *The Captain from Köpenick* [*Der Hauptmann von Köpenick,* 1906], a film dealing with the authentic story of the shoemaker Voigt, has been preserved. Carl Sonnemann starred as the main protagonist, while the other characters (as well as "the people") were played by employees of the Buderus Company ("Mechanical Manufacturer of Movie Apparatuses"). The head of the company, Carl Buderus, directed the film. Since the filming was an exceptional event that occurred outside of the routine of work, the man who plays the innkeeper at the inn in which the captain dines returns his gaze again and again to the camera in his excitement. However, in the shots of the wet streets, the camera is already handled with virtuosity: the police arrive in an open car to arrest the false captain. In 1908 several producers sought to film a documentary epilogue with the real shoemaker Wilhelm Voigt. The reproduction of the shoemaker's own written account testified to the story's authenticity.

Female Border Crossing

The shots of Sarah Bernhardt in *Tragic Actress Sarah Bernhardt as Hamlet in the Duel Scene with Laertes* [*Die Tragödin Sarah Bernhardt als Hamlet in der Duell-Szene mit Laertes,* 1898] and in *Salomé's Dance* [*Tanz der Salomé,* 1905] presented an exception to this male world. The female performer as attraction was also featured in *The Snake Dancer* [*Die Schlangentänzerin,* 1909] and in

Tilly Bébé: The Famous Lion Tamer [*Tilly Bébé. Die berühmte Löwenbändigerin,* 1908]. What makes these film scenes so interesting is the fact that each in its own way situates sexual attraction in a transcendence of a socially determined gender role rather than relying on the appeal of typical femininity. Sarah Bernhardt was chosen for a "trouser role," and she impresses the viewer with the powerful elegance that is evident in her "man to man" swordplay.

Salomé's Dance takes up a fin-de-siècle male fantasy that can be found in the poetry of Oscar Wilde, the operas of Richard Strauss, and the paintings of Gustave Moreau. In the imago of Salomé the excluded other—nature, sexuality, the feminine—returns as lure and as threat. By trivializing this imago, though, the film allows that which had become spellbound in this image to become independent; through a mixture of striptease and opera, the woman in front of the camera oversteps the borders of both "genres." One of the few actions in the film consists of the dancer allowing the black cape to slip from her naked upper body before she throws away the cape. As

she gestures and dances with clumsy lasciviousness, she moves her lips as though she is singing—apparently, the film was conceived as a sound picture. During the climax of the action, Salomé kneels next to the head of John, which was presented to her on a plate off-screen. She stretches herself out on the ground next to the head, caresses and kisses it. With respect to the realm of opera, the striptease oversteps a border; the female body not only exhibits itself to the male eye but also confronts it with hidden sadistic and necrophiliac desires.

In *The Snake Dancer* and *Tilly Bébé,* all literary and theatrical embellishments have been abolished. Female power and excess, and a transgression of roles, occur more authentically in the shape of artistic virtuosity and daring, especially in the case of the lion tamer. But the snake dancer also impresses the viewer with her physical power: dressed exotically in a sparkling dress with big earrings against her dark curls of hair, she handles the giant snake as though it were a scarf that she is winding around her neck, as though it were a lasso that she is swirling through the air. The sexual fantasy that she embodies breaks away

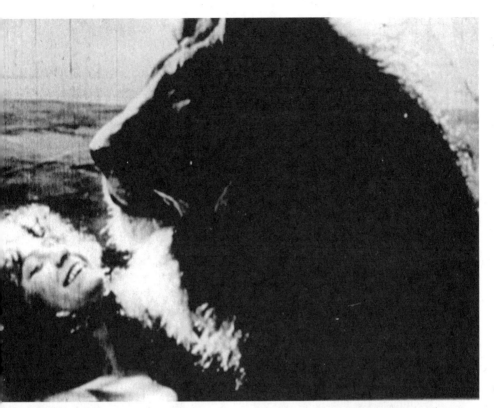

from male clichés and serves, on the one hand, aggressive, masochistic desires, but it also, on the other hand, thereby expresses female ambivalence. At the end of the film the acrobatic dancer drops the snake and raises her hands in a gesture of disgust, an expression she intensifies by picking up the animal, lifting it above her head, and throwing it to the ground again. But then, unexpectedly, she lies down next to it and draws the snake's body up between her legs and across her lower body, which thrusts upward.

Tilly Bébé plays with these contradictions in a different way. She wears a white lace dress, and her hair is set in dainty dark curls—in short, she fully represents the image of a sweet girl. She plays in jovial fashion with the wild animals, snuggling up to the lions, hugging them, and kissing them on their large snouts as though they were stuffed animals. But then she forces open one animal's mouth, presenting the enormous jaw and the dangerously gleaming teeth—and still laughs into the camera. Holding a whip, she steps in front of the tigers and dances for the tamed animals, which gaze obediently at her. The snake dancer and the lion tamer treat the beasts as if they were pieces of clothing or bedside pets, disregard and maltreat them, abusing the submissive animals to satisfy their own fancies and desires—at least, that is the fantasy they evoke. What kind of pleasure their artistic performances offered to the audience—whether the audience identified with the skillful female sadist or the maltreated animal—remains an open question.

Stories from the World of Women

Around 1909 the cinema of attractions obviously played with transgressive femininity. The films profited from the tension between a male fantasy, the images for which had been taken from other media, and the provocative "body art" [*Körperkunst*] of the female performer. Film set into motion that opposition between the sexes that had been stored, one-sidedly, in literary images and in painting. At the same time, other films from the years 1909–10 already revealed how the future form of narrative cinema was developing within the cinema of attractions in connection with a definite presence, even dominance, of women and their "stories." The shift from male hero to female protagonist as the center of the story indicates the degree to which, in the shift from a cinema of attractions to narrative cinema, the interests of a female audience were considered. With respect to this consideration, the perception of an emergent audience and an interest in regimentation went hand in hand. The advent in film of narrating stories drawn from a female world was closely linked to the necessity of canalizing that opposition between the sexes that had been set in motion in the cinema of attractions. The production of films for women, especially the formation of melodrama as a genre for women, certainly already implicated elements of a

later practice, namely, the attempt to anticipate reception and consequently inhibit the development of oppositional and diverse perceptions. At the same time, though, the films of the years 1909–14 present an incomparably open discussion about the reality and the fantasies of women.

A Mother's Love [*Mutterliebe,* 1909], *To Whom Does the Child Belong?* [*Wem gehört das Kind?* 1909], *Father, Your Child Is Calling!* [*Vater, dein Kind ruft!* ca. 1910], and *I Don't Want a Stepmother* [*Ich will keine Stiefmutter,* 1910] already signal, through their titles, a turn toward the family and the role of the mother, while the titles of the films *Cruel Marriage* [*Grausame Ehe*] and *Reason of the Heart* [*Die Vernunft des Herzens*] signal a concern with love and marriage and with the contradiction between social order and female experience. Each of the first four short films (none is longer than ten minutes) presents the love for a child in very different fashion with respect to both form and content, and they also present this love from different perspectives. In *A Mother's Love* one can see how the form of the "number," drawn from the cinema of attractions, becomes integrated into the still clumsy narration. At the same time, through this integration, reception is oriented toward women: in being addressed, they are at the same time defined.

The Petit Bourgeois Woman

A Mother's Love revolves around the child star Heinerle from the Theater des Westens in Berlin. Heinerle, who is called "Fritzchen" in the film, acts just as though he were onstage; for example, he turns away from the scene and toward the camera, as if that was the seat of the audience to whom he has to communicate an "aside." With his refreshing performance he is the only member of the "ensemble" who makes an impression. His appearance in a goat carriage constitutes the main attraction of the film. Dressed like a young gentleman, with a Prince Henry cap, he drives up in a miniature coach drawn by a billy goat. He stops, gets off, gives a sign to the servant, and hands the reins to him so that the servant may lead away goat and carriage. The mixture of parody and the dream of being a "gentleman" comes across as both funny and moving.

Taken by itself, this scene leaves it open whether the audience, taken in by the fantasy of "mastery," slipped back into its own childhood, or whether it smiled lovingly and yet with a sense of superiority, attracted by the young boy's charms. The former reaction on the part of the audience would have been that of the "child in man"; the latter reaction betrays that the erotic gaze constituted part of motherly love. The narration opposes the playful pleasure of both sexes. The documentary elements and the performances are both in the service of a simple story. A boy from a poor social background sees the daughter of rich parents, playing unattended, fall into the water. He pulls her out of the water, but she is already dead. The lady and the gentleman adopt the brave child. But the poor mother of the boy is suffering at home, and so finally the child decides to return to her: "Daddy and Mommy [the adoptive parents] are dear to me, but I want to go back to Father and Mother in the village!" states the farewell letter that the good boy has written. In the end, the child is again sitting on his mother's lap in the petit bourgeois living room where the story began.

The narrative introduces social reality into the performance on-screen and transforms the childlike fantasy of being a "gentleman" into the fantasies of power related to social advancement. At the same time, the narrative analyzes the conflicting elements of maternal love: the mother's selfish interest to keep

the child, on the one hand, and her altruistic interest in her son's advancement, on the other. Through the film's female protagonist of motherly love,
the female spectator is forced to deal with these psychical conflicts, and her
indulgence in the erotic charms of the boy is disturbed. Through its narrative,
the film engages the unsettled social position of the petit bourgeois wife and
mother. Her realm of influence, which had always been limited to the private
sphere, lost importance under capitalism. Children, especially male children,
alienated themselves from their living environment to a previously unknown
degree. Through their jobs and work, they were identified with a system of
power that tended to reduce the private realm to the reproduction of that
commodity called "labor." However, after the film's story has stirred up the
half-conscious worries of the female spectator, the happy ending is able to
calm her again with the illusion that there is still some power in a mother's
love: it wins out over the temptations of social advancement.

On the other hand, though, this illusion still left much to be desired, since the development of psychologizing depiction in film had yet to arrive; during the period under consideration here, felicitous moments of performance and mise-en-scène were only those based on "show" effects. These moments are supported by a "documentary" camera. A camera that simply records rather than treat its subjects in a sensitive fashion is of no help to the mediocre performance with which the narrative of this film is visualized. As a result, the effect of the film is dominated by those elements that have a show value [*Schauwert*]. The impressions that the film provides of a grand bourgeois world satisfied both curiosity and the pleasure that one takes in glamour. The parklike garden with its well-kept paths and pavilion and the lacy white dresses of the lady and her daughter, who promenade in the park, presented attractions especially for a female audience, attractions that ran counter to the morals of modesty, to which the illusion of female power in the family was tied. In the petit bourgeois living room a mirror presents the only attraction; it reflects back the image of the mother. Present in the first shot, this mirroring effect seems to hint at those for whom the film wants to be a mirror—but it remains undecided whether film will be a mirror serving a self-satisfied look at social roles or a self-reflection of one's fantasies.

The Maid

A Mother's Love contains a small subplot in which the servants are the protagonists. The nanny takes a walk along the lake with the daughter—an opportunity for the nanny's "fiancé" to meet her. The couple, busy with one another, leave the child unattended and fail to notice when she falls in the water. This episode from the life of servants represents the fears of nannies, but such a reference remained unimportant, since the film was primarily addressed to the petit bourgeois mother. Furthermore, within the narrative as a whole this episode is functionalized to tie the dramatic knot and to make possible a conflict between an emotional connection to the mother, on the one hand, and the appeal of a luxurious upper-class life, on the other.

In *To Whom Does the Child Belong?* produced in the same year as *A Mother's Love,* the perspective of the servants became more important. This perspective is connected to a kind of comedy from the cinema of attractions that is organized around the principle of repetition. *To Whom Does the Child Belong?* begins with an everyday episode: a nanny goes for a walk in the woods with the daughter of the nanny's masters and meets her lover at the same time.

For a short time the child is left unattended. Following this introduction, a mix-up comedy begins. A man abducts the child, who has been playing in the forest with her teddy bear. "Wait—I'll bring this back home with me for my wife!" he states in the intertitle. His wife is not at all happy with this present; rather, she suspects him of trying to foist off on her the result of an infidelity. Outraged, she hurries to a lawyer to get a divorce. At the same time, her friend, the lawyer's wife, is on her way to visit the woman. She finds only the husband and the child he found at home and begins to play with the girl. When the jealous wife returns home, she misinterprets the situation yet again: now she suspects her friend of being the child's mother and her husband's lover. The woman suspected of being the mother assertively grabs the girl—who is the reason for the domestic quarrel—and announces: "I'll bring this cute little kid to my husband!" At the lawyer's house, though, the appearance of the child serves as the source of a similar marital catastrophe.

The final scene again uses a bench in the forest as the setting. Quarreling

and obviously distraught, the two couples chance upon each other, dragging along the unfortunate child. While the four are still arguing, the child's nanny enters the scene, and the film falls back into its frame narrative. Relieved, the nanny hugs and kisses the child, who has finally been located. When the two couples see this, they follow the example: the women embrace each other, as do the men.

It is a popular theme in comedies to accuse the other of infidelity and as a consequence conjure up a marital argument and a divorce. The wit of this film lies in the contrast between the good intention ("Wait—I'll bring this back home with me for my wife!") and the bad interpretation and in the threefold repetition of this pattern. However, a sadistic pleasure in destruction is not the only reason for laughter. By erasing the good intention, the film also enables the imagination of a real "sidestep" and releases the fantasy of promiscuous sexuality. The film's humorous main part almost belongs to the category of "spicy films" [*pikante Films*], which were reserved for men's

nights. Curt Moreck's *A Moral History of the Cinema* [*Sittengeschichte des Kinos*] suggests that the censors intervened when the salaciousness of the story of the child became more explicit, deleting the "final shot, which shows how a naked little girl plays with the area below her stomach [*Unterleib*]."[5] In the preserved copy the little girl only busies herself with her plush fetish, the teddy bear.

However, the child does not simply play an obscene role in a comic context; rather, the child is above all at the center of a story about servants: a nanny, seduced by her lover, neglects the child who has been entrusted to her; the child becomes lost but is found unharmed in the end. This frame narrative is neither comic nor tragic but simply replays a conflict common for maids. Lack of spare time was a basic problem for servants before World War I—it was not intended that they should have a private life, and therefore one could not live a private life without a "neglect of duty."[6] Since the frame narrative catered to the perspective of maids, the comic story changes in its meaning and becomes more precise. The common relief function of comedy—which, in its commonality, is latently oriented at male needs—becomes more concrete in its turn toward a female gaze; this story is not about relief from a general sense of guilt that accompanies sexuality but rather about the maid's liberation from feelings of remorse that necessarily accompanied her attempts to have a private life. The incisive gaze of the servant fell upon the marital comedy, and the masters' "breach of duty" did not remain hidden from this gaze. As in *A Mother's Love*, the loss and return of the child brought the classes into a form of contact that allowed for comparison. The film thus served neither as the moral lesson of modesty nor as an astonished gaze at the world of the rich but rather as a defense against demands from above and stabilized the self-consciousness of the servants, especially the maids.

The Mother

To Whom Does the Child Belong? radicalized the class perspective that was also evident in *A Mother's Love* and actualized erotic imagination rather than puritan morality. While *A Mother's Love* sought to "disempower" the attraction of the luxurious life of the upper classes, *To Whom Does the Child Belong?* sought to put into perspective the authority of the master. In *Father, Your Child Is Calling!* the opposition between the sexes took the place of class conflict. By means of the child the position of the mother vis-à-vis the father is strengthened. The critique of parents who hand their children over to others—a critique that is concealed and relatively unimportant in the other two films—is essential to this film. This critique, however, does not reflect the self-consciousness of the petit bourgeois woman or the female worker; rather, the film attributes this critical stance to woman as such, thereby returning woman to a position as simply the custodian of morality. The conservative women's movement made similar attempts to strengthen the position of women in society. *Father, Your Child Is Calling!* revolves around the love of an upper-class mother who devotes herself to the care of her sick child—behavior that ensures her the sympathy of all mothers. The carelessness of the father stands in stark contrast and is finally punished by the death of the child, which confirms the rectitude of the mother, albeit unhappily. The film depicts female powerlessness and at the same time makes evident the concealed power of women. In contrast to *A Mother's Love,* this film did not produce, by means of a happy ending, the illusion that there was still social power inherent in the role of the mother but instead, by means of a tragic ending, affirmed women by making a moral demand vis-à-vis male reality.

In contrast to the way in which literature secured morality, the power of film to enlighten consisted in the more or less automatic communication of the differences of the levels involved in filmic representation, that is, the difference between the power of fiction and the validity of the real. The self-evident nature of such a double communication was only later expelled from cinema, primarily by means of the separation of genres. Without restraint, *Father, Your Child Is Calling!* switches back and forth between documentary, fiction film, and trick scenes. The film begins with a short dramatic episode:

an elegantly dressed couple wish to go out, but the news that the child has fallen sick causes an argument; as a result, the woman changes her clothes and sits down at the child's bedside, while the man sticks with his plan to go out. The following shot shows the husband leaving the house, and the performance of the actor gives way to documentation; we see shots of a street in a rich neighborhood with large villas and curious onlookers who observe the filming process. Next, we are provided with insight into the reality of a nightclub, though the flirtation between a "lady of the night" [*Kokotte*] and the man is staged. Both the death of the child at home and an invisible warning to the father are presented through trick shots: an angel who arrives at the deathbed does not enter through the door but rather suddenly appears by means of a stop trick. In similar fashion the dead child later appears, ghostlike, before the pleasure-seeking father and drags him away from the tantalizing woman of the demimonde.

The story of the child's sickness and death related to claims that female

spectators made on men and reinforced their argument. Through the dead
child's "magical" appearance, the moral claim became a wishful fantasy
[*Wunschphantasie*], and the magical aspect of female morality became apparent: the wife, tied to home and child, sends the image of the child out
into the public sphere of men in order to retrieve her husband. Ultimately,
the story weaves only a loose narrative thread around heterogeneous moments of attraction; these moments had something to offer to everyone in
the movie theater but were, for the female spectators, in tension with moral
tendencies.

Parallel montage was employed in order to keep those who accompany
the women to the movie theater entertained, despite the story's "female"
morality. The use of parallel montage in *Father, Your Child Is Calling!* has
as much to do with the organization of attractions as with the linearity
and suspense of the story. We alternately see the mother at the domestic

sickbed and the worldly amusements of the father. If these sequences had been edited to appear one after the other, female spectators would have been interested from the start and would have found their everyday experience reflected in the film, but the men who accompanied them would have lost interest; they were attracted by the documentary shots and the erotic flair of the nightclub.

Emilie Altenloh's empirical study *Zur Soziologie des Kino* is basically the only contemporary source of information about gender-specific differences in film reception; this study was conducted a bit later, though, in 1912–13. Beyond this text surveys were rare, and when they were conducted, it was only by teachers among children. An article by Dr. Fritz Auer from Berlin entitled "The Era of Film: A Survey on the Cinema" ["Das Zeitalter des Films. Eine Kino-Umfrage"], which was published in a 1911 issue of *Der Kinematograph*, could almost count as a precursor to Altenloh's study; yet this article does not deal with different preferences with respect to themes or genres, instead restricting itself to short characterizations of the particular attitudes toward cinema of children, (unsatisfied) teachers, mothers, businessmen, doctors, and office workers. What this article has to say about mothers already prefigures the aperçu on housewives that appeared in the *Dialectic of Enlightenment*, according to which cinema became a "refuge" for housewives:

> *Mothers*, especially working-class mothers, love cinema, since they can bring along the brat whom they are not supposed to leave alone at home; "children are free," they don't cost anything extra. And how many plagued and oppressed proletarian women in the nickelodeon forget, for a short time, their worries and sorrows. What is presented to them does not matter very much—they often feel so tired and worn out. They just want to rest and watch a little bit of the glitter of the big world dance by.[7]

This text comments in its own way on the film *Father, Your Child Is Calling!* It points out that the problem with childcare is that it ties mothers to the home; in contrast, fathers can simply exchange the movie theater for the pub or other pleasures. At the same time, though, the film refutes the thesis of this article that women only sought (and found) distraction in the movie theater. From Dr. Auer to Siegfried Kracauer and up to Theodor W. Adorno, statements of this kind represent, for the most part, these authors' projections onto female moviegoers.

The Little Girl

With *I Don't Want a Stepmother,* attraction once again won out over narration. This film's story also turned the child into an advocate for the wife's claim to power. Her husband should have remained faithful to her beyond the grave; otherwise, as the film shows, she would come and take the daughter. The story is as follows. A professor wants to remarry. The chosen lady comes in and seats herself upon a chaise longue, which is situated beneath a portrait of the professor's deceased spouse. After a ring has confirmed the engagement, the little daughter is supposed to greet her future mother with a bouquet of flowers. However, the child points at the image: that is my mother! The new family life follows the same pattern. The stepmother behaves in an unfriendly manner toward the girl, thereby encouraging the child's longing for the mother she has lost. At night the girl gets out of bed, walks into the salon, and with a candle in her hand climbs up on the chaise longue in order to look more closely at the portrait. The curtains catch fire, and soon the entire room is aflame. The fire brigade arrives, and though they rescue the child from the flames, she dies as a result of the accident. The mother appears to the dying child and, united again, they kiss.

This film is not concerned with the erotic interests of men, nor is it interested in those who are denounced by the moral claim of the story. The protagonist is a *Biedermann,* and his new wife—a plump woman with a lorgnette and a pointed feather in her hat—appears to be more a shrew than a complaisant lover.[8] Yet the female perspective, once it has been brought into play by the little girl, can stir up powerful waves of fantasy. For the moments of a cinema of attractions are not subsumed within the narrative; rather, the story provided a basis from which filmic effects could be presented to women. These special attractions consist of tinting, the mise-en-scène of the fire and the activities of the fire brigade, and the ghostly superimposition in the final scene.

The narrative is circuitous only in order to allow the film to play with the possibilities of tinting: the child awakens at night (the room is drenched in blue); lights a candle (the image turns yellow); leaves the room (which, as it is left behind, again is tinted in a night blue); enters the salon (the first shot shows the empty salon night blue like the bedroom, but the color changes to yellow as the child comes in); climbs onto the chaise longue; looks at the portrait; and sets the curtains aflame (the scene is now tinted a fiery red).

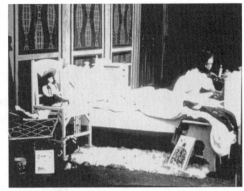

The next part of the film consists of an event that was typical for early cinema, the operation of a fire brigade. An interest in sensational events and an interest in technical detail were given equal weight in this sequence: the film depicts the use of the fire alarm and the unrolling of the water hoses as

well as the red-colored smoke and a fearless ascent of the fire ladder. In addition, the palpable attraction of these scenes provided nourishment as well for a phantasmatic turmoil of passions that oriented itself along the leitmotif introduced by the exposition: the motif of betrayed love or a virulent "Oedipus complex" on the part of the little girl. Through a dream that visualizes a rediscovery of the early mother-child relationship, the final scene offered relief in the form of regressive wish fulfillment. The slender appearance of the woman, dressed in white, is nothing but the wishful fantasy of finally attaining, once more, the good mother; she wears a transparent veil that she carefully lifts as she bends over to kiss the child. In its morbid eroticization of the mother imago, *I Don't Want a Stepmother* addressed a longing for a femininity that is unharmed by patriarchy. This dream lives off the memory of the narcissism and object love that were intertwined in the early mother-child relationship.

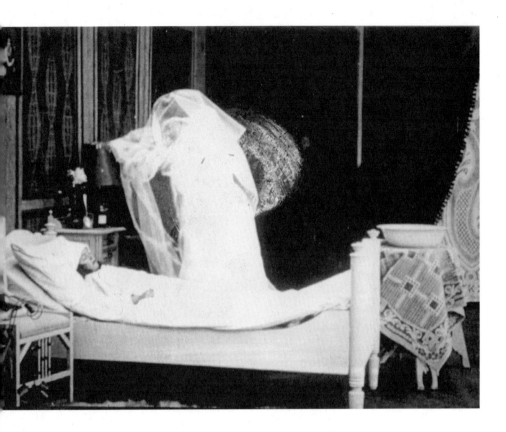

Female Narrative Perspective and Dramatic Frame

I Don't Want a Stepmother implicitly concerns the alliance of mother and daughter against the community of husband and wife. In the face of this alliance of female love, which was opposed to the social role demanded by marriage, it was of minimal importance whether the female spectator took on the perspective of the mother who gazes down at her daughter from the portrait or that of the child who carries her mother's image "in her heart." *Cruel Marriage* and *Reason of the Heart* (both 1910) each explicitly testifies to the fact that women experienced marriage as a constraint, as a repression of their living and loving. On the one hand, in these films a female perspective on the patriarchal order asserts itself; on the other hand, though, they also already introduced formal elements that ran counter to the expression of a female perspective—formal elements that prefigured a narrative cinema in which both the cinema of attractions and a female narrative perspective were repressed.

Cruel Marriage introduces the flashback, which constitutes the basis for the woman's narrative perspective with respect to the story of cruel marriage. At the same time, though, the flashback ties this point of view into a frame narrative that concerns a trial. This trial is obviously staged as a showcase for patriarchal power. The judges' bench, occupied by a row of men in black robes, is positioned frontally before the camera. A giant portrait of an authority figure (a man dressed in black, with a wig), which hangs centrally on the back wall, emphasizes the judges' seat in the center of the frame. Accused of second-degree murder of her husband, Anna Abel appears in front of this tribunal. She is asked: "Guilty or not guilty?" and she answers: "I don't know." She is thereupon urged to "tell us what happened!" and the main story begins. At the end the film returns to the courtroom, and the woman is acquitted.

In form and content, *Cruel Marriage* mirrors, as it were, the basic concept of so-called narrative cinema. In contrast, the earlier *Father, Your Child Is Calling!*—a film that still cleaves to the cinema of attractions, albeit with

narrative elements—concerned the "superior" morality of the woman. *Cruel Marriage* supported the woman's perspective on the family and, on the whole, gave itself over to scopophilia. However, as soon as the actions of a woman were no longer confined to the realms of matrimony and family but, on the contrary, destroyed these realms, as is the case in *Cruel Marriage,* films apparently had to make clear that such a woman lacked moral competence. She has no voice in the public sphere; her story can serve only as the factual material on the basis of which the men confirm their power of judgment.

The moment that a storytelling cinema was established as a public institution, thus moving beyond individual films specifically addressed to a concrete female audience, the form of this cinema had to be reflected and fixed as male vis-à-vis the contents of female stories. With respect to its content, the frame narrative in *Cruel Marriage* presents a court in which the patriarchy renders a judgment about a woman's deviation from her role. With respect to its form, the frame narrative is a dramatic "scene" into which the woman's story is inserted as a case study. The moment of generality inherent in the plot of the film—the form as a public mediation of individual experience—is negated through the frame narrative. This means, however, that the dramatic scene, copied from the theater, functioned entirely as a means to eliminate the woman as subject from the story and inform [*überformen*] her expressivity with the representation of male authority. Such a negation of filmic narration persisted as a property of later narrative cinema, with the consequence that not only was the latter dominated by a male perspective, but its narration also dominated the visuality of the medium rather than developing along with it. Sound film would seal the development of stories—subsumed under a positive dramatization of Oedipal conflicts—as bearers of ideology, while the problems that were the subjects of the narratives were reduced to the personal realm and became blind to the general conditions that were immanent to them. *Cruel Marriage* makes obvious how from the outset the culture-industrial form of the feature film was linked to a repression of female narrative perspective.

Nevertheless, the early form of "narrative cinema" still lived on contradictions. Within the general framework of patriarchal cinema a woman, at least as an actress, was able to communicate her story. The attention inherent in the cinematic means, though, could remain in the service of her story, rather than the representation of the patriarchal framework, only so long as she was still able to rely upon the tradition of the cinema of attractions. If one can trust the preserved copy of *Cruel Marriage,* the courtroom scene was depicted much more impressively than the rest of the film. The story revolves around a woman caught between two men; she loves one of them, but because he deserts her she is forced to marry the other. Both men "destroyed" her life— the intertitles allow the accused woman to express at least this much. When her husband wants to destroy his rival, old feelings resurface, resulting in the murder of her husband. The court questions neither the basic problem of a woman's self-determination in questions of love nor her social dependency on marriage, issues that become manifest in this story. Nor does the film itself care much about these questions, emphasizing instead the bad character of the husband, which becomes the basis for the court's verdict of acquittal; since the woman has saved the nobler of the two men, she is not guilty.

The framework of patriarchal norms need not always be represented by the film itself. *Reason of the Heart* (1910) is one of those stories of early narrative cinema that report a case "neutrally," that is, without the intrusion of morality. This case concerns two female friends: one, who is married, betrays

her husband with the help of the other. Rendezvous are arranged during group outings; during social evenings that involve all four people, the friend arranges for the two lovers to communicate without attracting attention. The friend covers up the relationship to such an extent that she risks not only her good reputation but also her life. During an evening rendezvous in the garden the couple is nearly discovered by the husband. Thinking quickly, the friend dons the wife's coat, thereby fooling the husband, who is wild with jealousy, and thus saving the situation. A shot is fired during the ensuing argument, and the friend collapses. Change of scenery: in the house the unconscious friend lies in an armchair, the wife throws herself upon her friend, and the husband broods over his mistake. Then the friend awakens and strokes the wife's back; she had hidden her face in her friend's lap. As the married woman looks up at her, the friend indicates, with a finger on her lips, that she should remain quiet. The husband fails to notice any of this, for he is still ruminating remorsefully on what has happened.

Reason of the Heart calls attention to a possibility only hinted at in *Cruel Marriage:* the story of the woman, which is not carried by her own judgment but controlled by male judgment, might be supposed to constitute only a singular case vis-à-vis the patriarchal order; however, since this order remains external to the film as a whole, the film is able to develop its own "reason." The female protagonists in particular resist the illusion that technical reproduction reduces the staged story to a collection of facts, that it "neutralizes" the story. The actresses become subjects of narration who have their own "reason of the heart." In the period that followed no one knew better how to use this possibility offered by early cinema—that is, of working, as an actress, against the grain of patriarchal culture—than Asta Nielsen, who shot her first film in 1910. What makes *Reason of the Heart* so remarkable is that the solidarity of women expresses an allegiance to love against marriage, such that not only does traditional morality fade into the background, but the figure of the husband comes to seem ridiculous as well. The film is narrated primarily from the women's point of view. The girlfriend keeps watch over the love affair, to whose arrangement she contributes, and, moreover, she maintains control over the husband. As the lovers meet in a park at night, she walks down a hallway to peep through the keyhole of the study. The following shot contains a keyhole aperture—a technical attraction—through which we see the husband walking up and down restlessly before grabbing a revolver.

This instantiation of the perspective of woman—which includes the mise-en-scène of the shot—reverses the patriarchal-moral judgment (the framework within which the film is located); it also opposes the morality that is found in the minds of the spectators. In the end the advocate of marital law—the potential prosecutor and judge—has been transformed into someone with a sense of guilt who sits contritely on a chair and does not even realize that he is being deceived by the two women.

Little more than the production company is known about early narrative films, and even this is not always clear. The names of female performers were vehicles for advertising, independent of whether the film included them or not. The first film actresses, in contrast, are nameless. Even direction and scriptwriting have not yet been registered as functions worth mentioning. In this respect, *Reason of the Heart* stands as an exception among the films mentioned here. In addition to the cameraman (Karl Hasselmann) and the main actor (Carl Wilhelm, who had already begun to work as a director around

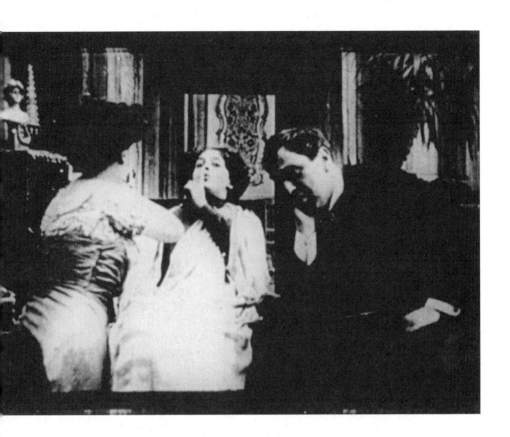

this period), the name of the director is known: Charles Decroix. An article by Walter Turszinsky in a 1910 issue of *Die Schaubühne* documents the contemporary interest in his work as a director for the Deutsche Mutoskop- und Biograph-Gesellschaft.[9] His ability to deal with actors and to communicate gesturally rather than verbally was of a special interest. The article tends to attribute the enjoyable "ease" of the film to a French influence. It comes as no surprise that the author omits the fact that this film offers more than an alternative to "Germanic stiffness"; namely, it offers resistance to the cultural and social order, not least the order of the sexes.

Charles Decroix seems to have been prototypical for directors of that period, whose careers took paths very different from those of the cultural bourgeoisie. Scornful of the prevalent cultural and social norms, these directors brought an openness to film production that also benefited the otherness of the actresses. In a 1913 article in *Die Lichtbildbühne,* Charles Decroix presents himself as a sort of occasional laborer in the field of cinematography:

Charles Decroix.

Author, director, actor, operator, photographer, machinist, assistant machinist etc., etc., etc.

A little French—fairly German—Alsatian—nothing else.

In addition to these primary titles—titles that I acknowledge and titles that I have been given by different personalities of the world of cinematography—there are others that my proverbial openness—after talking some sense into my well-known humility—cannot conceal. These titles, in their full simplicity, are as follows:

Ex–second sweeper for the Pathé Frères Company, Paris,

" brake attendant for the Film d'Art Français Company,

" mason for D. M. Biophon and Company, Berlin,

" cloakroom attendant for the Milano-Film Company,

" machinist for the Lux Company, Paris,

" head of the lost and found department, Gaumont Company, Paris,

and finally . . . simple pioneer of a future German-French entente.

I could add the title of a "subscriber to the Berlin streetcar system" to this beautiful list; however, my principle of opposing any kind of advertisement and propaganda forbids me from doing so.

For, I openly admit it, until now I have been the irreconcilable enemy of bluff advertising of any kind. Yet my friend Hanewacker (from the company Hanewacker and Scheler, Friedrichstraße 25; elevator, water, and gas supply on every floor) has been of a different opinion; for this reason, I now appear before the honorable readership to make, shamefully, the following embarrassing confession:

"I busy myself with cinematography."

Of course, you do what you can do!

I should have chosen a different career!

I could have become a good shoemaker, for example, just like my father, "Decroix senior, Shoemaker Ltd." Yes! but fate determined things differently! Poor butterfly! My wings led me to the stage, where they were soon burnt; from there I had to make just one more step to end up in cinematography.[10]

How could Decroix not have had sympathy for this step into cinematography by the actress "with burnt wings" and for the urge of the "subscribers to the Berlin streetcar system" to go to the movies? He presents himself as one of them who wants to remain one of them as well, an experimenter out of necessity and on a whim without any ambitions of professionalization. At the end of his self-portrait he writes: "Without question I will never understand anything of this unfortunate craft!" Around 1913 the trade was apparently still willing to adorn itself with such a profile.

Chapter Two

The Femininity of Men
Comedy

Jokes, humor, and the burlesque naturally played an important role in the early cinema of attraction, just as circuses could not have done without clowns, vaudeville without its funny numbers, and fairs without buffoons. The development of comedy also involved a turn away from the humorous scenes of early films and toward narration; this did not, though, imply a simultaneous turn toward female audiences. Rather, comedy developed in the direction of male self-reflexivity—and not least in the direction of his femininity. Until 1912 male protagonists dominated the scene, though by then humorous scenes had long since been integrated into narrative. The first step toward narrative consisted in connecting repetitions of a humorous motif; repetition was intended to increase the effect of the motif. *Willy's Pranks* [*Willy's Streiche*, 1909] and *Don Juan Marries* [*Don Juan heiratet*, 1909] are organized according to the principle of repetition, as are, to a lesser degree, *The Cavalier of the Rose* [*Der Rosenkavalier*, 1911] and *Fly-Hunting; or, The Revenge of Mrs. Schulze* [*Eine Fliegenjagd oder die Rache der Frau Schulze*, 1913]. This narrativization exhibits the male social character. The humor results from the contradictions to which man finds himself subject and that in turn reveal his compulsive side. *It Would Have Been So Nice* [*Es wäre so schön gewesen*, 1910] is about erotic fantasies in the barracks; *Leo the Ancillary Waiter* [*Leo der Aushilfskellner*, 1912] is about a good-for-nothing employee; *How Cinema Takes Revenge* [*Wie das Kino sich rächt*, 1912] is about a movie reformer's susceptibility to seduction; and *On a Man's Maidenhood* [*Aus eines Mannes Mädchenzeit*, 1912] is about a man in women's clothes. *Willy's Pranks*, a film by Heinrich Bolten-Baeckers that also appeared under the title *Everything Sticks with Klebalin* [*Klebalin klebt alles*], shows a series of pranks played by a boy.

The child acts as the agent by means of which male role-playing is subject to ridicule. Willy spreads Klebalin glue on the trouser seats of several children who are playing soldiers so that they stick to the wall; he glues a soldier's rifle to the sentry box while the soldier kisses his sweetheart; and so on. But little Willy, played by Curt Bois, is also representative of the child in the spectator, and consequently he satisfies, beyond the bare need for regression, the desire to gain mastery over the straitjacket of adulthood. The wit of *The Cavalier of the Rose* derives directly from the failure of so-called grown-up male eroticism. The film presents variations of coitus interruptus. A love-struck man who expresses his love with roses is regularly interrupted in his courtship by representatives of the forces of order [*Ordnungshüter*]: the father of the beloved, the doormen at the opera, his own father, and the police. The latter finally put him in prison, where he is restricted to drawing roses on the wall. Laughter about male courtship behavior could have coincided with both gleeful and grumpy consent with those forces that banish dreaming. But there is something oppositional in the "realism" with which the film reduces a romantic "high culture" figure to its problematic "lower" core.

However, the comic effect of *Don Juan Marries,* another Bolten-Baeckers film, is more differentiated and subversive. The film is a German variant of those slapstick comedies in which a man is chased by a number of brides, a theme that culminated in Buster Keaton's *Seven Chances* (1925) but that already had precursors as early as 1904 in *How a French Nobleman Got a Wife through the "New York Herald" Personal Columns* and *Meet Me at the Fountain.*[1] "Don Juan," about to get married, is chased by all of his former lovers. In the beginning we see how one woman after another reads his wedding announcement in the newspaper and sets out to the registry office, inflamed with rage: a maid, the laundry basket still under her arm; an elegant lady to whom a servant had passed the newspaper at the breakfast table; and a woman out promenading who received the news as she was sitting on a park bench. The deserted girlfriends unite to abduct the "Baron of Broken Hearts" ["*Baron von Herzenknicker*"]. The mass chase scene itself, however, is triggered by the abandoned bride, and it develops like an avalanche: she sets out with the entire wedding party in tow, tuxedos, top hats, and impressive robes included; they run after the carriage of the kidnappers, gathering up people on bicycles, children at play, and old women and carrying them along. Not only is the scene reminiscent of American models, but it already anticipates the absurd humor of the tumultuous funeral procession in *Entr'acte* (René Clair, France, 1924).

A scene portraying a battle of the sexes follows the chase. The baron—the aged heartbreaker—is now in the hands of the women. Spirited away to a villa, he comes to feel their power. One forces him to kneel down, the other brandishes an umbrella in threatening fashion above the humiliated man. However, he knows how to turn around the situation by shocking the other sex himself. Left alone in his "prison," he pretends to have committed suicide. As the women peep though the keyhole, he appears to have hanged himself from the ceiling lamp. Their curiosity and desire for control do not do them much good, for they become so panic-stricken that they carelessly enter the room and allow their victim to escape through the door.

In the final sequence, the police forcefully reunite the involuntarily separated bride and groom. The bride is arrested as she tries, with the help of a vagabond, to sneak into the villa in which her husband is being kept prisoner; the groom is arrested as he, finally free, tries to sneak into her house unnoticed. The prison cell unites them. This has the comic effect of reversing

the sense of police action (perpetrators whom the police take into custody now commit the actual "act"), and it also contains an allusion to marriage as prison—the prison in which the aging Don Juan finally ends up.

In the first part of the film, it is primarily the increasing repetition that provokes laughter, especially as it relates to the ritual of marriage; in the second part humor is connected to the inversion of roles, which enables, in a way that provides relief, an expression of the repressed power struggle between the sexes; in the third part, a crucial humorous moment is the literalization of the metaphor of the marital prison. These comic effects are, in turn, integrated into a narrative that unfolds the contradiction inherent in the role of the protagonist as he is presented in the first scene: an aging Don Juan. Despite a balding head and a wrinkled face, he turns himself in front of the mirror like a dandy, sticks a flower into his buttonhole, puts on a top hat, and reaches, eager for battle, for a bouquet of flowers. The humor begins with a gaze directed at corporeality, which undercuts the validity of the social character. The women in the film take up this gaze when they turn the panty-chaser into their prey. Eventually, that gaze is completely handed over to the audience, which sees this incarnation of corporeal potency finally become, via the body (the body that, in old age, makes one seek peace and security in marriage), a prisoner of the forces of social order. With its partisan look at corporeality, this comedy, despite its male humor and male heroes, keeps the interests of female audiences in mind as well. By initially emphasizing male weakness, the comedy destroys the image of a unity of corporeal potency and institutional power, that is, the personified patriarchal force as it confronts women particularly in the form of husbands and lovers. For men, however, this deconstruction of Don Juanism identifies the institutional force at the mercy of which they also find themselves.

It Would Have Been So Nice begins with an everyday scene in a military state: a little soldier has to perform exercises as punishment. However, the film aligns itself not just with the little soldier against his superior but also with the body against the institution. It illustrates the life of drives [*Triebleben*] in institutionalized rituals. After he has performed his rites of obedience the private retreats to his room, goes to bed, and falls asleep. He dreams of being a commander and of being able to recruit women for military training. He exercises with a group of full-bosomed beauties who must put on military jackets but whose skirts reveal their thighs as they goose-step. The "commander" retains the heaviest among the "recruits" for "penal exercises" that soon lead to a march into his room and into bed. Just as the motherly woman tenderly bends over the sleeping soldier, he wakes up: by means of a cross-dissolve, the film substitutes a sergeant for the woman, for whom the soldier, still sleepy, reaches out like a lover.

Through its exposition, the film reveals that sadistic male pleasure in a plump, exercising woman is a result of everyday repression that is part of

the military drill that shapes this sexual fantasy. In compensation for the harassment he has experienced, the little private dreams of himself as a commander who can make others exercise. However, immediately following this dream, which is motivated by the remains of the day, the actual image of desire, the woman, appears. Once she is in the dream scene she steers him away from his fantasy of revenge and toward the "primal fantasy" of the powerful good mother in whose good hands he wants to be. Aside from any homosexual associations it might evoke, his grasp for the sergeant as the soldier awakens points to the fact that the experience of being in the bad hands of the military is still mirrored in this "primal fantasy."

The Victory of the Pant Skirt [*Der Sieg des Hosenrocks,* 1911] betrays a masochistic longing for the phallic mother—a counterpart to experiences of sadistic violence in male society. At the same time, a film like this reacts to fashion phenomena that reflect the "New Woman." In *The Victory of the Pant Skirt,* the protagonist is magically drawn to women wearing clothes that resemble men's pants, to the chagrin of his girlfriend. In order to get the fetishist to the marital registry office nevertheless, she forces her corpulent body into a pantsuit. She is successful: now his eyes are tied to her legs and no longer wander to those of other women. The motif of the pant skirt seems to have been a popular one; there is another film by Eclipse from 1910 with the title *The Improvised Pant Skirt* [*Der improvisierte Hosenrock*].

Early comedies seem to have corresponded more strongly to a masochistic scopophilia directed at one's own sex rather than a sadistic voyeurism directed at the other. Desire for power is revealed as a fantasy of omnipotence that is itself the product of an oppressive reality. At the same time, though, the depiction of power fantasies represents a longing for a socially foreclosed desire and invites identification. "It would have been so nice," if one had been able to use this power for the satisfaction of one's fantasies. This insight, however, also hints at a repressed attachment to the feminine. Consequently, these comedies play not only with the social role of man but also with heterosexual or even homosexual possibilities for men.

Comedy develops into play with sexual equality and role reversal for the benefit of a male desire that is negated by the social separation of roles. This is especially true for *On a Man's Maidenhood,* a Messter production from 1912 that involved the participation of a number of then-prominent actors and actresses: Wilhelm Bendow in the leading role and Manny Ziener and Olga Engl in the female supporting roles.[2] The film presents a young man who dresses up as a woman in order to be employed as a maid. While the phallic woman is a fantasy construction that enables regression into male feelings of omnipotence when faced with a capitalist competition-society, the male body in women's clothes is a reversal of this fantasy, bringing it closer to its homosexual realization. Only for the audience, though; within the film the man in women's clothes remains fixated on the other sex and suffers the frustration typical of an omnipotence fantasy: disguised as a maid, he is able to approach a colleague whom he adores, but the moment he believes that she is "his," his sexual nature is uncovered, and, revealed as a fraud, he is doubly removed from her. The forces of social order lead him away.

The audience amuses itself with an inverted sexualization of society: as the man slips (back) into a skirt, the entire workplace turns into a sexual playground. While the master of the house seems to chase after every skirt, a servant dotes on a portly maid who has a hint of a mustache, and the "heroine" herself runs after an attractive young colleague. In the end the attendants throw a party in the rooms of the absent masters during which every desire presses forward but none is fulfilled. However, the pleasure of the audience is not exhausted by primitive Schadenfreude combined with crude sexual fantasies. Rather, from the beginning the film's narrator, the male protagonist, communicates with the audience in such a way that the audience is turned into an accomplice of his gaze beneath the cover of social order. In the opening credits the main actor addresses the audience, presenting himself with a wink in his disguise as a maid. Wearing a spotted dress with puffy sleeves, with a nice apron around his waist and a bonnet sitting coyly atop his black curls, he seductively catches our eye. Even though the protagonist fails in his attempt to fulfill his omnipotence fantasy "realistically" in the form of pleasure, for the audience the promise of pleasure is fulfilled through a gaze that perceives and enjoys the promiscuity of the sexes that occurs beyond social gender roles. *On a Man's Maidenhood* is the only known example from the prewar period that also shows a connection of the cinema to the homosexual scene.[3]

The narration in *On a Man's Maidenhood* exhibits an epistemological aspect, transcending pure amusement. While *It Would Have Been So Nice* marks a tendency toward masochistic regression as a reaction to the social institution of the military insofar as the latter is characterized by sadism, the homosexual pleasure in travesty in *On a Man's Maidenhood* refers back to a destabilization of the distribution of social roles. This destabilization is primarily caused by the increasing employment of women. In the realm of domestic services, decisive changes occurred over the course of the second half of the nineteenth century; attending to the household became predominantly a female job. In the first scene of *On a Man's Maidenhood* we see a man in a modest living room reading newspaper announcements as the landlady enters with a bill for the rent; excited by a sudden idea, he grabs her by the waist and whirls her around the room. The film derives its pleasure in travesty, which initially turns all women into accomplices, from a story of social hardship that results from female job competition; the female audiences are also implicated in this look at the sexual substructure of society. After the hero has decided to hire himself out as a maid, he goes to a barber, and, after a shave, he looks with delight in the mirror at his smooth skin. His coquetry with a feminine image is prolonged as he tries on different wigs. The landlady and her daughter form the audience for his disguise, which he stages exhibitionistically as a show.

The moments of a cinema of attractions nourish the libido and curiosity of the gaze of recognition and resist ideological occupation. A saucily inappropriate attraction emerges in the performance of the protagonist as a result of the clumsy attempts of early narrative cinema to substitute pantomime for words, which in this case create effects associated with a vaudeville act. When the man at first indicates to the women with gestures how he wants to dress in women's clothes, this is already the starting point for a fantasy on the part of the audience who sit before the screen; the man runs his hand down his chest, indicating a bulge, strokes his body from his hips down to his thighs, and then begins to move forward with little feminine steps . . . In the cross-dressing as such, a sadistic pleasure in dismantling masculinity breaks new ground: once the jacket is removed, the cuffs, attached with strips, appear; these are "tubes" that, once they are stripped off like the shirt collar and the stiff dickey, "stand" without their carrier and expose masculinity as an arsenal of accessories. Dressing in women's clothes works in a similarly funny

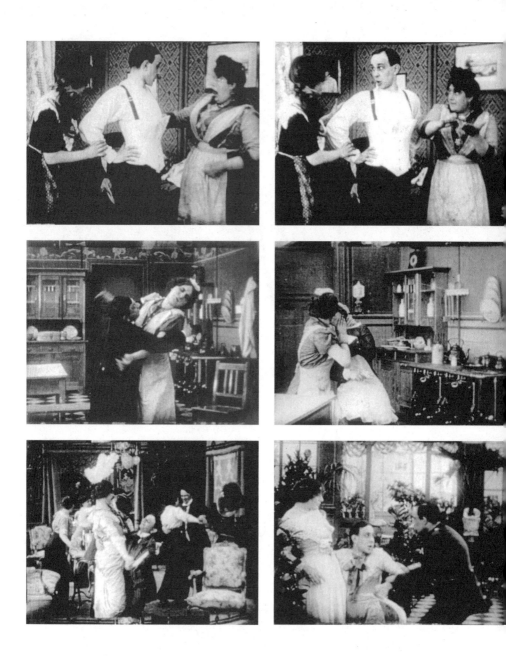

way: the reality of clothing is the illusion of sex, and the corsage provides the female sexual characteristic of a bust—no matter what kind of body and what kind of desire lie beneath it.

The integration of comic attractions based on sadomasochism includes women in the humor as well. They appear in these films as accomplices who

see through the game and enjoy male exhibitionism. In 1913–14 more and more heroines march into comedy. Cast in trouser-roles, they seek emancipation from paternal power, which threatens to deprive them of the source of their happiness, their lover. This play with desire, which in the case of male heroes is designed to work against a repressive social role, threatens to take a conservative turn for the heroines of *Hooray! Accommodations!* [*Hurra! Einquartierung!* 1913] and *Miss Piccolo* [*Fräulein Piccolo,* 1914], that is, toward the restriction of female roles to private and intimate realms.

This shift goes hand in hand with a "bourgeoisification": the milieu changes from that of the servants to that of the masters. However, in 1913 one comedy defends once again the voyeuristic pleasure of the "little people" against their cultural-bourgeois enemies. *How Cinema Takes Revenge* is a testimony to the effects of the movie reform movement. The intertitles put words into the mouth of Professor Moralski (the hero) that one can in fact read in the literature of the movement: "Thus, our people are being poisoned by filthy floods of immorality, which the cinematograph spews out over its audiences every night."

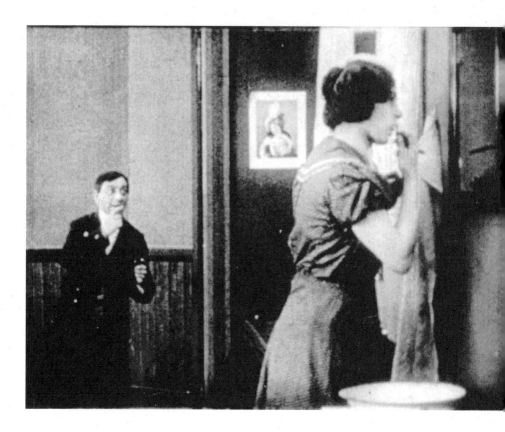

How Cinema Takes Revenge is one of the earliest films to show a "film in a film" in which the trade represents itself. The power of the medium to enlighten reveals itself in the double moral standard of the bourgeois citizen who wants to patronize the medium. An actress is asked to use the opportunity of an international congress on the topic "The Fight against Cinematography" to seduce Professor Moralski, who is traveling without his spouse. A camera team accompanies the actress to a seaside resort— the site of the conference—to capture and document the affair. The plan works. Director and cameraman observe the developing flirtation through binoculars in order to be on the scene with the camera at the right moment. "Back home" the professor is at first haunted by an "inner" manifestation of his resort "friend," who is set apart from the external run of events by means of a stop trick. She walks through the door of his study, he longingly opens his arms, and suddenly, confused, he recognizes the deception: his wife stands in front of him.

However, the cinematic depiction of the flirtation has wider consequences than just this fantasy image. The film producer passed the beach scene on to the professor as an example of the immorality of cinema. At the next meeting of the society the professor wants to show this "trash film" [*Schundfilm*]. The professor gives, as always, an introductory speech; he then sits down expectantly in the first row next to his wife. The title appears on the screen: "The Paragon of Virtue at the Seaside Resort." The first images follow, the room becomes agitated, the wife asks: "Josef—you are in this film as well?" The beach shots come next, first contact between the actress and the professor; he discreetly pulls his wedding ring from his finger. The audience becomes upset, his wife explodes, and Moralski, head drawn down into his coat collar, tries to flee, but his wife mercilessly keeps him in his seat. When finally the couple on the screen begin to cuddle, the outraged audience storms out of the room along with the professor and his wife. Outside flyers are distributed: "Zentral-Kinotheater. Daily, starting tomorrow: The Paragon of Virtue at the Sea Resort. Sensational

hit, amusing, instructive." Amused and satisfied, the director and the actress watch the professor and his wife make their escape.

It is in this light that the audience is supposed to view the movie reformers. Here, the filmmakers in the film are the narrators who communicate to the spectator their view of what lies behind the scene of this fervor to reform. The comedy itself proceeds in a similar fashion: it again exposes the hidden life of drives and sexual fantasies, but this time this exposure is employed not in the service of pleasure but so that the film trade can assert itself. The film thus not only brings to light a double moral standard, but it also presents the film milieu as "moral," in contrast to which erotic smut and spicy tidbits concern only the repressed desires of the antiprogressive cultural bourgeoisie. When the special assignment reaches her, the actress—wearing a clean white dress and seated in an armchair with a flowered pattern—was at home and just sitting down with a book. Her image communicates decency and propriety. *How Cinema Takes Revenge* reveals that cinema has effectively already lost, that it is willing to internalize censorship.

Chapter Three

Reaction in the Melodrama

The Power of Genre

A number of films have been preserved from 1911 that document the beginnings of melodrama in Germany. In these beginnings, the genre shows itself to be different than the broad Anglo-Saxon discussion about melodrama would lead one to assume.[1] On the one hand, German melodrama is situated within a history of the subjugation of folk art that falls under the claim of the bourgeoisie to "educate"; on the other hand, it is from the outset performing the function of "woman's film." Melodrama is the genre that the patriarchal cinema creates for female audiences, whose curiosity is not valued, even as their money is. One cannot talk about melodrama without mentioning the name of Oskar Messter, the entrepreneur and tinkerer who invested his technical abilities not only in the construction of the first German film production company but also in 1914 in military air reconnaissance.

The melodramas of 1911 considered here, *The Miller and His Child* [*Der Müller und sein Kind*], *Forgotten because of Happiness* [*Im Glück vergessen*], and *Tragedy of a Strike* [*Tragödie eines Streiks*], are all Messter productions starring Henny Porten and directed by Adolf Gärtner. In these films a newly emerging narrative cinema inherits the legacy of the *Tonbild* [sound picture], those filmed stage scenes that were accompanied by sound from a phonograph. In the production of sound pictures too the Messter company especially had built up a reputation, and Henny Porten began her career in these.[2] From its prehistory in the cinema of attractions, melodrama adopts a link between "lower" and "higher" art: the sound picture dresses the presentation of body art [*Körperkunst*] in the forms of classical opera and ballet; it orients itself toward images of bourgeois art history. In *Meissen Porcelain* [*Meißner Porzellan*, 1906] the attraction consists of allowing the movements of live bodies to appear as though they were the marionette-like dance steps of delicate rococo porcelain figurines.

In similar fashion, melodrama uses film to imitate an already existing art form. But while the sound picture consists of one scene or several successive scenes, in the melodrama one can already witness the beginnings of narrative linkage. And while opera and ballet are classical art forms, melodrama is a popularization of stage drama, a hybrid form even before it entered cinema. However, as in the sound picture, in which the cinema of attractions attempted to make itself fit into bourgeois culture by borrowing from traditional art, in melodrama narrative cinema subjugates itself to patriarchal cultural forms. It dispenses with the development of film forms taken from the presentation of female history/stories [*Geschichte*], and therefore it gives up its interest in aiding the self-expression of a female perspective. Instead, melodrama also employs music, though not in the form of specific phonograph recordings. In this case, music is not part of the scene that is presented but rather of the "scene" that is imagined: it facilitates the empathy of the audience with the events depicted on the screen.

Cruel Marriage allows one to identify a tendency to degrade the (female) story to mere content within a superimposed dramatic form, a tendency that operates through the establishment of "narrative cinema." To the extent that there is still a tension in the relationship between the depicted story and the dramatic frame, the film actress always has a chance for oppositional expression. She derives her power from the fact that lying concealed beneath the confrontation of two media—the literary medium of theater and the technical medium of film—is a confrontation of two "cultures": classical bourgeois culture and modern mass culture. The liberation of her acting style from prescribed forms is in keeping with the liberation of the mass medium from the prejudices of the prevalent culture, against which the medium could assert itself only with great difficulty. This tension, however, is exactly what is leveled in melodrama in contrast to "social drama." Social drama, which will be discussed later, breaks with the classical form through its proximity to the cinema of actualities (as Altenloh has observed) by means of documented reality: "Looked at from this perspective, an interest in newspaper articles or newsreels in the cinema is not all that different from an interest in cine-dramas. Surely, a strong reason is the devotion to the present. Film drama comes to the people by entering their everyday life."[3] In the form of melodrama, though, film is, on the one hand, cut off from the everyday life of its female spectators and, on the other, relates to them as a "folk mass"

[*Volksmasse*] as it is present in theater. In melodrama the audience finds again a familiar tradition, not a familiar reality. The promise of film to build a culture from below seems to be countered by this populist variant of drama. German melodrama did not succeed in destroying this semblance and working out the contradiction between a romantic concept of "folk art" and the modern concept of mass culture.

On the contrary, in its cult of the star the mass medium took up the romantic images of women that were carried along with this "folk art"—images that did not correspond in any way to real-life experiences within modern society—and enforced them as images that had current validity. Rather than validating the promise of cultural participation implicit in the involvement of female audiences in the cinema, melodrama, through the female star, communicates the illusion that woman is at the center of cinema. In this genre, therefore, it is primarily the concept of folk art—in its traditional sense—that is redeemed in mass culture; this means that film is art not *of* the people but *for* the people, in this case for the "female people." Not accidentally, this turn begins with women's film. In 1911 "The Name in Film Art" ["Der Name in der Filmkunst"] was still being discussed, as the title of an article by Gustav Melcher in *Der Kinematograph* no. 257 indicates. He writes, "Advertising with a name goes against 'folk art in the actual sense of the term.'" The alternative strategy for winning and retaining female mass audiences, however, would have been the involvement of women in all areas of production—though this probably would not have appealed even to a Gustav Melcher.

The relationship with dramatic form into which the stories of women are forced in film melodrama results primarily from the collapse—forced by the interests of capital—of inner tensions, of the opposition of the medium of film, and of women's will to expression as it was present in the actress. The introduction of melodrama into film makes use of the uncertain place of woman between "folk culture" and mass medium: on the one hand, melodrama promises to elevate folk art by introducing women and, at the same time, elevate the feminine into the higher spheres of dramatic art; on the other hand, it guarantees the nationwide or even worldwide dissemination of this upward movement by means of the technical medium. In Henny Porten's "self-presentations" her higher aspirations and sense of mission are unmistakable.[4] The dependence of classical tragedy on the individual, long since rendered obsolete, survives in melodrama, the heroine of which is at the center of the action, while the masses, the mob, belong to the evil powers of fate.

Film melodramas always seem as though they are secondhand. This is due not only to the mass cultural popularization of classical bourgeois art forms. Melodrama does not compose its tragedy from life experience but rather, so to speak, from the producers' experience with the presence of femininity in cinema. The tragic structure into which melodrama forces all of reality consists of nothing but the prescribed failure of a female narrative perspective, which had become possible in film, when confronted with the form of drama. Tragedy, therefore, is inscribed in the female protagonist prior to any narrative determinations; it develops neither from the reality into which the film places her nor from her story. Melodramatic heroines are static; they are not "narrators" but representatives of an always already determined femininity. Even their aura of suffering points not to a historical-societal experience that occurs outside of cinema (within which women around that time were becoming aware that a female character is not fate). Rather, this aura of suffering mystifies the repression of a female narrative perspective in cinema.

Confronted with such auratic representatives of oppressed femininity, the "reason of the heart" becomes speechless and is restricted to the inner reality of female spectators. No path leads from the ahistorical women characters of melodrama to the reality of the external world; photography becomes blind. Instead, an inner impact is organized along the lines of music. Emilie Altenloh has emphasized that female moviegoers are receptive not only to love dramas but also to musical accompaniment.[5] While the visual events on the screen remain empty, the melody stimulates dreams and memory. However, in the case of the latter every woman is by herself in the cinema. Melodrama was welcomed as the only true feature film form by those movie reformers who wanted to turn cinema into a synthesis of the arts [*Gesamtkunstwerk*] and who sought through this step to ban the emergence of an oppositional public sphere.[6]

And Woman Suffers Forever

Of the three Porten/Messter/Gärtner films from 1911 that were noted, *The Miller and His Child* is closest to the sound picture. It is the film version of an 1835 folk drama by Ernst Raupach. The story is simultaneously mundane and unreal. The daughter of a miller loves the miller's apprentice, but her rich and stingy father opposes their relationship. The apprentice leaves to work elsewhere for a while. The father falls ill, does not wish to leave his money to anyone, and sets out to bury it. Caught off guard by the returning apprentice,

he dies of shock. The daughter supposes that her lover has murdered her
father, and she sends him away. He returns only to witness her early death.

The film is produced entirely in a world of façades, with quite a bit of theater
whitewash and make-up. This aspect already prevents one from discerning the
topicality characteristic of social drama in this story. Additionally, this form
of love that opposes paternal possessiveness and the social powers of order
is granted neither a visual quality of expression nor a corporeal presentation;
rather, it is represented through music as an internal connection. A melody,
integrated diegetically as the sound of the apprentice's flute, signals the
meeting of the lovers. The film passes off as a higher virtue its negation of
its own medial quality, the visual, in order to reach inside by means of music:
dying, the woman asks her lover to step behind a curtain and play the love
melody from there, and as he plays she blissfully enters the realm of the dead.
In similar fashion melodrama veils reality and allows the female spectator to
sink into her memories and longings.

A similarly atmospheric death also awaits the heroine of *Forgotten because of Happiness*. This film, however, is not consistent. The first part unfolds the conflict between the sexes within a social context; the fictional love story is conveyed by a documenting camera. The story takes place partly in the unaltered reality of outdoor locations—the street, the station—and partly in indoor locations whose design documents the social milieu. In the second part of the film, the scenery changes; the sober quality of the gaze of the camera is not able to break through the theatricality of the acting, which is supported by the theatrical décor of the rooms. The crumbling plaster on the walls and the black make-up on pale-painted cheeks indicate an inner impasse and an attraction to death, both of which cover over the obvious lack of an externally plausible reason for the death of the woman.

The story is as follows. Engineer Brand is able to travel to the city to present his invention to a factory owner only because of the savings of his fiancée. The farewell at the station with petit bourgeois women (mother and

daughter) and the presentation of the novel arc-lamp at the grand bourgeois villa are both scenes that constitute documentary moments. The successful engineer meets the daughter of the manufacturer, and they become engaged. So far, this is a story from a world in the midst of social transition. The next intertitle reads "Forgotten because of happiness," and the melodrama begins at that moment in which a social drama would depict the role of woman in an industrializing society. The shots change their character: views of the squalid living room of the abandoned petit bourgeois woman, the cradle of the illegitimate child, and the sewing machine—the means of production of the female home worker—are obscured by the attempt to emphasize a humble life by means of a theater-like paint job on the walls and furniture. From this point on the main actress, Henny Porten, also becomes decidedly theatrical in her gestures of despair.

The presentation of the act of desperation itself, the jump into the water, once again profits from the documentary quality of the outdoor shot. The

sober quality of the shot points to the fact that illegitimate mothers have a difficult position in society. If the film were to end at this point, it could claim for itself the plausibility of a sad ending. But the suicide victim is drawn out of the water and carried to the bed in her squalid living room, and the unfaithful lover is brought to the scene of disaster, where he falls repentantly on his knees—and only then is she allowed to die. Her death is staged as a sacrifice that she makes for the redemption of the man. The dying woman, above whose hands the man bows his head, is transfigured into sublime maternity, beyond all bodily desires.

Forgotten because of Happiness makes clear how the "tragedy" of the female heroine originates in the "fate" of female narrative perspective in film. Clearly, the script by Luise del Zopp—author of about forty films between 1911 and 1914—succumbed to a production interest that placed the star at the center of directorial interest. In the first part the film shows the world of industrial progress and the possibilities for a man's advancement within it. The film does not evidence any doubt about the harmony of this society; doubt would necessarily enter the story if the woman in the film had had any chance to object. But the film systematically prevents this by separating the story of the woman from that of the man rather than, for example, using parallel montage to recount her case as being in tension with his ascent. Upon this separation, which is initially simply a fact of the story, the form of the melodramatic heroine is superimposed. The star, emphasized by her isolation, provokes the narcissistic sympathy of female spectators, such that they mirror their feelings of loneliness in the protagonist and lose sight of social conflicts. Finally, they find a happy end in the on-screen death, that is, a temporary transfiguration of their own reduced existence, a confirmation that justice will be rendered even without the effort of resistance.

The conservatism of *Tragedy of a Strike* is obvious: the woman who, from the outset, is for order and against the uprising is able in the end to convince the man—though at the cost of losing her child—that social conflict brings only disaster. Not only is the suffering of women in a male society glorified by melodrama, but the glorified image of the female victim is also utilized for a domestication of male oppositional perspectives. The actress—representative of femininity and a male projection rather than a reflection of female reality—no longer bears her own narrative perspective but enforces male order. The "reason of the heart" changes from a new narrative voice into the projective defense of reason brooding over changes in the name of speechless female sentiment.

Henny Porten, the embodiment of such sentiment, carried off the victory with her first screen appearance during the opening credits as a film star who takes a bow with a smile. The heavy-handed acting of the male protagonist cannot live up to this. He acts out the cliché of a Communist, with Russian shirt, proletarian cap, and wild mustache. This film also includes "realistic" bits: the first shot, for example, when things are still in order, presents everyday experience in a proletarian living room that combines living room, bedroom, female workplace, and child's room all in one space. The mother works at a sewing machine, and her little son plays at her feet. However, when the child gets sick, the film reverts to emotionalizing, suggestive methods. It conjures up the grim end by means of a camera that focuses on the nameplate of the casket maker rather than the details of an ambulance transporting the child.

The presentation of the strike must have appeared too "realistic" to the censors, and it by and large fell victim to them.[7] What remains is a single

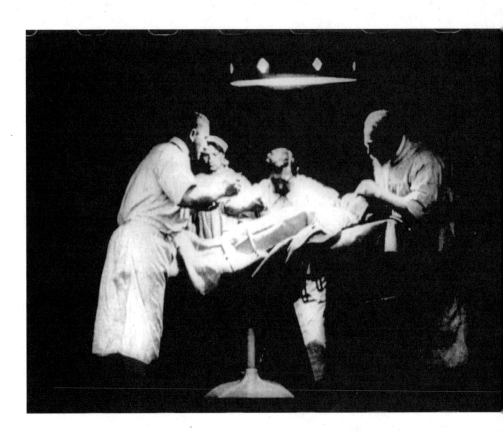

shot that shows the gesticulating body of workers from above: a gaze from a dominating position down toward insurgent reality. It is through an alluring image of woman that industrialization from above is supposed to be pushed through. "Light and Power" [*Licht und Kraft*] are indispensable, according to an intertitle that provides a textual version of the female protagonist's warning about the consequences of a strike. The writing appears on-screen as a text ribbon that flutters from the mouth of an allegory of Electricity that decorates the entrance to a power plant. The scene in the operating room presents electricity as a blessing—the operating table looks impressive in the cone of light thrown by the lamps. However, just as the text about the indispensability of this new technology does not come out of the mouth of a real woman, so too does the female protagonist over the course of the film fail to communicate the insight that technology could belong to women—or to workers. The mother, afraid for her child's life, waits passively outside in front of the operating room, a painting of the Madonna hanging over her head. When the lights go out, the "god in a white cloak" suddenly stands in the door, covered in ominous bloodstains; the workers' strike is first and foremost the defilement of a higher power. And it doesn't hurt if in addition a female spectator feels the presence of a higher law inside her vis-à-vis her husband, for whom everything is a matter of politics, a confirmation of her domestic concern for the private good.

Chapter Four

Excursus

Henny Porten, or,
The Realism of Melodrama

The beginnings of German film melodrama are inseparable from the star Henny Porten. The star phenomenon as such certainly contributed to a transformation of early cinema: the star interfered with the tension between performance and documentary mode. As the example of Asta Nielsen makes clear, a star performance could align itself with the capacity of the medium to discover and uncover. Henny Porten's performance, in contrast, never attempts to go beyond a patriarchal representation of womanhood. As a result, she fits into melodrama as though it was made for her. However, even early on Henny Porten was not just an essential support for melodrama as a genre; in addition, she became, alongside this conservative genre itself, the protagonist of German national film history. She persists unchanged from the German empire, through the Weimar years, into National Socialism, and up to the fifties as an example of *the* German woman: blond, robust, maternal, and pure.[1]

The Language of the Star

The "language" developed by Porten, from silent to sound film, is based on conventions, and it is neither derived from everyday phenomena (i.e., realist) nor expressive (i.e., originating in her body). Her conventionality stems from the trivial genres of oil painting prints, dime novels, and second-rate theater. Porten's stereotypical, repetitive expressions of shock and fear or of suffering blurred by light and her gestures of defense and heedless desperation strike one as outdated, and not just in her sound films. Her folklorelike touch is part of a culture that is itself borrowed, like the print hanging in the bedroom that derives its false glamour from its mimicry of Renaissance painting. The

affective rigidity of Porten's acting style is especially evident in those films in which camera and mise-en-scène evidence a tenderly observant sense of reality, situation, and story. *The Blue Lantern* [*Die blaue Laterne,* 1918] tells the story of the common life of a woman whose high expectations, caught between art and love, founder on the cruelty of patriarchal society. She ends up in the entertainment industry on the brink of prostitution. Focusing on interiors in which mirrors reflect certain moments and thus, almost casually, underline their significance, the film strings together episodes that mark a process of destruction. Henny Porten, however, walks through the film completely unchanged both physically and mentally; the story, her story, slides off the normative image of bourgeois womanhood. Her compulsion to communicate to the audience at every moment that, and how, she is a decent woman makes certain things incomprehensible, for example, why, of all people, this prudish, stuffy woman would be sought after as a bar hostess. Insofar as it persisted beyond the initial difficulties of the new medium of cinema, the rigidity of the appearance of the actress—the discrepancy between this appearance and the story that is being told—could on the surface be explained away by the star system. However, in the case of this "first German star," in which the genesis of a general phenomenon (i.e., a conservative form of melodrama) coincides with individual stardom, it is necessary to question what is apparently so obvious: is the rigidity of the commercialized image in accord with a certain content that is adequately communicated within this rigid form?

Henny Porten refused an entire field of acting roles, namely, anything that suggested an "unbourgeois" existence, such as the outsider, the "loose" woman, the prostitute, or the vamp. *The Blue Lantern*—a film in which she again withdrew from such a role, even though the story made it available as a possibility—raises the question of why she did not lend vivid expression to women with bourgeois moral standards, just as Asta Nielsen did for those living a marginal existence and for "escapees." Nielsen leveraged one of the primary potentials of film, the development of a language of the body. Béla Balázs described this from the perspective of film's opposition to the repressive literary culture of the bourgeoisie. The frozen corporeality of the Victorian woman signifies the way in which the expressivity of the body, along with its sexuality, is arrested. Victorian fashion—a corset, numerous pleats, long, heavy dresses—further underscores this. In the course of a reclamation of a language of the body, this repression of female expression cannot be represented directly. The content of the role—namely, a pure, maternal, robust woman who is not joyous but rather tends toward suffering and who lives within a corset of conventions, encountering sexuality only as something that comes from outside—is matched by the form of the role, its rigid, conventional gestures. The heavy-handedness and staccato nature of Porten's acting style reproduce the social limitations and isolation of the female body. A relationship to one's own body that is marked by a disturbance in the interrelationship between one's having-a-body and being-a-body also makes exchange with the outside world impossible. Such a correspondence between content and form does not have to constitute an effective affirmation; the film could, on the basis of its realist momentum, make the rigidity of the gestures appear strange [*verfremden*] and thereby point toward a female reality that is repressed. However, to become a star means to submit the realist potential of the film to the identity of the actress and thereby take the affirmative path of glorification: isolation appears as singularity.

The audience's love for Henny Porten is related to both the false glamour of the image of the star and its concealed history. The star was a mirror for women who, at the beginning of the twentieth century, modeled their life after the ideal image of the Victorian housewife; it was a mirror as well for workingwomen in the twenties who left the home under the sign of *social* motherliness. Unfortunately, though, it was not a mirror for recognition but rather for the perfection of one's own ego. The social roles of women, which women experienced in their own lives as increasingly impotent vis-à-vis the demands of industrial society, were encountered again in the cinema, on the screen, as a strength.

Henny Porten and the Women's Movement

The relationship between Henny Porten and the German women's movement is not explained away with the sentence "nor could she be stylized as an idol of female emancipation."[2] In much the same way, hints at "female productive force" that fail to take into account the political fight for this productivity, that is, the women's movement, are not enough to distinguish a recent appreciation of Henny Porten from an earlier celebration of "nature." Feminist analyses of female forms of resistance have also dealt with oppositional moments in the lives of Victorian women, for example, hysteria.[3] With her outré gestures, Henny Porten often bears more similarity to a hysteric than to female primal nature—also, and especially, whenever she plays the common woman "in the street." The conservative wing of the women's movement drew upon the fact that a denial of sexuality, as much as it might mean a repression of one's own drives and desires, could also present, externally, an independence from man and thereby the beginnings of personal autonomy. This attitude of the conservative wing traces an arc from Victorianism to the twenties, an arc that is also traced by Henny Porten's star imago. "Conservative" is the term for that part of the women's movement that insists on bourgeois sexual morals and uses them to fight against male privilege, against the experienced double standard. They condemn "free love" but, as early as the nineteenth century, advocate for the right of the unmarried woman who abstains from sexuality and motherhood to self-realization in her job and advocate for her as a social and spiritual person. In abstention the conservative women's movement also sees the possibility that motherhood, rather than being experienced in the context of the family, can be developed in society as social motherliness. In the Weimar Republic such modest ideas of sexual equality, of ways in which female characteristics could be included in male society in compensatory fashion, gained social influence beyond the scope of the women's movement.

Henny Porten fits squarely within the problem presented by the conservative women's movement. Early films like *Pearls Mean Tears* [*Perlen bedeuten Tränen*] and *An Artist's Love* [*Künstlerliebe*] thematize the moral double standard; however, and more importantly, the female nature that Porten is supposed to depict arrives at its "fulfillment" in marriage and motherhood only in rare cases. And even when such fulfillment is the case, disturbances occupy the foreground far more than the happy ending. The films are not concerned primarily with the joys of motherhood but rather with the social regimentation of the husband by means of the child: whether, as in *Tragedy of a Strike*, for example, this means that the husband's union activities are halted or whether, as in *Alexandra—Revenge Is Mine* [*Alexandra—die Rache ist mein*, 1914], this means that an illegitimate child calls into question the libertinage of the aristocracy—under the pretense, of course, that the heroine insists on moral standards herself and perishes when she makes a slip. Whether strict, educating, or nourishing-caring, motherhood—which, throughout Porten's films, is a substitute for equality between the sexes—is directed above all at man. In *Alexandra* an illegitimate mother orders her former lover to visit her after she has lost her child and atoned for this in prison: as a dark angel of revenge, she forces him to admit his guilt. In *Refuge* [*Zuflucht*, 1928] Porten depicts a nourishing-caring woman—a market woman—in relationship to Martin (played by Franz Lederer), the son of a factory owner who returns home from the Soviet Republic, tired of revolution. Comedies, on the other hand, enable orality to be presented as a direct displacement of sexuality onto eating, as in *Kohlhiesel's Daughters* [*Kohlhiesels Töchter*, 1920], in which love and the withdrawal of love are openly dealt with in the realms of chowing down and guzzling.

A protective shell against man functions as the condition for individual autonomy and even an uprising against patriarchy: Kohlhiesel's ugly daughter, made up to look like every man's nightmare, rules the house, including her father, who is unable even to throw a drunk out of his bar. As much as Porten's look of suffering seems false, she looks "right" whenever she isn't trying to act out inner movement and instead depicts an aggressive character by means of external movements and actions in space. A classic example of the combination of the (Brunhilde) myth of the aggressive woman, on the one hand, with Victorian reality, on the other (a woman shielded from love can stand up to man as an equal), can be found in the figure of the woman named Vulture Wally from the film based on the 1875 novel written by Wilhelmine von Hillern [*Die Geier-Wally*].[4] In Henny Porten, Vulture Wally found her first cinematic embodiment. There is only one step from the presentation of sublime frigidity and rigid sexual morals to the fantasy of a battle between the sexes, a step that leads closer to repressed reality. The compact nature of Porten's body, always "armed" with skirts and camisole and never articulate, here arrives at its genuine expressive sense: to prevent the appeal of the other sex from coming too close, and to prevent one's own feelings of affection from being expressed, affords a certain freedom of movement. She knocks down a presumptuously bossy suitor and sends a murderer after the lover who ridiculed her, only to save him later by means of the same strength with which she also defeated the vulture. The free, unrestricted movements of Vulture Wally amid the towering mountain landscape point beyond the love plot. Instead, what becomes manifest is a potential for action that is a result of a renunciation of domestic happiness and a rejection of the father's protection. Yet that freedom that the women's movement hoped to achieve was to occur within a social space. In the myth of Vulture Wally nature is a projection. However, in this 1921 film the mountain world is barely dramatized; the mountain is not yet "calling."[5] Photographic realism therefore breaks with myth in favor of a focus on the skill and audacity of the actress.

In her role as Vulture Wally, Henny Porten has retained, even into the present, her attraction for a female audience. An identification (mediated by voyeurism) with the strong, defensive woman—who essentially only narcissistically loves in man the mirror image of her own strength—condones the repression of sexuality. The adoration of Henny Porten by girls and young women—Marlene Dietrich admired her, for example—is the theme of films such as *The Scandal of Eva* [*Skandal um Eva*, 1930] and *24 Hours in the Life of a Woman* [*24 Stunden aus dem Leben einer Frau*, 1931]. Just as lived heterosexuality plays no role in this female character, so too does it lack a lesbian component. However, the asexuality of her appearance makes it available for pubertal projections. In *The Scandal of Eva*, Henny Porten plays a "Fräulein Doktor" adored by her female students. While *Vulture Wally* depicted the dream of the rebellious woman, Porten, in her role as a comradely girls' school teacher and sovereign governess of grown-up men, could also serve as an advocate for the conservative women's movement. Though directed by Georg Wilhelm Pabst, the film did not draw upon its potential for displacing repressed sexuality onto the sadistic manipulation of men. Aside from the initial scenes, the film collapses into boring and pointless episodes whenever the teacher acts as a judge of the love affairs of her male colleagues.

Masochistic Scopophilia

Strength based upon the renunciation of desire can transform itself directly into the sacrifice that lies at its base. Not just within her repertoire of women's roles but also within the films themselves Porten often switches from cheerful strength to suffering and collapse. Sacrifice is always presented as corporeal without ever being expressed as corporeal experience. Yet her conventional style makes it possible for immediate injury and denigration to be reflected as a metaphor for structural injuries to femininity in society. While a denial of love constitutes an important dramaturgic moment within Henny Porten films, the fact that she herself conveys the impression that an honorable woman has nothing to do with sexuality is even more fundamental. The maternal aura should be absolutely pure. This interest leads to a reanimation of the idea of immaculate conception—Lotte in the 1928 film of the same name gives birth to her child in a sacred space, close by people who are praying in the church in expectation of her child. "This child does not need a father," the film claims. Porten conveys the impression that she has little interest in love; often, she acts out sexual encounters as resistance to something terrible through which she must then suffer and the consequences of which she must bear like guilt. This is the case with her roles as Rose Bernd, as Alexandra, and as Christa Hartungen. For Helga Venroh in *24 Hours in the Life of a Woman*, sexual intercourse becomes an act of salvation and as such it is justified: she sacrifices herself to it in order to prevent a man from committing suicide (though even this turns out to be, finally, in vain).

Sweet litanies of renunciation, suffering, denigration, and self-sacrifice: not coincidentally, the iconography of this star finds a tradition in the colorful pictures of saints. Films, always new and always the same, become the text of redemption in the age of a new form of reproducibility—a text no less profane than the Lutheran Bible. Only now, stripped of its claim to revelation, the sociopsychic functionality of the filmic "text" becomes apparent in its reception. Henny Porten's stories of passion constitute a medium that enables one to enjoy one's own situation of miserable oppression. They affirm and support a tendency that is ambivalent in its meaning: to enjoy repression means to have come to terms with it, but it also means to develop a sense of self that establishes a distance from external violence.

The enjoyment of suffering constitutes itself through a voyeuristic pleasure that one takes in the star. Porten stands in for the suffering of the victim and she is at the same time a woman with beauty and power. The melodramatic mode conserves and intensifies such pleasure. Everything of understanding, everything of rational reaction, is absorbed back into emotion. On the one hand, this is achieved quite literally in melodrama by means of music. According to rumors, Henny Porten always acted her roles before the camera accompanied by music—and, of course, silent films were at that time shown with a musical accompaniment as well. On the other hand, "sentimentalization" is also created by camera work and editing. The realist element of film is reduced to linking the nonrealist performance with the experience in the mind of the female spectator. Consequently, the drama is not situated in a reality that film, as a photographic medium, discloses to the audience, as was the case in early social drama; rather, it is integrated into the world in the mind of the female spectator. Melodrama intensifies the interior world and regulates it as well. Alone with herself and her mirror image, a woman in the cinema can give herself over to the echo of feelings that are never lived out.

Backstairs [*Hintertreppe,* 1921] is the only film with Henny Porten that consciously rids itself of everything melodramatic. In order to accomplish this the film does not take the route of social documentary but rather that of a mannered overemphasis of conventions. *Backstairs* was not a success with the audience.

Chapter Five

Contradictions
of Social Drama

Around 1911–12 film producers made determined attempts to fit cinema into the aesthetic cosmos of bourgeois culture. This was their answer to the heavy assault by movie reformers. One attempt to gain respectability took the route of a different choice of material [*Stoff*]. However, the attempt by cinema to encompass classical literature was not immediately welcomed. Many self-proclaimed advocates of culture saw this as an insult to cultural treasures. German producers had just as little luck with film versions of national histori-cal events: *Theodor Körner* [1912] and *The Film of Queen Luise* [*Der Film von der Königin Luise*, 1912] received little positive response from the nationalist cultural bourgeoisie. The film adaptation was severely criticized:

> And now to the German film dramas, to the patriotic ones, which are supposed to sow good seeds in German youth: this is about the education of youth, a state's most important task; these are *Queen Luise* and *Theodor Körner*. In terms of technique, both are below average: the images lack both depth and breadth; one only sees chopped-up fragments, and never gets an impression of the whole as it is provided by reality. Everything seems obtrusive.
>
> The content—what shall I say? No one would claim that Germany lacks a poet, a director, and actors who could visualize the grand epic of the wars of liberation in a more worthy form and in all its essential moments. What we see here, though, are melodramatic pieces [*Rührstücke*] à la *Gartenlaube*.[1] Four times we see the queen amongst her children. Even the *Iliad* features a scene with children, but it comes up at that moment when Hector marches into a life-and-death battle. Filmed this way, without events, the scenes come across as shallow and obtrusive; it could be any other arbitrary mother who plays with her children here.[2]

**Familienglück.
Für diese Aufnahme wurde
uns die Benutzung des
Original-Kinderwagens des
nachmaligen
Kaiser Wilhelm I. gestattet.**

Certainly, the two films cited here exhibit a wooden clumsiness. However, at the same time, in these films the medium exhibits its democratizing and demythologizing effect. Malwine Rennert, whose critique is quoted above, finds fault with the technical limitations of the images; it is "depth" as an ideological quality, though, that she ultimately finds lacking in the films. The lives of the sovereigns in the film seem "shallow," trivial, like those of "normal" people. She emphasizes, as a contrast, a form of contemporary French production, the *film d'art,* which impressed people with its opulent décor and scenes of masses and encouraged the development of German art film production. This first female critic of German cinema, however, soon shifted her interests exclusively to Italian monumental films. For the patriotic cultural bourgeoisie, the impressive "emotionalizing" [*Pathetisierung*] of history in films such as *Quo vadis* (1912), *Cabiria* (1914), and *Cajus Julius Cäsar* (1915) was exemplary. History should be presented as a chain of great

"events" rather than being dragged down into the lowlands of mass cultural everyday life.

With respect to the material of "high" culture, "low" art is remarkable primarily for its effort to level; melodrama, in contrast, found a form to lend "event character" to the everyday. The social problems of women are stylized into the special tragedy of an exceptional woman, and they thus become metaphysical. The incorporation, by melodrama, of the "monstrous" [*ungeheuer*] power of the new medium is achieved by means of a "higher" form rather than a higher material. The development of a narrative cinema for female audiences must have seemed especially unsettling [*nicht geheuer*] for the bourgeoisie: what happens when women en masse see their own reality reflected in the cinema, when repressive gender roles are not only discussed by an enlightened bourgeoisie but represented to a mass audience by the disillusioning, "shallow" medium of film?

Melodrama asserts itself against the documentary quality of the medium, a documentary quality that is, little by little, forced out of entertainment cinema in general only to be tied more closely to war-related tasks during the war. Yet melodrama did not entirely dominate narrative cinema; in close proximity social drama increased in importance. In social drama dramatic form acts as an external censor that keeps the development of a female narrative perspective within bounds but does not yet force its resignation in favor of a representation of femininity within the dramatic form. The strength of the [female] narrative perspective is derived from its foundation in the cinema of attractions. This first cinematic form does not yield to the interest of bourgeois entertainment cinema as quickly as—from one film to another or even within a single film—documentary qualities disappear in favor of theatrical effects.

Social dramas might not transgress traditional gender roles, but they throw new light upon them. Like comedies, they own a subversive gaze at the body, at the life of the drives. However, social dramas are motivated less by the contradiction between body and social role than by their objection to an identification of body and role in the ideology of natural femaleness. Social dramas alternate between the depiction of stories of mistresses, on the one hand, and those of wives, on the other. In this way they unsettle the customary dichotomy between Madonna and whore; they comply neither with moral prejudices nor exclusively with the male gaze. Rather, they allow one to understand the social element of the "natural" function of woman— woman as sexual object—as much as they present, in the social position of the wife, her sexual "fate."

The Mistress: Mediation of Female Narrative Perspective through the Cinema of Attractions

Films such as *In Vain* [*Vergebens*, 1911], *The Way Home: Step by Step. A Model's Life-Confession* [*Heimgefunden: Von Stufe zu Stufe. Lebensbeichte einer Probiermamsell*, 1912], *Pearls Mean Tears* [*Perlen bedeuten Tränen*, 1911], *By a Hair's Breadth* [*Um Haaresbreite*, 1912], and *Madeleine* [1912] exemplify the fact that the form of melodrama is not yet dominant in this period. Amongst these films, *In Vain* and *The Way Home* demonstrate most clearly how the autonomy of the story, vis-à-vis dramatic form, goes hand in hand with a suspension of prevailing moral prejudices. These films are not about the contradictions of marriage, as are *Cruel Marriage* and *Reason of the*

Heart, but rather concern that quasi-institutionalized form of extramarital sexuality, "the mistress."

In Vain begins with a scene from "high society": the gentlemen gamble while the ladies, more or less bored, stand around. One gentleman seizes an opportunity to ogle one of the ladies; he then "abducts" her, taking her into the garden. While they sit on a bench outside, flirting with one another, one of the plump elderly men inside becomes nervous—but before he can make up his mind to interrupt the game and find out what is going on, a female friend fixes the situation and brings the lady back from the garden. The latter excuses her absence by claiming to have had a sudden migraine.

This flirtation has consequences: the next day, when the older gentleman comes to visit this same lady (who is apparently supported by him), she wards off his approaches by again claiming that she has a migraine. Even giving her flowers and reading aloud to her do not cheer her up. As soon as he has left the house, however, she jumps up, alive and well, to receive her new conquest. She tries to seduce the stately gentleman with lascivious gestures, but he remains stiff and demure. Eventually, it becomes clear why this is the case—he wants to marry her, "if you will lead a decent life during my three-month absence," the intertitle states. She is moved and impulsively agrees.

"Two months later" we indeed see her transformed in the direction of "decency." She wears a dark dress with a small lace collar, and the "evil bed" [*Lotterbett*] in her room is missing—yet absent as well is any attraction for the female spectator. Suddenly, the friend comes in: "Your old friend is downstairs—shall I call him up?" The lady does not resist for very long: "Back to her old life." A bit later, though, she receives a telegram from her

fiancé: "I have achieved my goal, I have become a rich man, I will pick you up tonight." For a moment this message throws the unfaithful woman into remorseful desperation until her friend calms her: "He doesn't have to find out!" In the evening the fiancée is in a state of "joyful anticipation." The gentleman arrives and joyfully greets her, but he also looks warily around the apartment. Not finding anything suspicious, he orders her to pack her belongings and promises to pick her up soon. Yet as soon as she is alone again, her old lover, who does not want to give her up, reappears. She begs him to let her go. He apparently agrees; however, instead of departing, he hides in the apartment, visible to the audience. In the moment that the fiancé returns he steps between the two and their happiness. "In vain" the woman tries to calm her future husband; she begs him not to leave her—but to him, the situation is obvious. He departs, leaving behind the former couple, now reunited. The "winner" fetches some wine and offers a glass to his mistress, who empties it in one gulp and then throws it away in order to open her arms in a gesture that is both reconciliatory and desiring . . .

The prosaic style of the narrative is a function of the fact that an interest in "attractions" is more pronounced than an interest in patriarchal morality. An "attraction" is constituted by a gaze at a world determined by sexual needs and desires. The relationship of this film to the spicy "gentlemen's films" is obvious: in both the actress is the object of their voyeurism. Yet this is not all. She is a narrative subject as well, since her perspective determines what we see, namely, what she is doing behind the back of one or the other gentleman. She seeks her own pleasure and advantage, and in the figure of her female friend the female spectator finds herself represented as an "accomplice." Yet those perspectives of the female protagonist that aim at having it *all,* sexual pleasure as well as social status, are restrained by the dramatic "superstructure" [*Überbau*] of the story. With respect to this superstructure, the male protagonist does not take voyeuristic pleasure in the female body but rather is bearer of the controlling gaze. The fact that this gaze produces the dramatic conflict has already been suggested when, in the first sequence, the portly elderly gentleman looks around nervously, thus prompting the woman in the garden to interrupt her flirtation and return to the party. Over the course of the rest of the film this gaze remains "off-screen": the friend comes in and says, "He is waiting downstairs." At this point the man does not appear as someone who exerts control, as in the first sequence, during which the friend took on a mediating role as well, but rather as a temptation, to which the woman gives in for the sake of her own desire. In this way *her* story asserts itself, and there is no particularly dramatic acting out of the conflict. The choice between lust and obligation has to be made by the female subject.

At the end of the film, in contrast, the controlling male gaze is once more visibly represented, now thwarting the woman's plans. She is even twice subject to this gaze: the returning fiancé looks around the apartment with a scrutinizing gaze but is deceived. The lover's form of control is more effective, for he hides, awaiting the return of the rival so that he can win back the woman by revealing himself. The controlling gaze, which produces the drama, is not yet directed at the guilt of the woman but rather at preserving her as the object of desire. Hence the circle is closing: the drama that restrains the narrative perspective of woman acts for the male gaze in the cinema of attractions. There, however, it meets the gaze of the woman again: the heroine of *In Vain* does not react dramatically to the failure of the marriage but takes the impossibility of attaining a "proper" social status as an opportunity to continue her "improper" story. The husband-to-be disappears from the woman's life as though he had never existed; what counts is the appearance in the flesh of her lover, whom she provoked into action with her story.

The title *The Way Home: Step by Step. A Model's Life-Confession* could have originated in contemporary enlightened women's literature. Likewise, the story of the film—a "proper" female employee is seduced to a life as a "mistress"—corresponds to cases that were described by the women's movement in order to set into motion emancipatory processes of reflection and self-reflection. Rehabilitation rather than social condemnation of "fallen" women was the goal of contemporary radical sexual politics; in 1914, for example, the magazine

The New Generation [*Die neue Generation*] published two series entitled "From the Life of a Prostitute" ["Aus dem Leben einer Prostituierten"] and "From the Notes of a Prostitute" ["Aus den Aufzeichnungen einer Prostituierten"].[3]

The Way Home also comes across as if it were "written down by herself." On the one hand, the film is shot with a documenting camera that savors the attractions of outdoor shots; on the other hand, it is staged with an eye for sexual curiosity and avoids melodramatic tendencies entirely. The female protagonist is seduced, but she is not stylized into a victim who awaits her inevitable death. Rather than representing patriarchal morality, she conveys sexual and documentary attractions to female audiences through her story. They look at the "world" along with her.

The Way Home is about Elise, who has an ordinary background and works at a dressmaker's shop. Her promotion to clothing model [*Probiermamsell*] brings her into contact with genteel customers. A count who visits the store together with his matronly wife is less interested in the latest fashion than in the girl who presents it. Elise agrees to a rendezvous and soon becomes the mistress of the count. He rents her her own apartment and spoils her with clothes and jewelry. These presents help her overcome the pangs of remorse over leaving her parents and fiancé. During an enjoyable evening at the "Maxim," she makes the acquaintance of Natas, an engineer, who courts her. When he comes to visit her, the count catches the two of them by surprise, and he not only throws out his rival but decides to leave Elise as well. She moves on to the engineer, who turns out to be a gambler, and eventually he also makes use of her jewelry. Disappointed in this way, Elise yearns for her home. Her father sends her away, but her fiancé runs after her and prevents her in her state of misery from throwing herself in front of a train. In the end her father must also reconcile with her.

As "confession" [*Beichte*], the story of *The Way Home* is comparable to the confession [*Geständnis*] in *Cruel Marriage;* however, the division between dramatic court scene, in which the question that is negotiated is that of "guilty or not guilty," and the nonjudgmental story of the woman, which just reproduces the facts, has been abandoned. Instead, the film begins with the story of the woman, and the moral authority, that is, the father, who appears at the end to turn the story into a drama after all, does not get the final word with his "guilty" verdict. At the only really dramatic point in the film, when the protagonist wants to throw herself in front of a train, it is her fiancé who intervenes; he, like the spectator, has a greater interest in the corporeal presence of the actress—in the life of the "heroine"—than in enforcing moral judgments. The female protagonist might not convey a new form of morality through her story (she comes back to marriage, after all), but the narration of her life story relativizes the prevailing morality and its dramatic representation, thus marking it as something that is life threatening and that puts an end to exhibitionist storytelling. The latter is rescued for the spectator by the actions of the fiancé. After her odyssey in the garden of earthly delights, the heroine walks, simultaneously, into the loving arms of her future husband and into the approving gaze of the spectator; thus, the spectator has had his fun, but not at the price of having to see the "whore" destroyed.

Narrative in *The Way Home* draws its strength from reflecting, again, the cinema of attractions; in doing so the film turns the initial formulation of the female protagonist's own standpoint itself into an attraction. In general, the story is presented by means of a plain sequence of scenes, each of which is autonomously arranged and shot according to its "attractivity" [*Schauwert*] rather than to its function within the film as a whole. "At home" Elise is "the sunshine of her parents" as well as that of her groom; but she is also attractive to the audience. At the tailor shop we get insight into the working conditions and means of production of this craft. Sewing machines stand in a row, cloth and completed dresses are everywhere, fashion sketches hang on the walls, and, at the center of our gaze, we see a mannequin dressed in the design that is currently in production. A number of women work as the boss, a man, comes in. A short dramatic scene is embedded in the presentation of the milieu, which is also produced by the controlling gaze of the man. The boss scrutinizes his employees—he is looking for a new model, and eventually he picks Elise.

The following scene again allows for insight into the working environment, since it shows Elise at work as a clothing model. The gentleman who accompanies his wife focuses more on Elise than on the dress that she presents, and thus he takes on the gaze of the assessing boss; but while the boss selected her for promotion on the basis of her attractive appearance, the gentleman chooses to make her his object of desire. For added piquancy, the count slips her a letter that requests a rendezvous.

The meeting takes place in front of a café. The camera looks over the shoulder of the man (who is standing on the other side of the street) as it focuses on Elise; she is standing, somewhat embarrassed and indecisive, in front of the café. On the one hand, the camera takes up the voyeuristically possessive male gaze, but on the other, it places the woman in the midst of the urban hustle and bustle of the big city; interest in documenting this "atmosphere" is thus

on a par with the formulation of the male gaze. The count is just about to light a cigar as she enters the field of vision: the pleasure in waiting. He crosses the street with the cigar in his hand, while the camera remains in place and records the two disappearing into the café.

Inside the café the man and woman sit, close to the camera, next to a window, which enables a view of the heavy traffic on the street and the pedestrians who walk by. Light from outside illuminates the faces of the couple. A street scene follows in which both leave the café and enter a carriage. This informs us about the further course of events, but it also gives in to the attractions of the street scenes, which were only vaguely visible through the window.

The following scene, in which the fiancé and the parents are informed by letter of Elise's new life, seems similarly informed by a consideration of the audience's interest in following the story. It is the only scene in the entire film in which Elise is not present—a seeming inconsistency within the subjective narrative structure of a confession. However, the shot centers on the written

note that the fiancé has received from Elise: "Forgive me, I have found happiness, I am not coming back home." The scene therefore actually strengthens the position of the narrative subject. The writing of the woman takes the place of her physical presence, and it refers—not simply with respect to its content—to her as subject.

The most elaborate scene of the entire film is devoted to the situation of the kept mistress; it not only characterizes the "milieu," but it also turns a glimpse of the subjective perspective of such a woman into an attraction sui generis. In dishabille Elise sits at her toiletry table, where she can look in a mirror and admire her new status. She gazes into a small hand mirror, but, rather than providing a general image of her external appearance, it presents figures from her inner life. Artfully, in the oval of the mirror a lamenting mother, wringing her hands, and a scolding father appear one after the other, each tiny like a little doll. The camera enthralls us exclusively by means of this little trick, and it presents conscience as a visual attraction rather than by means of gestures and facial expressions that reveal an agitated inner life. After this short trip into the arena of the trick film, the film returns to the milieu: the door opens and the count enters the room, laden with hat and clothing boxes. The apparitions have disappeared, and Elise takes delight in unpacking the presents.

The idea of using a trick is an example of how strictly the film bases its narrative on the "principle of numbers" rather than submitting narrative to dramatic form.[4] The film alludes to Elise's old ties—ties that create conflict in the protagonist despite her clear decision to embrace her new life—by means of an internal montage that leaves the frame of the scene untouched. At the same time, the autonomy of the scene supports the autonomy of the woman in the film: a parallel montage would have withdrawn the reactions of the parents from the gaze (and control) of the heroine and provided the audience with the possibility of turning against her emotionally and identifying with the parents rather than with the gaze of the "lost daughter" at her parents. The film would have endowed the moral superego with power over the female narrator.

Instead, in the next scene the film allows the protagonist and the audience a further taste of the pleasures of the world of entertainment. We get a glimpse of what goes on at the "Maxim." There the women enjoy themselves at least as much as the men; they drink wine and Champagne with exuberant cheerfulness and dance with one another. Elise enjoys the libertine erotic atmosphere as well. In the end she is accompanied to her carriage not just by the count but also by her "new acquisition," the engineer. When this scene was filmed, a large number of onlookers must have been present: they look at the camera with curiosity. Early films did not have to worry that attention not motivated by the story would break the illusion; as long as cinema drew its impact from the attraction of single scenes, the astounded people in the film only reflected a spell that is like that of the people in front of the screen.

Nor, when she is caught in her act of infidelity, is the woman presented as a helpless victim plagued by pangs of remorse. Exhibiting all the signs of rage that her count is throwing her out, Elise leaves the apartment. It is only two episodes later that she feels completely exposed, when the engineer dictatorially demands her jewelry, her only asset, in order to be able to pay his gambling debts. Intimidated, she hands over the casket. As soon as he is gone, however, she vents her anger and decides that she won't continue her existence as a mistress under these conditions. The memory of her old life becomes powerful, and "Elise longs to go home."

While the two older lovers—both portly and mustached—were essentially already reverse images of the father as moral authority, the end of the film brings his disempowerment to completion. "Go away, wretched one," says the father, as expected; her fiancé pleads for her in vain. She departs.

We see her leave the house and walk through the front yard; it is simply a normal late afternoon. In the next shot she crosses an open field in the direction of the train tracks. In the distance a train approaches, but before the audience can draw any conclusions as to why she is walking through the field, they already see the groom, who has followed her and who now takes her into his arms. The train passes by. This whole sequence derives its effect not by means of drama, that is, the creation of emotional tension, but rather, in this case too, by means of the attraction of the outside shot of the railway area and the passing train. The sober poetry of the gaze of the camera, in which technology and nature shine reconciled, also envelops the steps of the heroine until the end—she is the precise opposite of that suggestion of a higher power of fate that would, in the end, overtake those who have gone astray. At the end of the film, the pleasure of the men in the woman—who has moved on from the lovers to the groom—joins with her self-affirmation of her life against male authority. In early narrative cinema, which concentrates on "social drama," male voyeuristic pleasure is mediated by the assertion of a female perspective.

The Wife: Dramatization of the World of Things

The marriage that *The Way Home* does not end up depicting but only hints at toward the end would not restore patriarchal order but would instead seal the physical love between social subjects. Other "social dramas" deal with typical marriage in patriarchal society: depictions of the lives of wives are, like the narrative style of the stories of "mistresses," prosaic and attractive at the same time. *Pearls Mean Tears* (1911) narrates the development of a lieutenant's marriage: from nuptial infatuation to the boring marriage routine, to the husband's affair and the wife's patient effort to reestablish balance, up to their reconciliation. *By a Hair's Breadth* (1912) presents a grand bourgeois marriage in which a husband finds his club as important as his home, with his wife, child, and servants. That creates problems. Male friendship is disturbed by the friend's approaches to the wife. The husband's family life is threatened in turn by the relationship between the men, which has turned hostile. The safety of the household rests solely on the steadfastness of the wife.

Even though both films are Messter productions that star Henny Porten (one is directed by Adolf Gaertner; the other, by Curt Starck), they do not dramatize the suffering of a woman within her marriage. Rather, they recount scenes from a marriage and depict the milieu: the documenting camera works against the sentimentalizing perception of a staged, performed life-drama. As the marriage becomes more endangered in *Pearls Mean Tears,* there is a wonderful street scene. The shot shows a jewelry store (the shop display can be seen in all its detail); then the heroine comes into view and disappears into the store. The shot is, photographically, very precise, and at the same time it has a poetic quality as a result of the way in which light and dark values and the effects of reflections of light are handled; as such, it clarifies and concentrates our gaze at the woman's walk. A melodramatic sense of self-sacrifice ["*Opfergang*"]—she is selling her pearl necklace in order to settle the debts of her lover—cannot arise. In *By a Hair's Breadth* the depictions of the dramatic events between rivals—one dies from a poacher's bullet; the other takes flight, since he is suspected of murder—are stretched out in time rather than concentrated dramatically. The film loses itself in the attractions of landscape shots, images of seemingly endless flight and pursuit through forests and fields and across rivers.

Yet there is a formal change in these marriage films vis-à-vis the narratives from the world of the "mistress," even vis-à-vis a film such as *Cruel Marriage. The Way Home* relativized the dramatic form into a male frame of judgment that restrained the female narrative perspective so that it became part of the story itself. *Pearls Mean Tears* and *By a Hair's Breadth,* in contrast, develop a new dramatic effect through an element of the story. Both films feature objects whose meaning transcends the immanence of the narrative and creates tension, that is, suspense, with respect to the solution to the "puzzle." The newly married young woman receives a pearl necklace as a present from her mother-in-law together with a letter: "They always say 'pearls mean tears,' but they have brought only luck to *me!*" From this moment on the female spectator waits to discover whether the superstition will assert itself or whether an enlightened standpoint will be confirmed. It is the experience of the gift-giver rather than the popular saying that proves to be true, so that the "significant object" [*bedeutsamer Gegenstand*] creates a dramatic tension in the minds of female audiences, a dramatic tension that addresses traditional ideas of fate even as it criticizes them.

In *By a Hair's Breadth* the rival, as he is dying alone in the forest, writes a letter in which he admits that the husband is innocent. The wind picks up the piece of paper and blows it away. From that moment on the audience is in a state of tension: Will the letter be found? Can it fulfill its redemptive function? A playing child picks up the letter in order to wrap a bouquet of flowers within it. Thus, chance and the love of a child assist the word of reason

in preventing a threatening fate, that is, revenge. The pearls in one case and the letter in the other create an expectation that distracts from the story, which concerns the routine of marriage. The pleasure that one takes in the individual scenes, which are carefully documented and set up and shot in an appealing fashion, is overlaid by a desire that pushes toward the solution to the "puzzle." As forms of "puzzle-creating" ["*Verrätselung*"] suspense, the scenes themselves eventually tend to obtain a new quality that restrains the effect of the documenting camera.

This new quality consists in the stimulation of voyeuristic libido without anything explicitly erotic being presented on-screen. This is the case because in the marriage stories significant objects substitute for the spicy attractions that were otherwise offered in scenes with the "mistress." Since bourgeois marriage is not an institution of sexual pleasure (rather, it is taboo to take the wife as a public object of desire), the female protagonist cannot be openly presented as an attraction to the male gaze. As a consequence, in the marriage films a decisive moment of the cinema of attractions is missing, a moment with which the female story had affiliated itself in order to resist the establishment of bourgeois-patriarchal cinema. The suspense created by the process of solving the thing-puzzle substitutes for an erotic attraction that could have consisted in the heroine's negligee or in the hero's kiss on her mouth. However, by means of this tension of suspense, sexual excitement, even though it is repressed, continues to exert an effect. At the same time, and in a form that is detached from the female image, this excitement is generalized and also communicated to the other sex.

To watch everyday stories of marriage with a secret pleasure is more risqué for women than for men. Sexual pleasure [*Lust*] was not just a taboo in Wilhelminian bourgeois marriages; it barely existed at all for women. Because of the mistress and the prostitute, men did not have to forgo sexual pleasure. However, for women, repression of sexuality in marriage was equivalent to a repression of their sexuality in general. How much more it must have meant a break with their everyday experience, then, to watch the complications of marital life with lustful expectation in the movie theater. Thus, this form of marriage drama continues the development of a narrative cinema of attractions with an eye on female audiences. Cinema enables a gaze at the world of mistresses and prostitutes for women as an audience that can cast off money [*kapitalträchtig*]. A gaze at marriage not just as an institution for reproduction but also as a dramatic form of women's sex life is organized specifically in order to canalize the sexual curiosity that has been released.

In Wilhelminian cinema, men were able to satisfy their sexual desires with far fewer inhibitions. This cinema provided them with "separate presentations" [*Separat-Vorstellungen*] and "gentlemen's nights." Admittedly, *Der Kinematograph* claimed as early as 1908 that cinema had become "morally clean"

[*sittenrein*].[5] Yet the production of pornographic films seems to have continued, even though it was under the observance of the censors. An advertisement in the October 6, 1909, issue of the same journal, for example, seeks "spicy films (officially authorized)" for a cabaret. In contrast, issue 189 (August 10, 1910) reports on a "lawsuit against the producers of obscene films":

> This case is singular in criminal statistics, and it has caused a great stir. Eighteen films are incriminated, most of them shot in the Moritzburg forests, with titles such as *Harem Pleasures* [*Haremsfreuden*], *Stolen Innocence* [*Geraubte Unschuld*], *The Involuntary Bath* [*Das unfreiwillige Bad*], *The Ruthless Hoodlum* [*Der unbarmherzige Strolch*], *Lesbian Love* [*Lesbische Liebe*], *Monk and Nun* [*Mönch und Nonne*], *The Butterfly Hunt* [*Die Schmetterlingsjagd*], *The Blueberry Pickers* [*Die Heidelbeersucher*], and so on. The people involved received 5–10 marks to participate in the filming. The lawsuit does not serve the interests of an expansion of cinematography, since it [the lawsuit] is being exploited by many enemies.

Around this period economic interests had already begun to sweep pornography into the ill-lit dirty corners of mass society rather than bringing it from the closed "gentlemen's nights" out into the public. However, in self-conscious fashion one of the preserved pornographic films "takes revenge" on this entrance of prudery into cinema.[6] This short film has the title *Newly Married* [*Jung vermählt*], and it strings together three "couple scenes" that depict the progression from the arrival of the newlyweds at their home up to the consummation of the marriage in bed. Every scene is obviously played by a different couple, but the artful montage, by focusing attention on the course of the sexual events, makes one forget this fact. The first of these scenes, in which the couple, festively dressed, just as they should be, unpack a present from Mother, is simply taken from the Messter film *Pearls Mean Tears*. When at the end of the scene the couple leaves the room through a door to the right, the next scene, in which another couple enters a salon from the left, follows with logical consistency. However, now the woman begins to undress, while the man watches her, and in the third part we are in the bedroom, where the moving events take place beneath the covers.

Especially in the context of the displacement of pornography, attempts to canalize the sexual curiosity of women are not simply repressive but also productive. The integration of erotic attraction into stories about women lays open the social problem of sexual difference. The dramatization of the female narrative by means of an objectlike element inherent in the story itself reflects the social relationship, the marriage, back onto the repressed conditions of sexuality. Essentially, both *Pearls Mean Tears* and *By a Hair's Breadth* are simply films about men's decreasing sexual interest [i.e., in their wives] and the pleasures men locate for their spare time, which are grounded in homoeroticism. What one man finds in an officer's casino, another finds in a club; one relaxes with a ballet dancer, while the other goes hunting.

Social marriage dramas manage to not just convey a female narrative perspective by means of the cinema of attractions; instead, they convey both narrative perspective and cinema of attractions via the form of drama. It is in this mediation that the real importance of objects that advance to the level of actors is to be found. On the one hand, they are everyday objects that play a role as such over the course of the story. On the other hand, though, they have a fetish character insofar as they substitute for the openly erotic attractions of the "mistress" films. In this case they stand in for the sexuality that is repressed in the presentation of marriage. The happiness to which on the wedding day the mother-in-law—along with the pearl necklace—refers relates to the happiness of the sexes (to which the bride timidly looks forward before the wedding night); the rival's letter stands in for both the sexual desires that invaded the marriage from outside and a repair of the injured marital bond. In this way these objects occupy the sexual fantasies of the audience.

There is more to it than that, though. Just as the woman sells the pearls instead of holding on to the promise of happiness that is objectified in them, the film as a whole puts the fetishes into circulation, revealing their double character. The object produces not just that suspense within which the cinema of attractions persists. In addition, its importance in creating suspense is also to be found in the fact that, as an element of the story, it has at the same time a privileged position vis-à-vis the flow of the narrative. Through this structuring elevation, a moment of the dramatic frame—that is, the representation of patriarchal power—returns. This dramatic frame has disappeared as a form that enframes the female narrative perspective from the outside, but now it is present again in its threatening substance *within* the film: will maternal experience become productive for the daughter-in-law, or will it take on the repressive patriarchal mother role, which prevents the son from enjoying a happy relationship with the other sex? Will love reconstitute itself when confronted with the outbreak of an archaic power struggle for the woman, or will the marriage decay when it is confronted with the male claim to possession? The objects mediate erotic attraction by means of inhibition, and the id of the female spectator is mediated through the superego; they dramatize the gaze that falls upon the narrative.

The Way Home shows how a withdrawal into the story of a patriarchal "instance of censorship" makes possible an idea of marriage as a free union designed "for the reciprocal use of sexual organs."[7] The new medium of film thus responds to social changes that press forward toward a liberalization of marriage rights and toward equality in marriage as these were demanded by progressive social movements of the time, especially the women's movement. Patriarchal power is attributed to the past, and the film captures it as its prehistory in the form of the pearl necklace and the letter. However, patriarchal order does not just appear as something that has been overcome; rather, it is also present as something "internalized." Yet even as melodrama around this same period is already attempting to psychologize by turning external fate into internal fate, these social marriage dramas tie the persistence of past powers to that which is visibly material. The films place their hope for deliverance from a return of the same in the relationship between the sexes in the form of the visibly material. The function of the significant objects oscillates between releasing a desire for earthly happiness and blinding sexual desire through the fetish object.

For female audiences, for whom marriage dramas were primarily produced, these objects eventually stand in for the male sex as both patriarchal power and sexual object. This is what concerns the gaze of women as it searches for enlightenment and pleasure: the unknown that awaits them in marriage, that is, that which eludes wives, which looks for its satisfaction elsewhere, which threatens and lures one outside of marriage—that which is covered by social taboos. The cultural-bourgeois appropriation of cinema by means of melodrama develops a repressive mode of distraction that takes the form of a "sublimation" of the female gaze and its potency. In its early moments the dramatization of bourgeois living conditions—which occurs by means of the world of things [*Dingwelt*]—makes manifest how cinema, urged by its female audiences, develops toward a representation of male sexuality, of man as sexual object, while at the same time it encounters resistance from the structures of patriarchal society immanent to it. Eventually, cinema capitulates before this resistance, and the visual element of film that was charged with meaning completely takes on the role of taboo.

Initially, though, responses to this conflict between the voyeuristic interests of female audiences and the social maintenance of the status quo were not unequivocal. Among the longer feature films that prevail around 1911–12—that is, films of about 900 meters in length (in contrast to earlier 300 to 400 meter films)—three reactions can be distinguished, each of which I will discuss by means of an example taken from films that appeared in 1912. There is, first, a conservative reaction, that is, a reconnection of social drama to melodrama, as in the Henny Porten film *The Shadow of the Sea* [*Der Schatten des Meeres*]. Second, there is an emancipatory reaction, which consists in an exploitation of possibilities that bear on the actress in early narrative cinema, a reaction that was particularly exemplified by Asta Nielsen; as a contrast to the Porten film, I will provide an analysis of *The Sins of the Fathers* [*Die Sünden der Väter*]. The "auteur film" [*Autorenfilm*] presents a third reaction, which detaches a thematization of male sexuality from a realization of the female gaze. From this perspective *The Other* [*Der Andere*] establishes a caesura in film history. Film historiography, however, especially that of Lotte Eisner and Siegfried Kracauer, only allowed "German cinema" to begin with this "first auteur film."

Male Sex and Female Gaze

Dramas that deal with the lives of women, family, love, passion, and so on seem to have boomed around 1912, and almost every company produced these films: the Deutsche Kinematographengesellschaft (Cologne) produced films starring Lissi Nebuschka and Wanda Treumann; Vitascope produced films starring Viggo Larssen and Wanda Treumann as well; films produced by Deutsche Bioskop featured Hedda Vernon; those of Continental-Kunstfilm, Mia May; those of Deutsche Mutoskop and Biograph, Thea Sandten; and so on. It is difficult to assess the work of these and other actresses because of the limited preservation of these films. Early film drama might have included many more facets than the existing material suggests, though with respect to this extant material Henny Porten and Asta Nielsen embody extremes.

The Shadow of the Sea was produced under the direction of Curt A. Stark, starred Henny Porten, and was shot by cameraman Carl Froelich, who also had already participated in *By a Hair's Breadth*. The film used mythical elements—

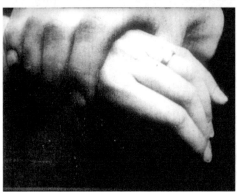

derived from the literary text upon which the film was based, the East Frisian legend "The Revenant" ["Der Gonger"]—in order to teach the curious female gaze a lesson. The camera work, however, is documentary throughout; filmed on the island of Kullen, the film excels in outside shots of ocean waves, rocky beaches, dunes, and the cottages of fishermen, and it excels as well in its cinematographic presentation of the urban environment. The heroine of the story is an emancipated woman, so to speak, a young painter. During one of her excursions she falls in love with a young fisherman; he saves her when, immersed in her painting, she fails to notice the approaching tide. Nor does the fisherman remain indifferent to her—yet he is engaged. Evelyn, the painter, retreats when she realizes that her love, if pursued, would lead to suffering. She leaves the island.

The gaze is ascribed to the woman in the film: she owns it as painter as well as in the considerate form of attention that she reveals in her treatment of the relationship. Her gaze is characterized by a love of nature that directs not only her brush but also her sexual inclination toward a man who is devoid of all traces of urban culture. The consequences for action that result from this gaze are less determined by a consideration of tradition and bourgeois morality than by solidarity with one's own sex. "You shall be happy," she says to the other woman and embraces her during their farewell. Thus, undramatically, a story from the life of a single woman, a painter, could end.

However, the woman was only able to end the story in this way because she used her foresight to deceive the man. When she confronts him with an engagement ring on her hand, he gives up. She misuses, so to speak, the symbol of a holy bond between man and woman in the interests of a profane solidarity with a woman. With this deception the protagonist loses her privileged point of view [*Blickposition*]. After she has left, the audience sees how the fisherman, rather than becoming reconciled to his fiancée, seeks his death in the ocean. The sequence that follows, over the course of which the story first becomes dramatic from the standpoint of the protagonist, is seen by the audience with a knowledge of the man's death.

Evelyn's natural inclination remains the same despite her decision for solidarity: after she has returned home she dreams of her "nature boy." We see her on the porch of her urban villa as she takes a bouquet of heather that he had given her from the wooden box in which she had stored it; she smells the bouquet and touches it with her lips. After evoking the one whom she loves in this way, she writes a letter to him. However, this letter, sent—like the letters in *Pearls Mean Tears* and *By a Hair's Breadth*—in the name of love, will not in this case reach its destination, as we know. In this way the suspended expectation that develops by means of the bouquet of heather and the letter works in the opposite direction for the audience than for the protagonist. While the latter hopes to solve the conflict between sexual interest and prohibition in happy fashion by means of the letter, the audience waits expectantly to see in what way she will be struck by the "stroke of fate." The gaze of the audience is already overshadowed by the punishing image of the dead man.

The loving gaze of the woman is doomed to fail because of the return of the patriarchal power of fate—which she, as an "emancipated woman," had overcome but which was reactivated in the female spectator. The third part of the film depicts how this failure is put into effect for the protagonist. When Evelyn receives back her own letter rather than an answer, she follows the dictates of her love, traveling back to the island. She finds the mourning mother and fiancée, and despite initial resistance she is able to win back their affection. However, the mother—subscribing to superstition rather than to the prospect of happiness, as in the case of the mother-in-law in *Pearls Mean Tears*—warns the young city girl against staying under her roof: there is a myth, according to which a dead man returns in order to take his loved one with him. The enlightened Evelyn does not heed this superstitious belief and thus learns a deadly lesson. At night the ghost of the dead man enters and forces her to follow him into a boat and out onto the ocean, where she drowns.

This third part of the film is melodramatic. The deadly fate of woman plays out its course. What strikes one's attention is how openly the film depicts the fact that it is essentially the emancipated gaze of woman that is doomed and an injured male potency that thus restores itself.

Evelyn sent the letter so that she could see her lover (again), without holding back. The expectation of the gaze is not only disappointed; in addition, the enlightened gaze is destroyed by the ghostly apparition, which seeks revenge. The violated taboo is reestablished. In contrast to the documenting camera of the main part, the ending makes use of stylized images and tricks to produce a gloomy and threatening impression of the return of that male power, which had been forgotten. The shot of the erect, dark male figure who stands up in the boat and presses to him the resisting woman, with her white nightgown and unbound hair, seems like a necromantic image, one that excludes reality. In the drama of the woman the body of the desired man appears only as shadow, and it causes her death. The "real tragedy" that stands behind the melodrama of the woman is a masculinity that has been shaken by the emancipated woman.

It may be important in this context to point to the return of the motif of "Death-as-Ferryman" in F. W. Murnau's *Journey into the Night* [*Der Gang in die Nacht*], which appeared in 1921. This auteur film, shot after the war, makes use of elements of early social drama in order to deal with a crisis of male identity and potency.[8] The impressive scene in which Conrad Veidt, in the role of a blind man, approaches the shore, standing upright in a boat, first and foremost evokes associations with romantic painting. If one sees this film side by side with *The Shadow of the Sea*, one begins to suspect that it might be a motif mediated by melodrama. The connotation of a form of masculinity that takes revenge, to which the female protagonist falls victim in Murnau's film as well, would then already be inherent in this motif.

As do marriage films, *The Shadow of the Sea* encourages an attention to

sexual relations in cases in which the façade of bourgeois life has rendered them taboo, especially for the female gaze. However, it is not immediately marriage that stands at the center of the film but the way of life of the unattached young woman, a state that—according to bourgeois ideas—is supposed to be temporary and lead naturally to marriage. On the one hand, the beginning of the film depicts this way of life in its autonomy; on the other hand, it makes visible the sexual desire that is behind but also in contradiction with the social desire for marriage: the painter desires the male body of the fisherman, whose strong arms carried her through the water; she does not dream of marrying him. For this reason the rivalry between the women does not turn into a drama. In its first part the film simply narrates; it only becomes dramatic when the painter, who has returned to her former social milieu, is reminded of her love by her lover's bouquet. Again, the bouquet of heather takes on the role of a fetish and bearer of a drama-producing prehistory; taken for itself, the scene provokes an antagonism between erotic curiosity and the patriarchal power of fate, which has already won in the gaze of the female spectator. The subsequent melodramatic action of the film therefore one-sidedly fuels fear and represses curiosity by dropping the dramatic object and allowing the dialectic of the gaze to crash along with it. Visualization of the feared inner authority takes the place of that materiality, which functions as a bearer of hope (i.e., the bouquet). The power of inner authority was already relativized, and it wins back an impression of superiority only through a technical manipulation of the image, which objectifies the male spirit [Geist] as a ghostly apparition [Geistererscheinung] on the screen. It subjugates the female gaze.

The Shadow of the Sea formulates a contradiction—that commercial cinema speculates on the female gaze yet, as patriarchal institution, cannot allow it—as tragedy and thus deprives it of an intersubjective solution. To resolve the contradiction in this latter way—that is, through intersubjectivity— was always Asta Nielsen's goal for film. In contrast to Henny Porten, Nielsen was a professional actress. She worked in theater—the Copenhagen Royal Theater—before she made her first film in 1910. Her autobiography makes clear her extensive involvement in the entire process of production of her films. From her account we not only know that it was left to her own fantasy to execute roughly sketched out actions; in addition, we also know that Asta Nielsen was the precise opposite of later stars that were "made" by directors. She determined her appearance down to the fabric and cut of her wardrobe. After the production of a handful of films in Denmark she signed up for eight films with Deutsche Bioskop in 1911 and then concluded a contract with the newly founded International Film Distribution Company [Internationale Film-Vertriebs-Gesellschaft], where she successfully pushed through a demand not simply for employment but also for shares. Among the other shareholders was Paul Davidson, the director of the film company Union, which around that period began to develop into a prestigious production company, the PAGU. The contract stipulated the production of eight films per year between 1912 and 1914.

In contrast with that of Henny Porten, Asta Nielsen's career in German cinema begins at the same time as the formation of monopoly film distributors [Monopolfilm-Verleihe], which separate film production from the sole responsibility of the production company (and thus also of the company patron) and place it in the context of the (international) market.[9] In this market the actress does not just represent a commodity; she is also on the side of the seller. These economic circumstances, together with the aesthetic development of film drama, were the conditions in which Asta Nielsen was able to implement and unfold her abilities. After some initial fierce attacks, Nielsen was greatly honored and admired by the male press of the period. Even as late as 1924 one can still read a hymn to Nielsen in Béla Balázs's film theory. However, by poetically elevating her unique abilities—descriptions ranged from the "Duse of film art" (in contemporary advertisements) to an "encyclopedia of the gestures of erotic language" [*Gebärdenlexikon erotischer Sprache*] (Balázs)—the importance of an oppositional female position, which was possible in early cinema and which Nielsen excelled in expressing, was displaced. This book is not least an attempt to remove Nielsen from this pedestal and to place her in a context that first makes visible her aesthetic-political importance.

Asta Nielsen played a decisive part in the formulation of social drama as well as the comedy of femininity. This development was interrupted by World War I: it was never again possible to retie the severed thread of that kind of film production within which the interests of female audiences were represented. In 1916, after a visit to Copenhagen, Nielsen was denied reentry into Germany. In 1919 she took up film work in the Weimar Republic but under the different conditions of the auteur film and with increasing difficulties. Before the war she had found in Urban Gad a director and scriptwriter who not only had a special affection for and understanding of her but whose work was also economically attuned to hers. Gad received his contract with the PAGU because Asta Nielsen was in high demand.[10] It would be interesting to consider the question of whether and how during this period a form of production that combined a private life partnership with a public work partnership benefited a woman's position. Henny Porten's situation was similar to and yet very different from Nielsen's. For Porten, work was not connected to "free love"; rather, her career began in the bosom of her family. Franz Porten, her father, was the director of many of her sound pictures. From her father's supervision and direction she then moved on to those of her husband and director, Curt Stark. The chances for emancipation were minimal.

When Nielsen returned to film after the war, though, her autonomy as an actress collided with altered structures of production. She found herself in disagreement with producers and directors, even when she acknowledged their capability, as was the case with Lubitsch, for example. In order to push through her own ideas, she founded her own company, with which she shot her version of *Hamlet,* in which Hamlet is a woman. However, the company only lasted until 1923. Looking back, Nielsen wrote:

> After all, I am still convinced that one needs a company of one's own in order to achieve both artistic and great commercial success. If the work is to thrive and bring praise to the artist, one needs to have in one's own hand and under one's own power everything that determines and is included in the artistic part of film production.[11]

In the prewar years, given a production structure that was much more accommodating to the self-willed aspects of female productive power, the problem addressed here was not yet as decisive.

Sins of the Fathers is one of many films that Asta Nielsen shot with Urban Gad as director—and, frequently, with cameraman Guido Seeber—during the few years before the war. Her films are certainly better preserved than the bulk of film production, such as comparable series with Wanda Treumann or Lissi Nebuschka. However, even with Nielsen films the situation is still pretty bad. The copy of *Sins of the Fathers,* for example, is incomplete, even though the available print gives a fairly coherent impression.[12] In our context this film is especially interesting because it implicitly addresses the relationship between film and the fine arts of *Jugendstil* and Naturalism, and it explicitly contributes to the theme of painter and model from the female reverse perspective.

Sins of the Fathers not only presents a female gaze directed at man; it also defends this gaze against the resistance that it met from society and cinema itself. The film addresses the denial and repression of the gaze, and it also destroys the myth of male genius. The way in which this film, in contrast to the Porten film, refers to painting—as the visual medium of bourgeois art—already betrays its radicality. Painting is not portrayed as a female occupation with beautiful landscape, the sublime quality of which—the elemental, threatening character of the ocean—can only take the painter by surprise; rather, painting is the representation of human beings by human beings. The film thus uncovers the gender-specific distribution of roles in the artistic process and thereby presents the latter not as accessory to the main action but rather as its core.

Sins of the Fathers rigorously develops the emancipatory implications of the form of the social drama. The central characteristic of the latter is the suspense-producing object. It reflects and stands in for the dramatic frame, which restrains the female perspective in early narrative cinema. The dramatizing effect of this object is not related primarily to the organization of the story that the film tells but to the gaze with which this story is perceived. In *Sins of the Fathers* this object is the painting, the female portrait. The film thus hits the mark. This object refers not only to patriarchal power as a social prehistory that also has an effect on the film's story of the present. This prehistory is referenced by the content of the painting *Misery of the Hopeless* [*Elend der Hoffnungslosen*], a misery for which—fully in the spirit of Naturalism—alcoholism and other excesses ("the sins of the fathers") are supposed to be responsible. Additionally, and above all, the film reflects in the painting a patriarchal prehistory as a history of bourgeois fine arts that overshadows the development of cinema and that needs to be overcome.

Something else becomes possible due to the choice of this particular dramatizing object: it allows the female spectator to avert her gaze from this fetish, which is clearly constituted by a male gaze, and direct her gaze against man himself. And finally, as a nontechnological image that plays a role within the technological medium of film, it not only provokes a contradiction between erotic curiosity and prohibition in the gaze of the female spectator but also reflects this provocation within the film itself: Asta Nielsen, who, in the film, stands in for the gaze of the spectator, takes up this contradiction and gives it expression as an opposition between the emancipatory possibilities of the new medium and those old conditions that the medium has not yet escaped. *Sins of the Fathers* takes up the old motif of painter and model, also a paradigm for feminist critique, vis-à-vis a discussion of the gender-specific organization of the gaze. The film criticizes the power relationship of traditional art from the perspective of the new mass medium as well as from the perspective of the object on display—which is ultimately the perspective that the actress Asta Nielsen assumes.

The story is simple. Hanna, a girl with a proletarian background, hires herself out as a nude model at an art school. She becomes the lover of a talented student, who portrays her as a female monarch of antiquity and then leaves her to continue his studies in Italy. The professor's family takes her on as a maid, but when her lover returns and becomes engaged to the professor's daughter, Hanna leaves the household. Naturally, an affair must belong to the servant class, while marriage must occur within one's own social class; yet this maid does not accept this self-evident rule. She becomes

a social outsider. In a rundown tavern the young painter again encounters Hanna without recognizing her; she has sunk into poverty. From a group of drinking and smoking young people he chooses her as a model for his painting *Misery of the Hopeless*. Over the course of this new work it is clear that Hanna is blossoming, and her engagement to a gardener seals her return to society. This disturbs the creative process of the painter, and he seduces his "model" in order to evoke again the old expression of hopelessness. He succeeds. However, after the painting has been finished, the model returns once more, and she throws the story of the creation of this masterpiece in his face from a woman's perspective: his fiancée and her father, who are present, are outraged and leave the house of this "unworthy" man. Hanna, alone with the painter, pulls out a knife and destroys her image, his work.

The first shot of this version of *Sins of the Fathers* can be read as an allusion to what is at stake in a story about painter and model: four students, three male and one female, are in the process of drawing a male nude study under the supervision of their professor. The half-finished drawings sit on easels, and the model himself sits in the background with a blanket around his loins. This scene also concerns the depiction of the male body from the point of view of a woman rather than the cinematic version of the Eternal Feminine as it appears in the gaze of man. As a result, the film rigorously dispenses with female erotic charms that would be hidden under the cloak of artistic or social problems: against this, Asta Nielsen employs a defiant exhibitionism and a provocative display of female sexual desire. Whenever *she* is not present in the depicted world of artists, the film returns to the male model from the first scene.

However, since the gaze of woman at man is repressed in society and thus also in cinema as a social institution, this film too can only act against the established organization of the gaze if it is in any way to express the interest of female scopophilia. The narrative is on the side of the female model, not the painter; the film follows her story, not his—as, for example, when he moves on to study in Italy. The camera is positioned vis-à-vis the portraits of the women; it targets them and simultaneously subordinates them to the flow of images that it produces. The living appearance of woman, which only served as a model for the paintings, merges into these moving images. By means of these images the entire film becomes a perspective on art from the standpoint of life, which traditional art had eternalized and rendered immobile; not the standpoint of life in general but that of the female individual who had never been able to express herself in art. A tension develops between Nielsen's provocative performance in the tale of "her" life and the dramaturgically and scenically significant paintings that seek to provide a framework for her life within which it can be seen but cannot see itself. Nielsen's exhibitionism is different from that simple expression of female sexuality that is exploited by cinema; it is a challenge to the other sex to become visible, to show itself. During the cinematic dialogue between painter and model the paintings turn into fetishes; for the man, they substitute for love: the actor who plays the painter remains erotically unexpressive. Suspense for the audience is focused on whether the heroine will succeed in seducing the man to become devoted to her, to loving her, so that we see him in an erotic situation. Such an expectation runs counter to the process of finishing the paintings and prevents the libidinous charge of the artistic creation. The finished painting simply disappoints this expectation. After his first painting the man travels to the land of "educational tourism" and only reappears in the film several scenes later. The second painting simply reveals a male inability to love.

The tension between image and life and between image of woman and female gaze that the film thematizes is also translated into the form of the film. Through her performance Asta Nielsen takes up the art of exhibition [*Schaustellungskunst*] from the early cinema of attractions, the art of Salomés, snake dancers, and lion tamers; she conveys the narrative of the film through the art of show, and thus she stands in contrast to the rest of the film. It becomes clear, in turn, that the film's dramatic structure, which revolves around the painting, is a framework that, in this case, does not restrain narrative perspective within the film but rather the scopophilia of female spectators. In contrast to the fetishizing cinematic image that orients itself at the frame of the camera and the screen [*Cadrage*], just as the painted image orients itself toward the boundaries of the plane, Asta Nielsen presents a different moving canvas—which, moreover, does not claim to be neutral but communicates her female sex. She wants to return the male gaze by virtue of her own female gaze. Asta Nielsen mirrors all the life situations that the film takes up once more with her body—the erotic charisma of which attracts the eye—through her posture, gestures, and expressions; through her choice of costume and the nuanced way in which she wears it; and so on. However, she does not simply reflect events; she also erases them in their "objectivity." Her ever-changing appearance—which does not develop along the lines of the narrative—insists that her story/female history [*Geschichte*] has not taken place so long as the female narrative perspective has not been integrated into the cinematographic organization of the gaze. The actress thus walks a thin line between the decline of narrative perspective that attends the sex appeal of the star and the "irrealization" of the story that attends the persistent presentation of a claim to express female sexuality in the events, which means in this case in the context of creative work. The heroine of *Sins of the Fathers* never gives up; even after the act of destroying the painting she turns to the painter, who has been existentially crushed, takes a step forward, and lifts her arms slightly away from her body.

In *Sins of the Fathers* she initially appears as the girl who takes her first step into the world of artistic bohemia when she wishes to become a model at an art school. Together with two other applicants she stands in the studio clad in a bright, striped dress and with her hair combed back and braided into a single plait. She stands around, bashfully bites her nails, plucks at her dress, twists her hands around one another, and eventually, helpless (what is one to do with one's limbs?), she allows them to hang down limply alongside her body: she is being observed and valued. She wants something, but she cannot do anything, and she has to wait, exposed to gazes. However, from the three beauties it is she who is chosen. A little later she appears to have grown into the frame in which she is put: "Hanna has become a perfect model." Now she allows her curly hair to hang freely, and she seems so grown-up that—as the next scene reveals—she can take on the role of a queen in the eyes of a student, a fantasy from which he creates his painting. With a headband and white stole, she invests the pose of the queen with the personal pride of the lover—yet the professor who enters the room overlooks the model. Still, this relationship separates her from her proletarian background. With a ladylike, decoratively patterned dress—it is tapered and, with its square neckline, seems a bit austere—she makes a marked contrast with the squalid apartment of her father. Shortly thereafter she has fulfilled her function: the glamour of first love has passed, the student is in Italy, and now she is simply "grown up." She wears a long, narrow skirt, a white blouse, and a broad belt around her slim waist, and her hair is drawn back and fastened at the back of her head; a feather boa gives her otherwise modest appearance an "unbourgeois" touch. During a fierce discussion with the professor she twists the end of the boa with her fingers—a gesture of insecurity as she protests that is comparable to the first time she stood in the atelier; now she talks, but she still cannot act.

Along with her father she assembles envelopes. At home she no longer wears the feather boa; there is nothing new in which she can dress. As she works she presses her chin to her chest so that a double chin stands out—a reflex of her surroundings, in which beauty does not matter. As a maid in the professor's household she lets her curls hang freely again, yet her dress is neither seductive nor elegant but neat and includes a white apron that emphasizes her position. Familial friendliness influences her only secondarily:

the next scene shows her wearing a ladylike, high-necked dark dress with a lavish velvet bow on its neck; overall, she appears more opulent and at ease. This changes as soon as her former lover returns. Wearing a slim, simple black dress with short sleeves and a square neckline and with the white apron around her waist, she seems to be constrained, gloomy, and forced back into the limits of her position as servant.

At the proletarian pub she appears completely alienated [*verfremdet*] with respect to both her clothes and her manners. Her appearance is contradictory: on the one hand, her hair is tied back into a knot, but, on the other hand, this draws even more attention to the unkempt bangs. She wears a long, dark skirt with a striped blouse, but the latter is unbuttoned at the neck. She smokes, burps, and laughs vulgarly, leans over the table with her upper body, and rests on her elbows. When her former lover enters the bar looking for a subject, she jumps up and assumes a provocatively defensive position: one hand rests on the table, her back is stiff, and the other hand rests on her hip. As he speaks to her she alternately reacts abrasively and with amusement; she presses her chin to her chest again and posits, by means of her face, *her* milieu against his. Now that she has reached the bottom end of the scale— the other end of which she once represented, as queen, for the painter—she has more female pride than ever. Now she determines the pose and the dress with which he will paint her, a masquerade she has already adopted in her life in order to hide her past injuries and her vulnerability.

The encounter at the tavern table is "Asta's great scene" (so say the laconic script directions for her films): the painter wants to capture her on canvas. The rest of the film shows how her life, lived in a different environment, again develops away from this moment and thus begins to stand in contradiction to the work of the painter, which is dependent upon a stable image. This discrepancy is acted out in excruciatingly long scenes; over and over again intertitles announce, through repetitious formulations with little variation, scenes in which the woman's awakening sense of happiness and vitality is in conflict with the professional interest of the painter. The film makes no headway; it seems as though the claims of reproduction [*Abbild*] also captivate the mobility of the film. The tension increases: the question is, *Who* or *what* will assert itself?

"The feeling of happiness has removed the model's expression of hopeless-ness." We see the half-finished painting, which presents an expression of fear and weariness and a look of skepticism, and next to it the "original," cheerful and relaxed, with a smile on her lips. The artist tries to adjust life

to the image. He indicates to her that she should appear more serious and tragic. She pulls herself together, but this does not last long. The painter steps up to her, grabs her by her chin to adjust the position of her head, and makes a hand movement that looks as though he would like to force her eyes into the right expression. She stands upright and looks into the distance but by no means with an expression of hopelessness. He makes another step toward the model, she listens to his advice, and she tries again. Eventually, he gives up, and she relaxes completely and slips away. A short scene in the garden with the engaged couple—Hanna and the gardener—follows. Then, once more, "Hanna's happy look makes it impossible to capture misery in the painting." A short scene with painter and model follows. Once more, "The model's face, transfigured by happiness, threatens the successful completion of the work."

Stringing together perpetually similar scenes that are separated by similar-sounding intertitles increases the tension produced by the contradiction, inherent in the scene, between male domination and a female desire for happiness until this comes to the bursting point. The last intertitle, however, initiates the seduction scene. In this scene the conflict becomes more relaxed, since the painter seemingly gives in to the desire of the woman, but at the same time it becomes radicalized. The film bluntly depicts sexual exploitation. The camera mediates the violent perspective of the painter by framing the model in close-up, while the easel in the background constitutes the point of flight. His movements create the connection between easel and model: he approaches her with wine and presses it upon her while remaining sober himself. In a calculated, intrusive fashion he slips his hand into the open neckline of her blouse, grabs her by her hair, and kisses her on the exposed skin of her breast—an erotic scene that emphasizes the relationship between the sexes under the conditions of a male claim to power. When she realizes that she cannot resist the doomed desire that is inside her, she closes herself off, scrunches up her face in such a way that it falls into strong vertical lines, and submits to his attack with a half-open mouth and a vacant expression. He lifts up the now defenseless woman as if he wants to draw her close to him, but in fact it is only in order to allow her to fall. Now he rushes to the easel and takes up the brush to copy this expression on the canvas. However, the painting was able to strike down life only for a short time: film returns "mobility" to the "model," passes the oppositional reply on to her gestures, and now she knows what to do with her hands: destroy the painting. At this point the film is already over.

The film could be perceived as a critique of bourgeois aesthetics, which arrogates to itself (i.e., in the movie reform movement) the right to regiment the new medium. The film points out not just the "interestedness" of the classicist art ideal of "disinterested pleasure." This social drama is also a critique of Naturalism as an "ratification" ["*Verkunstung*"] of misery. Both

artistic movements meet in the way in which, in both, woman becomes an allegory: an allegory of the greatness of antiquity, on the one hand, and of modern misery, on the other. The factitiousness of this art indicates that it relies upon and perpetuates a repression of life: the female monarch in the painting corresponds to a disrespect for woman in real life. Art that claims to depict reality in a way that is true to nature, that claims to take its motifs from real life, is doubly factitious and repressive, for the misery that the grand bourgeois painter claims to find is coproduced by him as well, only to be exploited yet again in its picturesque aspects; in this way it serves in the end the interests of his fame. Traditional art, which is obedient to power, is blind. Asta Nielsen speaks up not only for the female gaze but also for an opening up of the gaze and a liberation of fantasy in general, which film can provide when it resists bourgeois ideals of art and their repression of the other sex.

The specific quality of German "auteur films," of which Max Mack's *The Other* is an example, is to be found in the fact that they do not so much attempt to submit cinema to bourgeois ideals of art but rather seek to recognize and realize in this "lower" art form another side of bourgeois art. Thus, they seem to account for the fact that cinema is a bourgeois and not only a proletarian oppositional public sphere; at the same time, though, they bring cinema back to the familiar grounds of literature. It is characteristic of the auteur film that it is an adaptation from literature. In this way it finally puts an end to the oppositional development of early cinema, which had relied on both the primacy of experimenters and inventors and the autonomy of actors, especially actresses. In these first auteur films a modern science—psychoanalysis—provided the element of mediation between the traditional literary medium and modern technology. While the cultural bourgeoisie had emphasized again and again that film was already inferior because it could not represent anything spiritual [*Seelisches*], psychoanalysis had shown authors how romantic poetry of the soul [*Seele*] returns, in the technological age, in the notion of spirit [*Seele*]. The impulse of bourgeois culture, which is carried into cinema by films such as *The Other* and *The Student of Prague* [*Der Student von Prag*], is—despite literary references and despite the participation of Reinhardt actors such as Albert Bassermann and Paul Wegener—less that of art than of enlightened science. In the spirit of the latter, cinema is transformed from an oppositional public sphere to a representative of the social unconscious, which is how Kracauer then conceptualizes it much later in *From Caligari to Hitler*.

The Other is a cinematic study of the unconscious. After an introductory presentation of a still photograph of director Max Mack, scriptwriter Paul Lindau, and main actor Albert Bassermann, a text by Hippolyte Taine precedes the actual film:[13]

As a result of a fall, a serious illness, or exhaustion, a double essence [*Doppelwesen*] can form in man, a sick essence next to a healthy one. One does not know anything of the other. In a kind of twilight state, the sick one can commit actions of which the healthy one has no knowledge whatsoever.

The story begins with a small party at the house of Hallers (Albert Bassermann), a lawyer, during which this quote by Taine is discussed. Hallers disagrees vehemently with these claims; however, over the course of the film he becomes convinced of the existence of this other essence due to firsthand experiences. Along with the protagonist, the audience is taught this lesson as well. The film is directed at those "Hallerses" who feel safe in their bourgeois, well-ordered life, and it seeks to make them think.[14] By informing audiences about the dark side of human individuality, the auteur film also implicitly reflects its own mission: to encourage the bourgeoisie to change its attitude toward cinema; cinema is the "Other" of one's own culture. *The Other* connects two discourses, a semantic one—a reflection on the male life of the drives, made possible by reference to modern science—and a pragmatic one—the proof that cinema represents not simply a low-culture and morally devious form of pleasure for maids.

The story of Hallers the lawyer has the characteristics of a psychoanalytic case story. The lawyer clearly has tender feelings for a young unmarried woman, Agnes, who lives in the same house one floor above him. Enraptured, he listens to her play the piano night after night and expressly asks her not to stop playing; however, he does not declare his feelings for her. A detour is necessary in order for him to reveal to her his sexual interest. As the result of a fall from a horse, he begins to divert himself every night in the lower strata of society and life without being aware the next day that he has done so. After thus familiarizing himself unconsciously with sexuality and crime—and, moreover, after his nightly excursions begin to leave more and more traces—he is one day forced to remember his "other" life. Eventually, he is able to narrate scene after scene to his doctor. After a period of convalescence in the countryside, the first thing he does upon his return is to ask Agnes to play something for him. As she had feared, he initially falls back into his old state of melancholy, but then, happily, he shakes his head, goes up to her, hugs her from behind, pulls her up to him, and, when she turns toward him, kisses her mouth.

Beneath this case story is another, more primitive story of a maid. This case does not concern a particular neurotic disturbance but everyday parapraxis.

One night after an exhausting day, Amalie, maid of Agnes, absentmindedly pockets her mistress's watch as she puts her to bed. Accused of stealing, she must leave the house. She then works as a waitress in just that bar to which Hallers is attracted every night. He arouses her affectionate attention, especially because she recognizes him immediately. She shows him a photograph of herself, at which he stares, and then he lets it slide into his pocket. She mends a tear in his jacket sleeve for him, and, when she unintentionally pricks his wrist, she kisses the injured spot. She tries in vain to keep him from falling in with crooks. A burglary at lawyer Hallers's house is planned and executed. The thieves are discovered, but naturally the lawyer is not identified as an accomplice. The next day his servant, puzzled, shows him not only the mended coat—which Hallers used to wear during his nightly excursions—but also finds the photo of Amalie in the coat pocket. Shortly thereafter, Amalie herself visits Hallers to return to him precisely that watch which Agnes had given to him and which he had left with the waitress. He initially responds to her visit with dismissive incredulity, and it is only when Amalie begins to cry that he devotes more attention to her. She proves the truth of her story not only through the mended coat but also by taking his hand to remind him of the needle prick (and the kiss). This is when it all "dawns" upon Hallers, and it is then an easy job for Dr. Feldmann, who had been called in, to elicit the entire story from him. When Hallers returns from his trip in order to become engaged, Amalie has been reemployed at the house.

This social drama that surrounds Amalie is reduced to fulfilling simply a function in a story about men. Amalie is the only one who perceives Hallers in his other form, and her loving and understanding gaze enables the man to become self-conscious. The man's process of cognition, the perception and recognition of an "Other" inside him, results in a different relationship of the citizen to the other, the servant class. They are human beings as well, they have a bourgeois consciousness, and a "trespass" on someone else's belongings can result from parapraxis; it does not have to be a crime. The auteur film puts an end to the perspective from below, of the Other (ideally of the other sex), in favor of a seemingly liberal perspective from above, which, however, prescribes to the Other its own, albeit psychoanalytically enlightened, image of humanity.[15]

The gaze of women at men, toward which social drama strives, was taken from woman in the auteur or "art" film before it had a chance to realize itself. It becomes a moment of male self-representation, which in turn is communicated to female audiences as well, as a representation valid for all mankind, as a "humanism." The "humanity" of woman in general consists in being as attentive to and understanding of man's "lower instincts" as had previously been the case only for women of the lower classes, such as Amalie. The humanity of upper-class women, however, consists in responding in an enlightened fashion to the problems of servants in a way that was earlier possible only for the psychologist. The female perspective is also subsumed under the male in the sense that real community, which was established across class divisions in the female perspective, is turned into an ideological community—"femininity" as a quality that complements man—and thus the bourgeois woman is de facto relegated back to her class standpoint.

Formally, *The Other* works, just as in the case of social dramas, with the objective gaze of the documenting camera, which resists sentimentalization. However, the performance of Reinhardt actor Albert Bassermann gains importance vis-à-vis this camera work. In addition to the figure of the lawyer, he also depicts the invisible unconscious as it has taken possession of the body of this person. This is not the psychologizing performance of melodrama that hints at an inner life but rather a new attempt to show, expressively, the otherwise hidden inner life that has become visible on the outside. This performance confers on the human being the role of the "co-acting" object of social drama. In the role of the nonperson—the "id" that has been separated off—the actor takes over the dramatization of the story of the lawyer Hallers; at the same time, as an achievement of its own, the acting performance constitutes the central attraction of the film. The fact that this famous actor was starring in a film had already created a sensation in itself, and it provided a reason for contemporary critics to consider, finally, the case of cinema. Bassermann himself, however, did not simply have his theater-style performance filmed, but he instead used the objectifying medium in order to represent an objectification of man—a topic that exploded the frame of classical drama.[16] The so-called Expressionist film of the Weimar Republic would take up this topic again. Bourgeois actors initially loathed the cinema because performing in it meant descending into the lower realms of "physical performance" [*Artistik*], in which man does not mediate himself as a spiritual being through his corporeal art but rather exhibits himself as an attraction.[17] Paul Lindau's script made it possible for Bassermann to give meaning itself to a reduction of acting to the level of a corporeal art of disguise. Yet this film thus inverts the meaning of "attraction": instead of presenting the libidinal [*Triebhaftes*] for the purposes of erotic pleasure, it is presented, filtered through science, as an object for study.

Just as the female perspective—the story of the woman and female scopophilia—has been reduced to fulfilling simply a function, so too has the dramatizing object. In many guises the dramatizing object accompanies and supports the central drama around the nonperson and mediates it with the narrative. Yet it no longer possesses in any of these guises an autonomous power of dramatizing the gaze of the spectator. The coat and its mysterious transformations play a role that produces suspense and pushes forward toward its resolution. The watch also plays an important role as an objectification of identity that persists even when a person loses his identity. The watch stands in for the loss and the (re)gaining of identity. Because of the watch Amalie loses her position within the context of bourgeois society and ends up in the outsider context of quasi prostitution (which waitressing was at that time regarded as being). By means of the watch she identifies the lawyer in his "other" form, and in order to give the watch back to him she returns to the bourgeois apartment building, which initiates his process of healing and her rehabilitation.

A third, dramaturgically relevant object is the photograph of Amalie. While the coat belongs to a mystification of life during the day by means of what occurs at night, and while the watch insists on identity by objectifying it, the photograph stands on the side of enlightenment and clarification [Aufklärung].[18] The discovery of the watch in Hallers's coat pocket, followed by Amalie's appearance in person, leads to a solution. At the same time the photograph, as an object that conveys the drama of the no person by means of the story, serves to banish erotic associations into a form of latency and thus keep the story of psychoanalytic enlightenment free from them. To the extent that the photograph is erotically charged when it first appears in the pub, it becomes at the house of the lawyer a pure medium of male self-awareness, interpreted in its function as image. As an image purged of all sexual associations, its fetish character is not abolished but instead simply repressed.

The ambivalence in the image of woman in early cinema was also repressed; in this image female narcissism is as much present as subject to the objectifying grasp of a male "desire to possess" [Habenwollen]. Amalie shows her picture to Hallers because she wants to awaken his interest in her through this exhibition of her beauty, of her "more perfect" self; however, she does not provoke his affection but only a primitive desire to possess: he pockets

the photograph. In that moment the photo becomes a dramatizing object: What if he as a bourgeois person finds it? the audience asks itself. With the photograph, though, no enlightenment as emancipation from the drives occurs. Rather, an enlightenment that attaches itself to the mimetic character [*Abbildcharakter*] of the photographic medium becomes one with a method that aims to reconstitute control in the face of an always possible relapse into the world of drives, of the lower classes, and of woman, which are controlled. With this kind of male self-presentation, not just female scopophilia but scopophilia in general is stripped of its autonomy and functionalized. The auteur film puts an end to the cinema of attractions not simply by negating the latter but by absorbing it for its own means.

Chapter Six

Perspective "from Below" or Perspective "from Outside"

The Detective Film

The previous chapters tried to show how a consideration of female audiences played a constitutive role in the development of narrative cinema. A similar influence of proletarian audiences cannot be determined for German cinema on the basis of the existing material. In the films presented—with the exception of comedies—women's topics predominate and female protagonists play central roles, while the milieu ranges from petit bourgeois to grand bourgeois; real proletarians are as rare as aristocrats. Insofar as it can be inferred from Lamprecht's list of titles, in 1912 the emphasis of film production is on dramas focused on women's topics, while in 1913 and 1914 the offerings are already more mixed: detective films [*Kriminalfilme*], sensational films [*Sensationsfilme*], and comedies are equally represented. Nor do early comedies seem to support the hypothesis of a "proletarian cinema"; however, in these films cinema presents itself as a pleasure of "the little people." The stories take place in the countryside or in the milieux of the petite bourgeoisie and servants, but beyond that they manifest a tendency toward eccentrics, outsiders, and "lumpen proletarians."[1]

The beginnings of narrative cinema stood entirely in the tradition of a lower art excluded from the bourgeois cultural world. It is the experience of a similar exclusion that attracts women to the cinema. The social drama stands at the end of a development in which cinema, opposed by the cultural bourgeoisie, accommodated the interests of women in feeling included in the cultural public sphere. By addressing female audiences, cinema already attempts to enter bourgeois circles. Thus, alongside all the attempts to assimilate to bourgeois cultural forms, an aesthetic emancipation of the cinema of attraction occurs of which the social emancipation of women is a part.

With the auteur film the entry of cinema into the bourgeois art world has been achieved (at the premiere of *The Other* all art critics were present), but a social interest in emancipation has fallen by the wayside. The auteur film dispossesses women's perspective of its aesthetic base, located in elements of the cinema of attraction, and appropriates it for the presentation of the male Other. A matter purely of male art production, auteur film integrates elements of low art—from which the social dramas still derived their oppositional power—into the "modernization" of bourgeois culture.[2]

Around the same time, however, cinema begins to assert itself within a much broader framework, which is that of capital. The movement of cinema toward a victory over bourgeois prejudices announces itself in a new aesthetic self-consciousness of the medium. Indicative of this are detective films. They still reflect the standpoint of the outsider, of one who is excluded from bourgeois culture—but one who will not be for much longer. Progress and enlightenment, which are both inherent to cinema as technological medium, will prevail. The detective film also claims internationality for itself as a specific quality of cinema—a claim it sets in contrast to the limitations of national culture. German crime film [*Verbrechensfilm*] was originally a foreign, especially Anglo-Saxon import, and it does not deny this origin.[3] Detectives and other protagonists have English names, and the stories sometimes take place in England as well.

The gaze from outside, which is inherent to the detective film, is not one that has always already been excluded from the bourgeois public sphere but rather the gaze of modernity at an antiquated world. Women participate in this gaze as well as long as they "stand their ground like a man." In addition to male detectives, there are also female detectives (in fact, entire series of this female variant), and their play with the trouser role is part of the attraction of these films. However, the fact that female protagonists star in these roles is not simply a sign of modern sexual equality; rather, their presence initiates the expression of a dialectic of progress. Kracauer was wrong to shrug off German detective film so quickly as an imitation of English detective film.[4] Aside from an enlightened beauty that is peculiar to all these films and that deserves to be appreciated in its own right, there is a dialectic of progress inherent in them: the female protagonists especially force the pathos of progress to reflect upon itself. The formal equality of the sexes does not yet abolish the centuries-old, internalized power relationship between the sexes [*Geschlechterherrschaft*]. As a result, female detectives do not just play the role of the active, professional woman, but, in the unfamiliar image of the female gaze, something archaic returns within modernity. From this phenomenon springs a genre of its own: the sensational film. At its center is not the enlightened and enlightening gaze but rather the gaze of woman, which in its unfamiliar power [*Mächtigkeit*] at once attracts and frightens. Another variation of the detective film is a hybrid form of detective and love film that combines the aesthetic elements of detective film with those of social drama; this form is a result of the same contradiction that the detective film, with its tendency toward a presentation of woman as equal to man, encountered.

Like social drama, the detective film is a type of narrative cinema that has retained and further developed aesthetic elements of early film. Technology is the main attraction of these films: procedures of criminalistic science, modern means of transportation, energy production, and so on. However, these technologies are not simply attractions before the camera but rather associate themselves with the latter. Eventually, the camera itself and the film as a means of technical reproduction become the most interesting and exciting elements. This emphasis still informs the dramatizing element of the story, the enlightening detective gaze, without subsuming the camera's curiosity and mobility into this inner-diegetic gaze.

Social Mobility and the Mobilization of the Camera's Gaze

It is primarily the emancipation of man that motivates aesthetic emancipation in detective films. By this I am referring not just to the concrete emancipation of man, which had already been the demand of contemporary women's movements and without which an emancipation of woman is impossible, but rather to the general bourgeois emancipation from prejudices and institutions of power.[5] The directors of these films, for example, Joseph Delmont and Harry Piel, were outsiders themselves, adventurers and internationalists who entered Wilhelminian society through film in order to stir things up. Harry Piel started his film career in Paris, and Joseph Delmont worked in the United States as an animal tamer before he entered German film production in 1911.[6] Originally performers, they not only threw themselves into the experimental field of film directing but frequently also starred in their own films. Curiosity and the spirit of adventure, together with experience in show business, transformed them into apt mediators between film's technical pioneers and the employment of acting performance now demanded by audience and industry.

However, their films testify not only to an experimental interest in the phenomena of modernity—which run from film technology to new means of transportation to the fascinating dynamics of metropolitan life—but also to a relationship with actresses that was different from what was customary in theater. This new relationship is based on collegiality among performers, but it also partakes of a sense for the transformations of modernity with respect to the relationship between the sexes. Early detective films thus do not exhaust themselves in male self-presentation, that is, the exhibition of male abilities and achievements. The heroes of these films are by no means strong men but rather clever men. They make use of and misuse [zweckentfremden] for their own means the technologies that they come across in order to escape threatening social powers. In so doing they place their trust in a solidarity with those who are socially weak: women. Women not only protect the hero but set out themselves to support him. Additionally, this trust does not just express itself in the content; it also determines the way in which these films relate to women in the audience.

Early detective films are only superficially purely films for men. In fact, in their own way they take up an element of social drama: the interest of female audiences in perceiving men. The heroes of detective films are not just simultaneously weak and clever; they also give themselves over, just as do the heroes of comedies, to scopophilia. However, in contrast to early comedies, the exhibitionist aspects of detective film speculate on a scopophilia in which the female element is present as distinct from the male element. While the clever use of technology in detective films protects their modern, "effeminate" heroes from ridicule in the eyes of men, in the eyes of women technology occupies the place of the suspense-producing object that social drama introduced. Except that now this object is in a much more obvious way conveyed by the male main character: through its misuse [Zweckentfremdung], technology clings to man's physical potency and acrobatic accomplishments like a sheath.

In detective films the gaze of the female spectator at man is—in contrast to the Nielsen films—not directly represented by the actress. Woman's gaze in film is one that she shares with the male protagonist or that she takes over from him, as in the case of the female detective films: she also knows how to use technology. The position of the female spectator finds itself represented in the film first of all on the side of the "invisible," especially in montage. Montage connects chases between men with the presentation of women's stories, scenes from the life of woman. In these scenes a libidinous charge of the one who is pursued occurs in place of the power of the pursuers. But the world of woman is also set in a different light. The beginnings of technologization and modernization manifest themselves in this world, and it appears, above all, as a world changing in the name of autonomy and self-awareness [*Selbstbewusstwerdung*]. Thus, women who master the gaze make their appearance in the detective film. Femininity is no longer the harbor into which man enters after long odysseys. The *First International Film Newspaper* [*Erste Internationale Film-Zeitung*] no. 37 (February 1913) reports the following about an appearance of Joseph Delmont at the movie theater ["Vereinigte Theater-Lichtspiele" in Hannover] on the occasion of his film *On Dying in the Woods* [*Vom Sterben im Walde*]:

> Herr Delmont has set himself the goal of striking new paths in cinematography. In his explanation, he emphasized that his films possess opinions [*Tendenz*], logic, and psychology. A film needs to make sense, and Herr Delmont listed the dramas shown so far, in which the protagonists almost always end up with one another in the end, and mentioned that in his films couples do not get on each other but on each other's nerves.

Even though the director's—or the journalist's—joke does not apply to Delmont's known films (which constitute only a fraction of the total production), it at least hints at the fact that Delmont had a better sense of the battle between the sexes than of the common clichés of happy love, which he avoided reproducing in film.

Early detective films, developed in the Wilhelminian empire, do not simply rely on capitalist progress; they are still produced from an outsider position that wants to enforce enlightenment and knows how to affiliate itself with the outsider position of women and their claim to emancipation, even if it is not fully committed to the latter. No film depicts this more clearly than *The Right to Existence* [*Das Recht aufs Dasein*, 1913], in which the drama is a consequence not of the detective's gaze but rather of an impossible relationship between a released convict and the daughter of a bourgeois citizen. Just as in the case of every regular detective film, this one deals with an illumination [*Aufklärung*] of a crime and the identification of the criminal. The story therefore consists mostly of flight and pursuit, both of which offer ample opportunity for dynamic camera work. The film is set primarily in the development areas in West Berlin. Rope winches and scaffolding offer routes and means of escape beyond the usual means, such as cars, motorboats, and trains. The camera participates in the flight: an external elevator on the side of a factory building seduces the camera into performing a vertical tracking shot, and its position on top of a moving train not only takes one's breath away because of the cameraman's audacity but also mediates dynamism as such. A scene that seems almost experimental is created when the camera hangs vertically above the wagon bumpers and focuses on the ground that rushes by beneath the speeding train.

Modern criminalistic techniques of persecuting and solving a crime are impressively staged from the beginning. The forensic methods of the police enter the picture: fingerprints are photographed, and plaster casts of footprints in wet soil are taken. In a darkroom we see how photographs are developed, while the tinting imitates the red light of the development lamp. Glimpses at bureaucracy—criminal files and a "dactyloscopy"—follow. The organized search is aided by a map on the office wall as well as by a wanted poster on all advertising columns throughout the city that publicizes distinguishing personal characteristics, such as a tattoo on the forearm and a deformed finger. Yet in the end, the "crime" that they pursue dissolves into thin air. The released convict, a social outsider, is finally, through the detour of a second chase, rehabilitated for real and admitted into society. Seen in this way, the protagonist is a means for the film to unfold the miracles of modern technology; his story, as movement from outsider to citizen, stands—like film—on the side of rational social development. It is perhaps not without significance that director Joseph Delmont not only stars in the role of the hero but also has almost the same name.

The "reason of the heart" brings the story to its happy ending and thus helps the film to depict the social reason [*Vernunft*] inherent in its story. Moreover, the love story is not simply an entertaining addition to the detective film; rather, the relationship between man and woman, as a relation of gazes, constitutes the actual "dramatizing" element. Through the latter the exciting and attractive aspects of the medium represent themselves at the level of the narrative: the liberation of the gaze, which is always, in addition, a mobilization of the forces of the drives [*Triebkräfte*]. In social drama, the object produces suspense in the gaze of the spectator. In place of the object, the detective film places the gaze within the film: this conveys the narrative through the technical attractions in front of the camera and especially through the camera work itself. This gaze, however, is not unified [*identisch*] but contains the difference between the sexes.

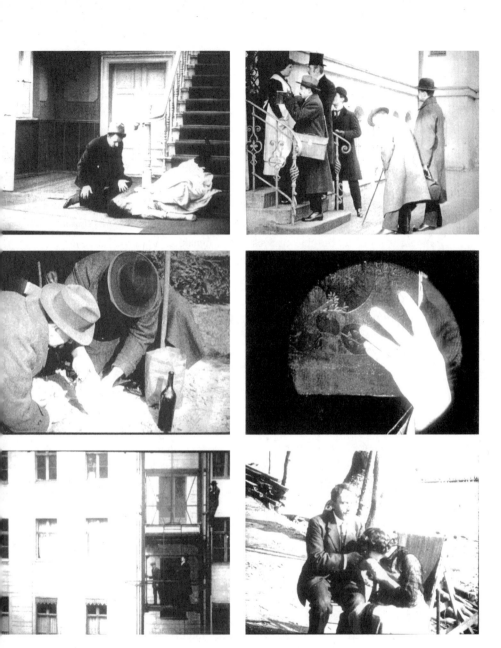

The fiction of crime in *The Right to Existence* begins with a man's gaze at an unconscious woman and ends with a woman's gaze at a man who is marked as a "criminal." Joseph Dermott, the released convict, sneaks into a villa, but as soon as he enters he nearly stumbles over a woman who is lying unconscious at the bottom of a staircase; after this discovery he immediately flees the house. Shortly thereafter the mother comes in, discovers her daughter Edith, and suspects that a crime has occurred. She calls for the doctor and the police. Both go about their work, but since Edith cannot remember anything after she wakes up, the illumination of the crime initially lies in the hands of the police. The suspense caused by the first encounter between outsider and unconscious woman is grounded in the question of whether she will remember and absolve him of the charge. For the police's circumstantial evidence testifies against him, and the fact that he has a criminal record appeals to prejudice: someone who does not value the belongings of others does not value the lives of others either. The audience is aware of Dermott's innocence, just as the unconscious of the female protagonist knows it; the suspense of whether there will be a happy ending works against prejudices, which the bourgeois audience, at least, shares with the police and with the parents in the film.

There is no other on-screen advocate for the audience's desire for happiness than the woman's unconscious; the spectators are thus in a similar state of suspense: will she regain her ability to remember? The man's ingenuity—which the audience, thanks to the achievements of the camera, follows breathlessly and, like the camera, by his side—might protect him from the pursuit by the police, but it does not return to him the bourgeois "right to existence." Only the woman can do that.

In the house of a prostitute (a *cocotte*), the innocently persecuted Dermott is granted an initial respite from his attempt to escape. Entirely in keeping with the attractions with which the detective film plays, this scene foregrounds not so much erotic details—in the background one can see the painting of a naked Venus, just so one knows what is going on—as technical ones: a "spy," attached to the window from outside, makes it possible for the maid to survey the entire street inconspicuously so that she can warn the fugitive in time. Along with her we see the police approaching in the mirror. This scene does not just consist of a clever mise-en-scène but mediates as well the audience's gaze by means of the gaze of the women who protect the fugitive; it makes explicit a solidarity that has been implicit from the beginning. In the following escape scenes, which occur across rooftops, streets, rivers, and railroad tracks, the camera's gaze is again on the side of the escapee, whom the police are, for the moment, not able to catch.

However, this is only a temporary delay. The fugitive is granted another break: injured by a jump from a train, he is discovered by a sympathetic

gentleman, an American, who harbors him until he is recovered. The escape attempt would have continued after that if Dermott had not unknowingly remained close to his only savior, Edith, during his recovery. The film had informed us about the further development of her story once before through shots quasi parallel to the scene of his stay with the prostitute; a scene with Edith—who is, to all outward appearances, recovered—was cut in between the chase scenes and those of his convalescence. Now we find out that she has been visiting a sanatorium in that area into which Dermott has been cast; an operation is supposed to give her back her memory. Before the fugitive finds his savior the film first lets him do something for her. Dermott answers a call for a blood donor in a newspaper ad, even though he compromises his disguise by doing so. The blood is intended for Edith's convalescence, but he does not know this yet. For now the film simply confirms that the male and female spectators' wish for happiness has justice on its side: someone who is not very particular about the belongings of others can nevertheless set the

lives of others above his own self-interest. At the hospital a doctor observes a tattoo on the arm of the blood donor that reminds him of that possessed by the wanted criminal. The police in Berlin are informed. However, before they arrive, Edith and Dermott become friends. We see them sitting at the beach together; he carries his arm in a sling, she thanks him for what he did.

In this sense he helped her to recover completely, that is, to regain her memory, for whose loss he was not at fault. She is now able to use her memory for his rehabilitation. The police arrive and transport the wanted criminal to Berlin. Edith finds out about this through her father and becomes agitated, since she knows now that she received her injury during a fall and not by Dermott's hand. Freed from his cell, he is brought back to Edith, who thanks him again; again, they sit at the beach together, where he pulls up his sleeve to show her his tattoo, and she bends over his naked arm and kisses it: "The voice of love." In the end even the social drama of erotic love has returned, with the tattoo playing the role of the suspense-producing object—the tattoo separated him from her but also united them in the end. Responding to Edith's kiss, Joseph Dermott takes her hand with both his hands, leans forward with his upper body, bends his right knee, slowly goes down on his knees, and buries his face in her hands, in her lap. This time he not only was released from prison but also arrived in a society without prejudices. Those aspects of the new medium that are exciting to a new society—represented by the suspense that stretches from the beginning (the man's gaze) to the end (the woman's gaze)—consist not least in the fact that technical mobility in the cinema also signifies a mobilization of the relationship between the sexes. The speech of the woman, who is now able to remember, stands above the controlling gaze of the representatives of the state, and her gaze not only returns to the outsider his innocence but also initiates his happiness. However, in the detective film *The Right to Existence* the cause of woman's loss of consciousness, memory, and ability to speak is no longer present as a prehistory but taken as an accident.

The film *The Adventures of a Journalist* [*Die Abenteuer eines Journalisten*, 1914] is directed by Harry Piel. Not only was he popular up until the 1920s and 1930s as an actor who aspired to the image of a "German Douglas Fairbanks," but he also was one of the most successful directors in the genre of the detective film, and among his preserved films are *The Bear of Baskerville* [*Der Bär von Baskerville*, 1915] and *The Castle at the Hillside* [*Das Schloss am Abhang*, 1919].[7] *The Adventures of a Journalist* establishes an explicit connection between the dynamization of the camera's gaze and an engagement with the bourgeois prejudice against a modern, mobile lifestyle, as the protagonist's detective gaze forces the patriarch to withdraw his claim to power. The rivals are a journalist named Harrison and a professor in the natural sciences named Cleavaers. The latter has a daughter, Evelijne, who is in love with the journalist. The father, however, forbids the relationship on the basis of the claim that Harrison has no proper, steady occupation. In the eyes of the professor, free-lance journalism is idleness. While *The Right to Existence* allows the outsider and the daughter of the bourgeois citizen to fall in love only after persecution and suffering, the loves of those who are not completely recognized as responsible citizens stand at the beginning of *The Adventures of a Journalist*, and they find in film a language that cannot be overheard even by the patriarch. Although it is more about the occupation—which has been misjudged as a useless scribbling—of the man, who liberates the woman from her dependency, whether marriage with a modern husband will allow the woman greater autonomy is not, in the end, of interest to the film.

The Adventures of a Journalist was shot during the year World War I broke out. Its shadow looms over the film: the professor is not just any representative of the patriarchal bourgeoisie. Even before the film shows him from this side it introduces him as the inventor of a new technology of strategic importance for the war for which the navy department had offered a high premium. The ensuing entanglements, however, are not of a military-political nature; they do not concern competing national interests but rather money. Yet the end of the film, like the beginning, deals with "the problem of wireless landmine ignition," and we see a successful "wireless" explosion. This is staged as an interesting attraction that accompanies the happy ending, and the suspense that it so visibly discharges is, in the context of the drama of the story, the tension between the sexes. However, the fact that the spraying water produced by the ignition of the landmine almost presents a metaphor for natural "relaxation" points toward future ideological ways of proceeding in which all relations between the sexes are in the service of a "naturalization" of political interests. But since this is not yet the case for this film, it makes sense to look at it from the perspective of a still visible politics of the sexes and subsequently to reflect upon the film's relationship to the war.

The order of the introduction of the characters and therefore of the sectors of life is as follows. First scene: a man (Harrison) reads in the *BZ [Berliner Zeitung] am Mittag* about Professor Cleavaers's invention; second scene: the professor in his laboratory is handed a newspaper that reports on the navy department's prize; third scene: Evelijne in her room looks out the window and waves at someone.[8] The mass medium of the newspaper is thus explicitly depicted, while the invention is only mentioned in an intertitle: it circulates from one scene to the next, from one room to another. Next we get a glimpse of the realm of research and, finally, of the private realm of a bourgeois household. Yet the woman in this private sphere looks outside, and in the next scene she follows her gaze out into the garden, where we can see to whom she was waving: the journalist Harrison. The movement of both the gaze and the film thus leads, after the short introductory scenes, from her to him, from the woman under the roof of a patriarch to the man coming from outside—a representative of a modern, mobile public sphere that, as we saw, knows how to transgress the boundaries of private rooms.

However, this movement is answered by a long, static sequence, introduced by an intertitle that informs us about the professor's prejudices against the newspaper journalist. This sequence expresses movement only as the minimal amount possible within a statically framed scene and expresses the switch from inside to outside only through internal montage. The sequence is informed by the presence of the patriarch and represents his power, which dominates the external world, in this case the love that develops outside, through a controlling gaze that originates from a stable, inner standpoint.

The camera is positioned in a dim laboratory. The professor stands at the window; his figure is shot from behind as he starts to open the blinds. Along with his gaze, the gaze of the camera looks through the blinds out into the garden, where the couple is in the middle of an intimate conversation.

However, in this shot the professor is not reduced to the function of being a bearer of the gaze; the camera's attention is also focused on the appearance of the patriarch. The camera follows his gaze but does not identify with him. Through the opening of the blinds, light from outside falls upon the man inside, and the window, still in half-darkness, reflects his figure. The bulky body, clothed in a white coat that concentrates all the brightness upon it, dominates the foreground of the image. When the professor discovers the two, he pulls the blinds up all the way in order to have a better view, and by bending his body back he clearly takes care not to be seen himself. Outside, Harrison bends over Evelijne's hand and kisses it. Thanks to the camera's deep focus we can see this as clearly as the professor sees it, but we also see how the professor's body flinches at the sight. The audience learns about the father's class-related prejudice through the text in the intertitle—the audience is familiar with such prejudices, and there is almost no need for the intertitle. However, by means of the camera the audience is also able to see what is otherwise, even when encountered in reality, invisible, namely, the father's resistance to his daughter's marriage. This resistance is stripped of all verbal and social reason and appears as an involuntary physical reaction. The fact that this is the movement of an actor does not diminish this attention to corporeality. The camera not only objectifies the patriarch but also uncovers the "optical unconscious," as Benjamin called it, while film disassembles, between text and image, the complexity of this power. Cleavaers not only winces but also twitches his arm, in the form of a reflex movement, only to let it drop again abruptly and use it to support himself on the windowsill, with his face almost touching the windowpane. Finally, he detaches his gaze and carefully retreats. The scene is over.

Thus far, the law-making [*statuarisch*], controlling gaze of the father is not only opposed to that of the daughter, whose gaze looks and rushes outward and welcomes in a loving fashion, but also depicted in this scene as standing above and superior to her gaze. However, her gaze is caught by another gaze that develops its own language in opposition to paternal control. That which would remain mere cliché in every dime novel—since the latter would be unable to do more than simply state the difference between the two men— does not remain cliché in this film. Film is able to impart to the gaze of the journalist a language different from that of control: a curious, enlightening, world-opening language of which film was only now becoming conscious in the genre of the detective film.

There is, however, yet another issue that is only striking when one thinks through the film more thoroughly. The protagonist of modernity not only picks up the gaze of the woman, which strives outward lovingly, in order to help it to realize itself in its opposition to the patriarch. The oppositional language that he employs is also itself an answer to the expression that woman's protest finds in film. Without this expression his language would be impossible. Just as in *The Right to Existence*, this film also displays at its base a gender-specific dialogic structure of dramatic form.

This dramatic form begins immediately with the father's prohibition; in order to deliver it he had ordered the couple into his workroom. The suspense begins: will the female gaze at the man assert itself against the forbidding gaze of the father? Will the advocate of modern mass culture assert himself against the champion of traditional order? A crime occurs. A gang known as Medusa desires Cleavaers's invention so that they can collect the prize. The head of the gang, Baxter, has sneaked into the professor's house disguised as

a gardener. The professor, after having been lured away on a trip by means of a telegram, is kidnapped, so the gang is able to carry away the device without any trouble. As they break into the house at night they accidentally start a fire in the lab. While Evelijne is sleeping peacefully amidst scenery that has been tinted pink, the next shot of the lab presents it in a threatening red color, and smoke billows up. Through a montage that runs parallel to the events at the researcher's villa, we see the professor himself confined in the house of the criminals.

This backstory to the actual story about the methods of criminalistic science is not just sensational; it has the character of a wishful fantasy. As soon as the film succeeds in activating in the audience a resistance to the patriarch, that is, a desire to get rid of paternalism (a resistance upon which the film can draw due to the female audience's patterns of viewing social drama), the crime ends up being nothing but the fulfillment of this fantasy. The audience need not feel any more guilt than the female protagonist, who sleeps peacefully while

the criminals remove the patriarch for her. "Medusa" is exactly the right name for this criminal behavior: it names the terror to which bourgeois male society fears it would be subjected should woman raise her gaze against it.

After this dreadful night, the path is open for Harrison the next morning: he visits Evelijne, discusses with her in the salon what to do next, and investigates the destroyed lab. The hour has come in which he can prove the social relevance of both his abilities and his medium. To begin with, Cleavaers's continued absence arouses Harrison's suspicion, since, given that a newspaper report has spread nationwide the news about the lab fire, Cleavaers should have become alarmed. Harrison begins to figure out the crime and pursue the criminals, and he remains at the center of the action until the happy conclusion. In the end the crime is solved, the father is again present, and love and the modern way of life have asserted themselves—one could say through a clear negation of the return of the archaic, that is, patricide. When the camera accompanies Harrison's enlightening gaze, it works in opposition to those shots that cling to the father's gaze and at the same time observe him. In the case of these latter shots, the camera made use aesthetically of the stability of the position inside the house, not least through a careful choice of mise-en-scène and framing, differentiated lighting, the control of deep focus, and an observation of even the smallest movements in front of the camera. In the shots of Harrison, in contrast, the camera savors all the attractions of movements that occur outside. The camera is interested in depicting the wonderful variety of technological means of transportation, in catching the speed of modern life, and in taking on this speed, mobilizing itself as part of a world-conquering technology. Against the background of the powerful, acrobatic dynamism of the chase scenes, in which Harrison snatches success away from the criminals, the aura of the patriarch fades.

After a few shorter scenes around the villa of the criminals—whose hideout Harrison soon discovers—as well as in the city streets, the Wuppertal suspension railway is displayed as a means of escape and pursuit. Enthralled by the attraction of this special transportation device, the cameraman and the director of this film delivered wonderful documentary shots. The pursuer and the pursued stage a race between car and suspension railway—who chases whom is unimportant for the attraction of the shots. What is interesting, though, is the fact that throughout, as in *The Right to Existence,* the camera takes the side of the fugitive. Harrison might not be a wanted criminal, but he shares with the latter, as the beginning of the film made clear, the position of outsider. As Harrison chases Baxter in order to prevent him from delivering the invention, two criminals in turn try to catch up to Harrison in order to thwart his plans. Only Harrison's success will negate his position as outsider. However, the construction of the chase scene depicts something else as well: during his breathless chase—which is a chase that is both for the future and after the impersonator who is trying to capitalize, undeservedly, on the results of modern science—the man of the media, in looking back, still needs to know himself how to withdraw from the grasp of the Medusa. He is moving along the turning point between, on the one hand, a return of the archaic and, on the other, a future in which the old culture of sovereignty is sublated in the new mass culture.

Following the scenes of the suspension railway, Harry Piel allows himself a trip to the western: cowboys on a field lend their horses for a race across the heath and through a hilly karst region. Soon, however, a river comes into sight, and motorboats prove to be a faster means of transportation. Here especially the standpoint of the camera, positioned close to Harrison as he is pursued, is shown to advantage. The camera looks over Harrison's back toward the riverbank, which the persecutors approach on horseback; later in a similar shot the camera observes their boat, which follows Harrison. Following this there is a risky ride on the running board of a car and a small shoot-out. Yet a sign at the side of the road—"To the airport"—implies excitements that exceed those depicted so far. This expectation is rewarded: Harrison jumps on a plane that is just about to try out a new type of bomb. Aerial shots are edited in, a fight with the pursuers' plane is hinted at—but the release of the bomb takes care of them. Harrison jumps out with a parachute and prevents Baxter's presentation of the wireless landmine explosion.

The end is short and compact. Baxter dies during his attempt to remove the landmine. The father is liberated through the help of the police. "Eight days later" the legitimate delivery and presentation of the invention by the professor to the navy department take place. Harrison and Evelijne, now engaged, attend to and kiss one another underneath the blooming branches of a tree, while the rescued father and successful researcher Cleavaers, appearing benevolent, stands by their side.

The film clearly is not shot with the intention of furthering the audience's interest in the national war; the war-related invention, its successful test, and its appropriation by the navy do not constitute the film's moment of suspense. At the same time, though, the invention does serve as the external framework for situating the detective film within society; after all, the film promotes the navy minister and the landmine explosion from a mere mention in an intertitle to a visible appearance at the end, enriched by rudimentary images of an air fight. Within a different context this can alter the reception of the film. After the war broke out the allusions of the frame narrative must have gained sweeping importance for the perception of the entire film. A pseudodrama [*Scheindramatik*] develops, Harrison becomes a national hero who saves the strategic invention, and the dynamics of the relationship between the sexes recede into the background.

The Adventures of a Journalist allow us to reconstruct how, due to the external circumstances of the war, a different interpretation is forced upon the self-consciousness of the new medium—a self-consciousness it had just gained in the detective film that turns the emancipation of the medium into its opposite. In retrospect, it might seem as though the self-confidence of the medium shifted smoothly from an internationalism to an awareness of its importance for a military state—an importance with which *The Adventures of a Journalist* also already plays. If this had been the case, however, the explicit enlistment of cinema would not have resulted in the aesthetic leveling that commercial cinema experienced during and after the war. In order to grasp the extent of the leveling, one must recall the complexity of ordinary entertainment film before World War I. Cinema was triumphant, but only on the basis of the functional interests of capital and the military. Its own emancipatory interest as well as that of the audiences with whom it interacted fell by the wayside. Yet both film itself and the audience were involved in this development. *The Mysterious Club* [*Der geheimnisvolle Klub*, 1913], another film by Joseph Delmont, differs from the previous two detective films in that it includes a woman in the dynamic of the enlightening gaze. She leaves the house and becomes the protagonist of fast-paced scenes of flight and pursuit. The emancipatory tendency of the detective film unfolds in this film with decisiveness and clarity.

A precondition for this development is the choice of material, no trivial story but rather a literary work entitled *The Suicide Club*.[9] Its author is Robert Louis Stevenson, who provided, with his novel about Dr. Jekyll and Mr. Hyde, the model of the doppelgänger for his literary successors as well as and especially for filmic representations of this topic. However, Joseph Delmont had a take on the Stevenson story very different from those of auteur directors such as Hanns Heinz Ewers in *The Student of Prague* and Max Mack in *The Other*. Delmont does not take on the role of an artist in his film production but rather that of a craftsman, a technician. As a result, his film conveys, by means of the literary story, the self-confidence of the technical medium rather than that of the bourgeois auteur: when the film begins, literary production is relegated to a past that is still under the spell of magic. *The Mysterious Club* takes up motifs from Robert Louis Stevenson's *The Suicide Club*, but the film does not concentrate on providing images for those uncanny elements

in Stevenson's work that reflect the identity crisis of the bourgeois citizen. Rather, the film deals with the literary source altogether as though it was an earlier work, the enduring presence of which in the film produces an uncanny effect. This uncanniness is from the beginning the subject of the camera as it demonstrates its enlightening power over the former; it does so with the pathos of certainty that the literary text itself is only a relic that the visual language of film will not have to sustain for much longer. The old magic will be sublated in a new aesthetic miracle.

The Mysterious Club shifts Stevenson's uncanny story from foggy, gloomy London to the clear light of authentic locations in Holland. The film contains technically brilliant shots of Rotterdam's main train station, a steel structure, city promenades, banks and stores, canals, the beach of Scheveningen, seaside facilities, turn-of-the-century hotels, and the then still new sport of bicycling. They all appear as locations of modern life, independently from the fact that they also serve as locales for the fictional plot.

That this bourgeois, enlightened world might also contain relics of uncanny criminality initially appears only as a suspicion in the mind of Gerhard Bern, the young son of a merchant from Berlin—and it appears this way as well in the mind of the spectator. Through a letter that the audience is also able to read, Bern learns of the suicide of his brother, who lived in Rotterdam, and about the latter's will, which leaves his fortune and the rights to his expensive life insurance to a secret club. Bern decides to travel to Rotterdam along with a detective in order to clarify these murky events. By establishing that crimes have been committed—that is, by uncovering and thus resolving the uncanny as that which persists as a threat amidst the bourgeoisie—the film essentially presents its abilities to enlighten by means of technology, abilities that shine even more brilliantly because they bear the dark background that accompanies the confirmation of uncanny suspicions.

In Rotterdam the male protagonist encounters a woman who immediately becomes the center of his world there for him. While the suicide constitutes

the prehistory that provides the foundation for the story of the enlightening gaze, the story itself unfolds between Bern and the woman. The resolution of the enigma that the brother's suicide presents becomes, even before it begins, a function of the emancipation of the woman. Ilse Verstraaten is the daughter of Consul Verstraaten, an acquaintance of the detective whose support Bern and the detective seek when they first arrive in Rotterdam. She is courted by the "salon hero" van Geldern, who soon becomes the object of suspicion. Though Bern wins her heart in a snap, she, in order to separate herself from her deep-seated affinity to van Geldern's mysterious appearance (of magic power, of the dark side of capital), must first recognize and identify this power herself. This process of recognition [*Erkenntnis*] is initiated by Bern's entry into her father's house and into the garden, the favorite place of both mother and daughter. In the end her recognition in turn enables his salvation as well, for he must enter the criminal alliance in order to be able to break it apart. The positions of the sexes shift, since their love allows them to complement

one another. At first, the young man arrives from Berlin in order to alert the Rotterdam merchants, and especially one merchant's daughter, to the dark danger that surrounds them. However, he is then imprisoned in the dark rooms of a building in Rotterdam that is accessible only through a courtyard, and the woman comes to his rescue by taking a train from a seaside resort; a carriage from the station to the detective's hotel; and finally, along with the latter, a boat in order to reach the hidden locale on the other side of the maze of the canals.

It is interesting to note how the film places contouring side tones and shades amidst its depiction of a bright, bourgeois world, such that it suggests that one has escaped an abyssal conflict. The female protagonist, Ilse Verstraaten, played by Ilse Bois, presents herself from the beginning as a modern young woman who, dressed in sporty fashions, moves without restraint around the large park that surrounds her father's house. In the midst of this cultivated central European milieu, her constant companion and playmate, a fully grown ape, creates a bizarre effect. His presence can certainly be read as a reference to the Dutch colonies; it can also be explained by reference to the director's capacities as an animal tamer. Yet at the same time, the ape that accompanies the woman is the tamed figure of her fascination with the Other—the irrational and uncivilized, according to then-current Darwinian theories; the prehistoric past of human beings themselves. The contours of the female protagonist are produced by this "accessory"; the entire film works with the black-and-white values of moving black-and-white photography. Yet it does so not in order to stage romantic images but rather to create, by means of twilight, a transparent and moving plasticity in clear outdoor shots. The first encounter between the "enlighteners" from Berlin and the fake "gentleman" from Rotterdam is captured in a cleverly arranged shot: the carriage in which the antagonists (the detective and the suspect) both disappear from sight is filmed from the entrance to a store. Like the audience that views the bright screen from a dark room, the camera is directed from a dark place toward the light—an unobserved, observing gaze that occurs precisely in that moment when the carriage rolls away. Like an echo of the sudden insight that the illumination of the uncanny has begun to move forward, the carriage, which had left our field of sight on the right, reappears for a moment on the left, reflected in the dark surface of a shop window that is to the side, in the shadows.

As "enlightenment" comes close, the criminal elements are, at the same time, granted pictorial momentum. Entire shots are now dedicated to them, and these shots alternate with tracking shots of a penetrating gaze. The criminal headquarters is a hermetically sealed interior, overladen with rugs, heavy curtains, and dark furniture. No daylight enters the room. Gerhard Bern has become a member of the club in order to reconstruct the fate of his brother. During a card game he is, like his brother before him, dealt the seven of spades, and thus he is supposed to kill himself with a pistol, as outlined in the contract of the alliance. By himself he would hardly have been able to turn things around and capture van Geldern. However, the film offers us a shift back and forth between scenes of the club, tinted in brown, and outdoor shots in which Ilse and the detective hurry through streets and canals to his rescue; these latter are tinted in a cool blue.

Following the successful liberation of the captured Bern and during a brawl, Ilse ends up in the hands of van Geldern, who manages to reach a boat and flee with her. After all the different trips through Rotterdam that occur as the criminals are pursued and following Ilse's hasty departure from the seaside

resort and her arrival in the city and at the center of dark machinations, the film now arrives at its crowning finale, an impressive chase sequence. The pursuit leads through the narrow canals up to the more open area around the harbor. Two boats, one containing the police and one containing Verstraaten and Bern, pursue van Geldern and the abducted Ilse. The camera remains close to the pursued criminal and his victim, which means that the suspense of escape is constructed not just from the gaze back toward the pursuers but also from the close-up of the woman's struggles to free herself. In the end it is even necessary for her to fight against the naked violence of one who has by now lost all other forms of power. As the boat rushes along Ilse tries to wriggle out of van Geldern's grip, while the camera keeps the boats that follow within the horizon of our view. Looking toward the front, the boat presses forward between the façades of buildings and beneath bridges. Beneath the bridges the fighting bodies merge to form huge, dark silhouettes, but, just as these figures almost merge into the shadows of the vaults of the bridge,

the arch opens the camera's gaze to the bright background against which the boats become visible. The constancy of this view at the boats provides a support for the woman. The suspension of the camera between dynamism and photographic fixity is thus finally directed at the desire for freedom, that is, a distinct self. As they reach the spacious harbor area Ilse Verstraaten is able to liberate herself through her own means: she jumps to the shore, where her father and her lover can reach her. A Dutch drawbridge mechanism causes the criminal to fall into the water, making it possible to capture him. The technical object steals the show from the persecutors.

Female Detectives

The mobilization of the gaze by means of the mobilization of the camera is, in its technicity, also a social mobilization. Yet the social movement that finds expression in this mobilization should not be confused with that of the rising bourgeoisie that is conquering the world. The male protagonists are outsiders who oppose the established bourgeois reality of high capitalism by means of bourgeois ideals of enlightenment. However, detective films do not have their basis in such obsessions; rather, they have their basis in the self-consciousness of film technology. As a result, they do not illustrate "positions"; instead, their dynamic expresses the fact that the position of enlightenment itself has begun to shift. Prior to World War I the ideals of humanity, freedom, and equality had become subject to the loosening up of the petrified relationship between the sexes; only the emancipation of woman and of the relationship between the sexes can, in the context of a sublation of class oppositions, return a lost social meaning to these ideals. The social mobility that is reflected in the mobilization of the camera in detective films is the mobility of a relationship between the sexes that has begun to shift.

The detective films discussed thus far illustrate this in the way in which the mobility of the male gaze, which already exists, must be linked to the female gaze, which still needs to win both itself and its freedom. Even though these films include the "detective-like" gaze, they do not center on the figure of the detective, as in the case of the classical detective novel. There were equivalents to the latter in German film as well. Stuart Webbs was the name of the hero of an entire series of detective films. *The Man in the Basement* [*Der Mann im Keller*], the only film from this series with which I am familiar, lacks the usual chase scenes. As far as one can tell from the fragmentary copy, the film consists of a rather wooden stringing together of episodes within which the detective's gaze proves its abilities by engaging hideouts, secret doors, and disguises. The female gaze might also play a propulsive role, but it does not play a mobile one. The film is about Stuart Webbs returning a missing fiancé to a woman. He does so—but twice: "Good heavens, which of these is my groom now?" asks the intertitle, and Stuart Webbs must first lift his mask before she can fall into the arms of the correct man. It is as though, because of the dominant position of the detective in detective films, the mobility of the relationship between the sexes—as a game of covering and uncovering that circulates around itself—becomes arrested once again.

With the introduction of female detectives, in contrast, the detective film achieves a new quality in the reflection of the female gaze. In German film the female equivalent to Stuart Webbs was named Nobody, played by Senta Eichstaedt. In the role of the detective, woman already occupies the position of the equal, free gaze, which the female protagonists of other films still

needed to develop to a greater or lesser extent. Consequently, this character is marked as a fictional one through and through: even though she can be interpreted as an example of a professional woman, just as the Ilses, Evelijnes, and Ediths can be read as examples of upper-class daughters, she is essentially the male literary stereotype turned female for the narrator of the detective story. Through the figure of the female detective the genre of the detective film thus becomes self-reflexive.

Aside from the Nobody films—of which I was able to see only two: *The Mystery of the Château Richmond* [*Das Geheimnis des Chateau Richmond*] and *The Chase for the One-Hundred-Pound Bill* [*Die Jagd nach der Hundertpfundnote*, both 1913]—there is a type of female detective beyond that embodied by Nobody, namely, the detective Ellen Gray in *The Wanted Poster* [*Der Steckbrief*, 1913]. This type exemplifies the fact that once the female gaze, mobilized by the enlightenment pathos of detective films, has been achieved, it turns into the imago of a threat, which questions from inside out the self-consciousness of the new medium and the form of the detective film along with it. Female detective films no longer begin with the emancipation of the female gaze; rather, the self-reflexivity of the genre achieved by these films reflects an arrest of the mobility of the relationship between the sexes—that is, the historical moment in which the latter either transforms into a complete emancipation of society or virtually falls back into the archaic spell of the battle between the sexes.

The Mystery of the Château Richmond unfolds, in all its liberal power, the role of the woman who owns the gaze, who spies, and who illuminates things. The film employs a motif that is like that of *The Mysterious Club:* an alliance between men that has its own mysterious rituals and from which one can withdraw only through the loss of life or fortune. In this case Farley, the hero, must sign over his entire fortune, including any future earnings, to the alliance. Naturally, he immediately receives an unexpected inheritance, and since Farley doesn't even entertain the thought of adhering to the agreement that was extorted from him, complications begin. Fortunately for the hero, though, his lack of loyalty to the alliance is the subject of observation not only by his former alliance brothers but also by an entirely different factor. The Dresdner Bank sends a female detective after Farley, since he had just received a generous inheritance from them. For one "party" it is a matter of fulfilling an unlawful contract; for the other it is a matter of being certain about the legitimacy of the heir. On one side we see, in much more exaggerated fashion than in *The Mysterious Club,* an antiquated world that makes use of the subtle terror of magical practices (they convene in candlelight around a human skull); on the other side, there is the modern world, in which enrichment not only is rationalized as the business of a bank but must also be legal. Both of these worlds compete for the hero. The role reversal of the sexes, which in *The Mysterious Club* was still tied to the basic fact that this is a matter of the emancipation of woman from the influences of dark beings, has now been radically completed: even though the protagonist withdrew from the alliance of men, he remains under the threatening shadows of this past, while the woman, who belongs entirely to modernity, is able to help him ban the spell completely. Toward the end of the film she herself steps into the midst of the dangerous conspirators in order to put an end to their spooky activities.

The uncanny places belong entirely to the male protagonist not just because of the alliance but also in a way that is independent from this. Farley lives in an old castle that contains secret doors and suits of armor within which enemies

can hide, and nightmares haunt him at night, appearing alternately in the guise of his alliance confederates and the detective. The masculine trauma, constituted by a return of the threatening shadow of the past in the guise of modern woman, is represented by means of a stop-action trick; still, the film answers this trauma with documentary shots of realms that belong together in reality: by splitting the image, the film depicts Nobody as she phones the banker. The left third of the image presents the head of the Dresdner Bank on the phone; the right third presents Nobody; and intertitles in between the two let us know what they are saying. This scene employs the trick image differently than was the case in the mise-en-scène of the dream. In the former case the film produced an illusion, while in this case a relationship to reality is established precisely because the film conveys, through its technical trick, that the shots it combines are filmic records of reality. Through technical means it connects things that are visually distant, just as the telephone, which is presented on-screen, connects things that are acoustically distant. In this instance, the

content of this scene, in conjunction with the text panel in the middle of the screen, renders the form of the film self-reflexive.

The Mystery of Château Richmond includes the chases and shots of urban scenery as well as shots of cars, motorboats, and so on that are typical for this genre. Bound up with these attractions are plot elements such as concealment, detection, and disguise that belong to the classical figure of the detective. Because of the female cast these plot devices become significant in a specific way. In the Nobody films what is striking is the pronounced mise-en-scène of the gaze in everyday, rather than exceptional, situations and the emphasis on clothing in general, not just disguises [*Maskerade*]. It is as though the fact that woman appears in public and maintains power over the gaze is excitement enough, that is, as though there is no need for further attractions beyond this gaze.

The female detective is depicted not only as observant and as spying in her professional role but rather as focusing her gaze on man more generally.

In one sequence Nobody follows Farley into a bank, maintaining a distance from him as he stands at a counter in order to process his transactions. Both people are shot from the side and from the same distance from the camera: he stands frame-left, and she is near the right side of the frame. This shot emphasizes how the detective story enables women's gaze at man, and at the same time the situation is captured with a strong emphasis on the vertical lines of the frame. In other scenes the female gaze distinguishes itself from a masculine background. During the first fleeting encounter on the street between Farley and Nobody, both protagonists turn toward one another as they pass: his is the typical gaze at a woman, but she is able, in unusually active and self-confident fashion, to return the gaze because of her role as detective. In the chases near the end of the film, gaze and countergaze are even expressed by means of a kind of shot/reverse-shot montage. The band of criminals pursue the detective; the camera captures her in the foreground and looks back toward the pursuers along with her. The next shot works the other way round, adopting the gaze of the men at her. The identification of the perspective of the camera with the pursuers is, as I have demonstrated, not common in detective films of this time. As a result, one can assume that this deviation is based on the gender of the main character and that it presents the first instances of a shot/reverse-shot montage that already possesses precisely the ideological significance that it will assume later. The emphasis on the mise-en-scène of the female gaze in the Nobody films cultivates an attraction, but it also already domesticates a transgression.

Nobody represents the New Woman through her posture and clothing. She wears a black woman's suit with a long, tapered jacket that emphasizes her strong but slender figure; velvet lapels, a white blouse, and a white feather in her hat lend her a vivacious elegance. In another scene she wears a long, sporty, white scarf around her head that is also tied around her neck and that is complemented by a light coat with dark lapels. The (photo)graphic effect of her outfit is in the foreground; even in the final scene, a festive ball that takes place after all the excitement, the simple cut of her dress, over which she wears a translucent dark jacket, the cut of which is reminiscent of her "professional clothes," makes her stand out amidst all the other ladies in their frilly and lacy dresses.

The care with which clothing has been chosen facilitates, on the one hand, her characterization as an emancipated woman; on the other hand, though, it focuses attention on clothing as "costume," which enables the implicit suspicion that her professional role might also be just a masquerade. The film

dilates on this notion of masquerade by playing with gender roles. In order
to outwit her persecutors Nobody slips into the role of a man: in a checkered
suit and cap and with a mask in front of her face she looks with contentment
at her image in a wardrobe mirror, a wardrobe into which Farley will disappear a moment later in order to escape his pursuers. For a moment the real

man stands before the false one like a mirror image. As she flees, Nobody dupes the pursuers a second time—with lightning speed, she dresses up as a farm maid. She pretends to be someone else yet again when she comes to a meeting of the alliance dressed in a man's suit and a hooded cloak. There she tears off her disguise and turns the men over to the police. The following scene, that of the ball, depicts her as even more "feminine" than before yet still differing from conventional femininity: she takes Farley by the hand. After playing with gender roles, this is a confirmation of sexual difference [*Geschlecht*].

The Chase for the One-Hundred-Pound Bill depicts Nobody once again in the context of chase scenes and depictions of voyeurism and masquerade; however, the film adds to this the attractions of an exotic ambience. Since these attractions are produced primarily in the studio, they displace the photography of everyday life, of unstaged reality. The film moves through a series of references: Cairo, Bombay, and Nagasaki appear as if they are illustrations from travelogues and adventure stories; an attack on a train by Native Americans could have come from an American western. The film makes reference to itself as well in the sense that, as a sequel within a series, it has at its command a filmic existence of the protagonist that extends beyond its own context of action. A scene in the Orient is introduced by the following intertitle: "When necessary, Nobody carries on her profession everywhere." The episode that follows has almost nothing to do with the main plot. Nobody uncovers an opium den. She again makes use of her skills of masquerade: Turkish trousers and a velvet jacket transform her into an "Oriental."

The disempowerment of the female gaze through a countergaze—which, as a consequence, brings into play sexual difference—seems even more pronounced in the second Nobody film. There are honest-to-goodness duels between gazes: at the New York harbor, she observes the male object of her investigation through binoculars in a shot that employs a binocular matte that represents her gaze; however, the young businessman observes her gaze and reaches for his field glasses as well. In the end the detective loses the duel into which, to a greater and greater extent, the film develops; she is not able to complete her assignment. However, she fails less because of professional incapacity than because her job does not remain unaffected by her private life. Over the course of events the young man liberates a woman from a harem; now Nobody must observe two people. This alters the character of her gaze; it changes from a gaze that enlightens to one that is clouded by

passion and jealousy. Her defeat in the end is thus double: instead of *her* finally being able to hold the hand of the male protagonist, he gives his hand to the dependent woman whom he was able to liberate, heroically, from her slavish existence.

The transformation of the enlightened and enlightening gaze of woman into an agency of wrenching passion is also depicted in *The Wanted Poster,* a film produced by the Luna Company and directed by Franz Hofer. Yet this film also realizes that the interests of modern man cannot be readily amalgamated with those of female emancipation. During the attempt of detective film to establish an equality of the female gaze, the old battle between the sexes enters the picture again. Hofer was one of the most exceptional directors of the time, though he also is almost unknown today.

He was Austrian and early on was enthusiastically active in theater, as we learn from the article "Art and Literature in the Cinema" ["Kunst und Literatur im Kino"], which was part of the 1913 special edition of the magazine

Lichtbild-Bühne entitled "The Movie Director" ["Der Kino-Regisseur"]. The fact that he had an opportunity to contribute to this issue illustrates his prominence at the time. He claimed that his disillusionment with theater—"my dark, theater-hostile soul, which had once held theater so dear"—contributed to his decision to switch to film. It can be verified that from 1910 on he was working as a scriptwriter in German cinema, and in 1913 he directed what was—presumably—his first film with the newly founded Luna-Film GmbH, a company for which he had, by 1914, shot at least twenty-five films. The title of his first film is *The First Signs of Age* [*Des Alters erste Spuren*]; it is already 826 meters long.[10]

Hofer worked with then-prominent actors and actresses such as Rudolf del Zopp, Franz Schwaiger, Manny Ziener, Frieda Richard, Doritt Weixler, and Mia Cordes, to name just a few. Emerich Hanus, who himself became an interesting director during the war, also starred in Hofer's films. Hofer's last work as director for Luna was *Chamber Music* [*Kammermusik*], which was produced

in 1914 and which premiered on March 12, 1915. During the war Hofer col-
laborated with a number of different production companies, Messter-Film
GmbH among them, only to try his hand at his own production company—the
Hofer-Film-GmbH—for a short time after the war.[11] In the following years he
produced films less frequently than in his early productive years; in 1925 he
directed a remake of one of his first films, *The Little Pink Slipper* [*Das rosa
Pantöffelchen*], and in 1929 he directed what is apparently his last film for
German cinema: *Madame X, the Woman of Confidential Advice* [*Madame X, die
Frau für diskrete Beratung*]. From the films that he directed during 1913–14
at least two comedies have been preserved, *Hooray! Accommodations!* [*Hurra!
Einquartierung!* 1913] and *Miss Piccolo* [*Fräulein Piccolo*, 1914], as well as a
"home front" film from the first year of the war, *Christmas Bells* [*Weihnachts-
glocken*]. There are three other films from 1913 that I wish to analyze in more
detail: the "thrilling detective drama" *The Wanted Poster* and the "sensational
films" *The Black Viper* [*Die schwarze Natter*] and *The Black Ball* [*Die schwarze
Kugel*] (the latter is also called *The Mysterious Sisters* [*Die geheimnisvollen
Schwestern*]). Hofer seems to have been a virtuoso in multiple arenas, as his
movement between genres in 1913 suggests. The handful of films noted here
already reveal an unusual variety. However, in general he seems to have passed
on melodrama and social drama. At the same time, though, the theme of social
drama reappears in all these different genres. *Hooray! Accommodations!* for
example, a "woman-in-pants" comedy, could also be read as a comical version of "woman's struggle between her feminine-sensual instincts and social
conditions," which is at the center of social drama, according to Altenloh. A
comical version, but not one that holds up this struggle to ridicule. Hofer's
films do not retreat from the unmistakable manifestations of the female gaze
in cinema that are characteristic of social drama. Rather, these films constitute
different versions of a sympathy with the rise of women in modernity and
with the intimidation that such emancipation triggers in men. This social,
or sociopsychological, interest is reflected in an aesthetic interest in border
crossing and in a pleasure in travesty, whether of images of women—*Miss
Piccolo* is a trouser role as well—or genres.

   The Wanted Poster revels in excess with respect to both; the film not only
casts the detective as female, but it also pursues the consequences of a
transgression of traditional sex and gender roles for the form of the detective film in general. While this genre celebrates the modern gaze associated
with technology, science, and the enlightened world, *The Wanted Poster*

problematizes the pathos of enlightenment. In taking its departure from romanticism, modernity has not automatically thereby achieved rationality [*Vernunft*]. Even though that which is inscrutably libidinal [*Triebhafte*]—which the spectator of Hofer's film encounters in the character of the emancipated woman—springs from projection, this projection itself reveals a real insecurity that has entered man's optimism, his enlightened gaze at modern society. Hofer's detective is a female "detector" who presents guilt not as the result of a violation of the prevailing order but rather as something that springs from the rationality of the latter.

In the first part of the film the protagonist, a man of the city, finds himself carried back to but alienated from a romantic nature-world. Wanted by the police and tired of life, Egon Valier finds in nature peace and relaxation from the stress of the escape, and through the love of a young countrywoman, Nelly Ferron, he finds new courage. Detective Ellen Gray goes into action only in the second part; she locates and identifies the alleged criminal (whose crime, incidentally, will never be cleared up). At the start of the third part she attempts to arrest him; he is able to escape, but there is no happy ending. The story of this man is tragic because the woman is able to offer him only refuge, but she is not, as in *The Right to Existence,* able to return innocence and a bourgeois existence to him. Instead, the mighty gaze of the emancipated woman tears apart the veil of love and makes the man conscious of the fact that he cannot escape the stigma of guilt. The film does not end with Egon Valier's capture but rather with his resignation—"no more fleeing"—and, parallel to this, a depiction of the suicide of his lover.

In all its parts *The Wanted Poster* offers brilliant outdoor shots, among which the landscape portraits in the first part and the images in the third part of a fairground, the site of the flight and pursuit of Valier, stand out. However, the character of these outdoor shots differs from that of those customary in detective films. In the latter a pleasure in documenting everyday urban life and the modern, technological world plays a central role. In *The Wanted Poster,* in contrast, nature replaces the city. The shots are stripped of everything accidental and incidental that are consequences of the pleasure of discovery; instead, they are determined by a stylistic intention [*Stilwille*] clearly influenced by the tradition of romantic landscape painting. Take, for example, the gaze from a steep slope out toward the vast countryside: in the foreground the silhouette of a lonesome man stands out against the bright sky. Or an immersion in a river valley: against a background of softly rolling fields, a splashing waterfall, and bright eddies of water the wanderer, world-weary and deep in thought, plays with a bouquet of flowers given to him by an unknown young woman as she passed.

Even the customary scenes of flight and pursuit do not act out a fascination with technology; they do not serve as a way of presenting the latest means of transportation (cars, trains, planes, etc.). Rather, in these scenes film returns to the world from which it developed as an entertainment medium: the fairground. There too technological processes of modernization have occurred; the film does not make a detour around these but rather employs them in order to mobilize the camera. A Ferris wheel constitutes the main attraction in the chase scene; in several shots attention is directed at the movement and scale of this wheel. However, as the camera takes a ride on the wheel in one of its cars, there is no shift from a fascination with technical objects to a pleasure in the mobility of the camera. Rather, what occurs is a reflection on the subjectivity of technical reproduction, an expression of a division [*Brechung*] of nature by the subject. In this sense a different gaze—i.e., different from the gaze at the "old world" in the first part of the film—falls upon the landscape: one that is fragmented and unstable, clearly dependent upon the standpoint of the camera [*Aufnahmestandpunkt*], and lacking a stable frame.

The Wanted Poster does not—as clearly was the case in *The Adventures of a Journalist,* for example—oppose static with powerfully dynamic camera work; rather, over the course of the film it replaces stylizing/harmonizing camera work with camera work that fragments and that is unstable—an expression of skepticism rather than self-confidence. Nor does this difference in the way

the camera operates represent differences between traditional and modern masculinity; rather, it represents an inner conflict of the modern male character himself, a conflict that concerns the contrast between "natural" and emancipated femininity. In order to distinguish the past or doomed world of the traditional woman from that of the "new" woman, the film resorts to the formal means of traditional visual art. These means go beyond those of the stylization of landscape mentioned above. The first part is framed and interlaced with the "myth-turned-image," which initially, with respect to content and form, stands in contrast to the combination of enlightenment and visuality in the detective genre. As the second part begins these images are omitted; the world of the female detective is the world of enlightenment beyond myth. However, from the beginning the film does not align itself with the mythical; rather, it uses the latter as a source of attractive images in the style of historicist, neoromantic painting. Through this aestheticizing transformation the idea of fate already presents itself as a life-giving illusion. After the first shot, which depicted the fugitive's exhaustion with life, an intertitle states: "At the forge, though, they had determined his fate differently," and after this, the "forge of fate" enters the picture. Pixielike figures with floral wreaths in their hair whir around the anvil and forge not swords but rings. This intermediary scene is tinted red.

As the mythical beings swarm out into the landscape scenery of the first part, they bring an element of unreality into the presentation of the harmony of nature. Amor, clad in a little white coat, shoots an arrow at Valier, who immediately afterward encounters the countryside beauty, Nelly Ferron. The secularization of myths and the fictionalization of technically reproduced reality extend further: by means of a double exposure, Nelly appears, dream-like, in the place of Amor, whose ghostlike appearance and disappearance are achieved through a stop-action trick. She seems to step behind the man, who daydreams and plays with the bouquet that she gave to him. He jumps up as though he felt her touch and turns around; the apparition, teasing him, shifts position in order to remain behind his back and touches him again. He shudders; the flowers slip from his hands, which he turns toward the imagined lover as the apparition disappears: still completely occupied by his desire, he opens his arms. Then, in close-up, he slowly comes to his senses and touches his forehead; a smile comes over his face, he takes a deep breath, bends toward the flowers on the ground, picks them up, and presses his face into them.

In its visualization of body *and* imagination, real landscape *and* romanticizing gaze, the film overcomes the banality that such a story would have in a novel. At the intersection of an aestheticization of myth and an enlightening-realist mode of photography, the romantic love of the bourgeois citizen as outsider, that is, of the lonely subject, is depicted in its tension between the physical intensity of desire and the creation of imagination—an imagination that profits as much from the attraction of reality as from its exclusion. As a result, the destruction of romantic love does not come from outside, as might seem to be the case from the narrative constellation of the protagonists (i.e., the female detective breaking into the lovers' idyll). After the lovers' first walk together, the forge, tinted red, is edited in a second time: the pixies forge the rings into a chain. A scene that provides a segue into the second part follows: Ellen Gray reads the wanted poster. Subsequently, this "realistic" scene is interpreted "mythically": in the forge of fate the rings break under the hammer. With this scene the forge is referenced for the last time. For now the second part of the film starts, in which the work of the female detective begins. The film thus introduces her at the interface of the romantic and the modern worlds. As heroine of enlightenment she presents the negative power that is itself part of what it negates. In this sense a moment of mythical force returns along with her, even though myth itself had already seemed to yield to the beautiful semblance.

The film depicts the figure of the female detective in such a way that she resembles an archaic (male) fantasy in modernity, a Medusa. Yet with her appearance at the beginning of the second part the narrative perspective of the male hero recedes into the background behind the gaze of the woman in the

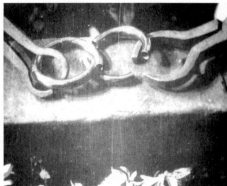

film, enabling an unmediated voyeurism on the part of the film's spectator. The audience can watch the fugitive along with the detective, but, above all, it watches this woman and her gaze. While Nelly Ferron, the lover aligned with nature, appeared to poor Valier as a tantalizing daydream, Ellen Gray presents herself to the man in the movie theater as a perverse eroticist. While in the first case the distinction between dream and reality was obvious, at least at the level of narrative (even as this distinction excluded the character of the woman), the figure of the detective oscillates irresolvably between the realist image of an emancipated professional woman and the fantastic image of a sensually destructive, devouring femininity. *The Wanted Poster* is an incomparable example of the cinematic depiction of the relationship between the sexes as in transition, between a romanticization of the traditional roles of femininity—taken entirely from the imagination of man—and the staging of the attraction and the threat of the New Woman, a staging in which the gaze of woman is involved.

Detective Gray has a broad face with a strong chin framed by black curls, dark eyes, an ample mouth, heavily painted lips, and sensually large nostrils. Her occupation—which involves observing, investigating, and monitoring—always seems erotically charged, as though it were ultimately a perverse satisfaction of the drives [*Triebbefriedigung*]. Close-ups reveal her facial expression of satisfaction whenever she is in control of "enlightenment" and lust in her eyes whenever it is a matter of capturing a fugitive. The sexual foundation of her activities as a detective is especially evident in two scenes. As Gray approaches Valier for the first time in a pub in order to determine whether he has a mark on his neck that was noted in the wanted poster, she takes on

the body language of seduction. This "eroticization" of the act of sneaking up on him is *her* performance, her cover—the woman in the film thus has male fantasy "in her grip," and she does not intend to satisfy this fantasy. This power in turn constitutes part of her attraction for the audience in front of the screen. With a flower in her mouth she comes close to Valier, her victim, in flirtatious fashion; she pours some wine for him and forces him to make a toast with her. Stimulated, he begins to fantasize; she strokes his neck; with a sudden shock he realizes that someone other than the romantic woman of his dreams stands behind him. Using force, the detective still makes an effort to see that toward which her controlling gaze is directed (the mark on his neck), but the man is able to escape.

But not for long. After the poor fellow has tried in vain to see his beloved once again—on the side of the beloved, the mother acts as a cruel obstruction to happy love—and, in addition, has been accused of murder, the detective is able to strike. Clad in a shimmering, dark blouse, with a black band adorning

her neck, the detective sneaks into Valier's room at night. She lustfully rolls her eyes before she knocks. Valier opens the door in his shirtsleeves—she makes a suggestive and provocative step toward him, is already across the threshold, closes the door from inside the room, and draws her gun. She drops her mask of smiling sweetness, and her face takes on a serious expression. He tries to wrestle the pistol from her, a shot is accidentally fired, and the fight is continued on top of the bed. At the same time Gray's assistant climbs across the roof and observes the action from a heart-shaped opening in the window shutter. At this point the film shifts from the gaze of the woman—as an exhibition of female potency—to the gaze of the man, in which the voyeurism of the audience as well as the gaze of the camera and the director find representation. The detective drama of flight and pursuit constitutes, in the dramatic climax, a primal scene [*Urszene*] of masochistic scopophilia.

The Wanted Poster allows a dream of love at the beginning of modernity to shift into the image of an archaic battle between the sexes. At the same

time, though, this cinematic procedure signifies a displacement of the male position. The representative of this male position—the protagonist in front of the camera—is negated by the female gaze that controls the screen, and in its negation it facilitates the position of man/men behind the camera and in front of the screen. *The Wanted Poster* reflects upon and transcends the standard role of the pursued man. This is possible because there is no close reciprocal relationship between director and male protagonist, as had been the case, for example, with Joseph Delmont. The man who is pursued is introduced as "world-weary," unable to make clever use of technology. Only the images of a romantic landscape, of a wonderful lover, awaken him to life once again. In a similar fashion the cinema offers to men, exhausted by the hustle of modern professional life, a place that meets their desire for regression. However, in the midst of his devotion to dream-life [*Traum des Lebens*] he is, like the hero on-screen, confronted with the female power of the gaze. Unlike the hero, though, he remains in his seat, fascinated, rather than running away. The actress at first leads him only further into the labyrinths of his unconscious. Yet in the end he finds himself there and awakens—not as the hunted hero but as the little assistant of the strong woman. Directors such as Urban Gad took on the role of assisting the self-performance of woman before the camera, a self-performance that was directed at provoking man, producing self-surrender, and creating erotic and social exposure. The scene of the battle between the sexes, observed through a peephole, conveys the position of a director, who aligns himself with the interests of women, to the audience: against male indifference toward, and fear of, the emancipation of women at that time. In the last scenes of the flight across the fairground,

the figure of the detective begins to become lost amidst the landscape, and at the end she disappears entirely. Her gaze, however, which the camera has supported all along, has now been taken up by the gaze of her "assistant," the spectator. In the end the hero is at the mercy of the latter.

The detective has disappeared because her job is done: the hero has been "discovered." Gloomy and exhausted, he sits at a table in the garden of an inn and allows his head to rest upon his arms. At the conclusion of his movement through the world there is no salvation; the spectator sees no redemptive woman who waits for him. At the same time as the romantic lover—and not, as the logic of myth would have it, the woman who makes the man justify himself—throws herself into an abyss far away from him, the modern Oedipus gives up. He tears up the letter, in which he affirms his innocence, and throws it into the same river in which Nelly Ferron seeks death. On the shore stands a large rock onto which Valier had once engraved a sentence for Nelly: "Your love is my life." Before she threw herself into the water, his despairing lover inscribed the antithesis below this: "Your love is my death." When, finally, in close-up, the pieces of the ripped testimony of innocence are carried away by the swirling water, the end of romantic love is linked to the end of literary culture. This image of the forces of nature devouring writing reflects the failure of the desired reconciliation between technical visual reproduction and text [*Schrift*]. Yet the spectator, "living without books," has been released from his Oedipal blindness by gazing at Medusa in film.

Chapter Seven

Uncanniness of the Female Gaze
Sensational Drama

In Feuillade's *ciné-romans* an actress appeared who was celebrated by the avant-garde of the 1920s as well as by female French cineasts of the 1970s for whom she became their leading figure: Musidora.[1] Her first big-screen appearance was *Les Vampires* (1915), a detective story in several installments in which she—as the head of a gang of criminals—is the real adversary of a journalist who is determined to illuminate that which is hidden. Her "professional outfit" consists of a black bodysuit that envelops her from head to toe, stressing her female figure in an obscene way but also emphasizing her uncovered face, her gaze. This figure of the artistically mobile female body, the movements of which are directed by a powerful gaze, also embodies the shift from a modern presentation of a highly technologized world to a mythical image of libidinally motivated [*triebhaften*] crime—a shift with which *Les Vampires* plays more generally.

A genre related to the detective film, sensational drama seems to have developed in German cinema, and it employs a similar focus on the female power of the gaze. The pathos of enlightenment of the detective film is especially evident in Eiko Company productions, a company for which Joseph Delmont was working, while Franz Hofer, working at Luna, had already depicted the shift from enlightenment to myth in *The Wanted Poster*. He also dedicated sensational dramas such as *The Black Viper* and *The Black Ball* (both 1913) to a female gaze that oscillates between enlightenment and the return of that which is archaic.

The detective film had a tendency to place the consummation of its inherent enlightening movement—which manifested itself in a fascination with technology—in an emancipation of the relationship between the sexes, which means first and foremost the emancipation of the female gaze. The female detective represents this aim. In this respect it is in fact not the mobile camera and its fascination with technical mobility that finally constitutes the most advanced moment in cinema but rather the appearance of the female gaze on the screen. Hofer's sensational dramas are especially devoted to the latter, and in this way they develop their own form, which is different from that of the detective film.

In the detective film, the self-consciousness of the technical medium of reproduction finds expression, while in the sensational dramas mentioned above, a self-consciousness of cinema—which includes these films themselves—takes shape. As a new, modern public sphere, cinema distinguishes itself by including the participation of women. Just as detective films emphasize the relationship of film to the "technologization" of society, sensational drama reflects the fact that cinema is embedded [*Verortung*] in show business. It is set in the milieu of the circus (*The Black Viper*) or vaudeville (*The Black Ball*). What the cultural bourgeoisie had regarded as the stigma of cinema's origin—namely, its emergence from low forms of art rather than high culture—is deployed proactively by these films as the attraction of new female characters and of future female autonomy. Cinema had developed as an art of attraction alongside other arts of exhibition [*Schaukünsten*]; sensational drama now, in turn, employs this realm of entertainment itself as an attraction that conveys the main achievement of cinema, that is, the female gaze, as an attraction on the screen—albeit one that exceeds the framework of regular entertainment and that excites but also shocks the audience, especially men.

The Black Viper is set primarily in the milieu of the circus, the attractions of which are relished by the cinematography. An additional locale is provided by a castle, which, with its Old World, unilluminated rooms, presents here as well a site of the uncanny and magic in contrast to the technical mastery of nature that the acrobatic performances represent. The cinematography is less successful in its depictions of the castle, for its heart belongs to the circus. The film concerns a rivalry between two women over one man; the latter plays a subordinate, passive role. All attention is focused on the women and their development in contrasting worlds. The contrast between them, however, is not that of traditional and emancipated femininity, of "little woman" and bluestocking, but rather that between an archaically uncanny and a modern but no less unusual femininity.

One could say that the protagonists of *The Black Viper* embody the two sides of Ellen Gray: on the one side, there is the passionate, destructive Ladya, the "black viper," a snake tamer; and on the other side, the coolly controlling Blanche d'Estrée, the "feared patron" [*Patronin*]. Blanche d'Estrée and Iwan Karloff fall in love with one another, but the viper plots against this new

love, spirits Iwan away to a castle, and ensures that Blanche is arrested by the police. The police remain suspicious and send Detective d'Olton to the castle. Just as Ladya, already in her bridal gown, is about to marry Iwan, Blanche d'Estrée enters unexpectedly and, with a gun in her hand, forces her rival to surrender. A happy ending for Blanche and Iwan.

In terms of the narrative, the fight between the two women is about a man; however, in terms of the emphasis that the film places on its settings, it is about the disempowerment of the magical world by means of the enlightened world. In the beginning, and still within the world of the circus performers, the space of the snake charmer presents the "Other" sphere, in which the force of nature and human reason combine in a murky mixture. The film begins with her: the "black viper" is stretched out upon a divan; she is a black-haired beauty wearing exotic clothes, a headband circling her hair, necklaces looped around her neck, and gleaming bracelets decorating her arms. A snake and a dark-skinned servant constitute her company. Later, she presents herself as the mistress of the uncanny castle.

Blanche d'Estrée, the leader, is dressed like a dominatrix; she wears pants, severely cut black riding clothes, and high black boots. These are combined with a white blouse and a flat straw hat, which rationalize her attractive look. The whip in her hand betrays the fact that she keeps the animals under control by means of the practices of dressage rather than through magic. The atmosphere in her dressing room is not lascivious and erotic; instead, the room is bustling with male and female performers. When Blanche is chased by the police, the film takes this as an opportunity to depict the acrobatic performance skills of the dominatrix. She flees through the arena and swings herself up onto a trapeze and from there into the dome, only to escape through a small, high window. The chase continues outside across rooftops and between the stands and carousels of the fairground. Eventually, she is captured and put into chains. This image is able to occupy erotic fantasies at least as well as the image of the richly adorned "viper" on her divan.

The detective takes up the circus performer's case. He makes his way into

Ladya's realm, the castle. D'Olton makes use of a clever technique of observation: when he takes off his cap, he is able to observe, with a mirror that is attached to the inside of the cap, what occurs behind his back. This "trick" initiates an unusual shot: we see a close-up of d'Olton from behind as he thoughtfully tips his hat; the mirror inside it reflects Ladya's face so that it is clearly visible to us. Only the camera—and the spectator—are able to decipher d'Olton's posture as the result of a concentrated effort to read the facial expression of the schemer, who believes that she is unobserved. Additionally, this scene is also a self-reflection of the medium.

While Blanche suffers in chains, the "viper" enjoys the devotion of the enthralled Iwan. Outside, snow is falling. However, the showdown soon arrives, staged and filmed with great finesse in the form of an effective finale. Ladya prepares her bridal outfit in front of the toiletry mirror; clad completely in white, she fashions herself as an image of innocence. She places a white lace cloth upon her hair, and she is just about to place the wreath upon it when Blanche d'Estrée comes up behind her. In panic Ladya almost automatically smashes the mirror—shocked by the sight of the female gaze on the screen, a similar reflex might overcome the spectator. However, the spectator would thus be, like the "viper," under the spell of dark, unconscious forces, while the detective demonstrates a conscious use of the mirror (and thus of the film): he uses it in order to read that which occurs behind his back. Ladya confuses projection with reality—Blanche d'Estrée still stands behind her. Her machinations have failed—the decisive weapon, the gun, is in the hands of the circus performer. Had cinema dreamt in 1913 that woman would get hold of the camera?

The sensational drama takes up in the audience the female gaze that the social drama developed and enforces it on the screen; the representation of this gaze in the film, however, refers to women in the cinema not only as recipients but also as producers. These interconnections are even more pronounced in *The Black Ball* than in *The Black Viper*. *The Black Ball* begins with a reference to a social drama that constitutes its prehistory and from which the actions of the sensational drama, or rather the female protagonists, draw their motivation. The film ends with a joint gaze of the protagonists at the camera.

The first shot depicts two women who look similar to one another, one blond, the other dark-haired. The latter, sterner one holds the blond one in her arms, and they earnestly gaze into one another's eyes. This is not yet the beginning of the plot of the film but a prelude that shows the two actresses

in sisterly agreement. Their agreement signals that they are not going to represent a rivalry over a man, like the women in *The Black Viper,* but rather will be allies against him.

The story itself begins with the sisters Violetta and Edith returning home from the funeral of their other sister. Dressed in mourning clothes and wearing veils, they hug each other and cry. A nun gives them the suicide victim's farewell letter, and the photo of a man falls out. We discover that he cheated on her and drove her to death. The sisters swear, on the image of their beloved dead sister, to revenge her.

The sisters are artistic performers who star in vaudeville shows. The film is set mainly in their milieu, though this has two sides: the private side of living together and the public side of professional performances. To show women in this tension between two realms of living is new: the heroines of social dramas and melodramas did not engage in activities outside the house, nor did the female detectives have a private life. The exceptional camerawork provides a lucid presentation of both realms, the intimate situation of living and sleeping together and public situations in the dressing room and onstage. The inevitable castle, equipped with the usual characteristics such as heavy velvet draperies in front of doors and windows, trapdoors, and a deep cellar, constitutes the sphere of the male antagonist, or victim. However, the film is less interested in old forms of uncanniness than in the new one that the sisters bring into play.

The two women, gazing in unison, not only present a threat for the man, as we can see from the first scene; they also stage themselves as this threat. By staging as their own aura that uncanny aspect of the female gaze that pursues crime, the women preserve the self-confident clarity of their gaze from traumatic male projections. The persecution of the guilty man is, at bottom, just a masquerade in which he is conquered by his own fears without need of any other weapons. This masquerade takes place first onstage and then within the filmic "scene," which stands in for life.

As "The Uncanny Sisters," the performers star in an intimate theater frequented by the seducer, the Vicomte Geron. The show begins with a rococo idyll: two women in hoop skirts swing back and forth on swings while two cavaliers dally with them. This beautiful semblance of a lighthearted dalliance is followed by a number entitled "The Uncanny Sisters," as the program—shot in close-up—informs us. This number is shown in its entirety as an attraction in itself, just like those first films shown at the Wintergarten, which depicted the Grunato family's gymnastics, a boxing match, or the boxing kangaroo. The actresses, clad in black masks and covered by large black coats, enter the stage and present themselves to the audience, their arms folded across their chests. They resemble each other in the way that doppelgängers do. Rotating their bodies, they turn their backs to the audience and spread out their arms so that the coats unfold into giant bat wings. This is only for a moment, though. Then the coats glide off their shoulders, and in the background the curtains are lifted to reveal an alpine landscape. In the middle of the scenery a red fire flares up, and on the left and right sides two monsters sway their grotesque heads while the performers in the proscenium calmly perform their juggling tricks. They throw burning torches at each other across the fire as though the torches were balls. The number ends with a small explosion that makes the infernal manifestations disappear behind thick smoke.

It is only then that the film deals with the audience. That is, it first reflects the fact that the scene was performed for the male gaze: the two performers

appear again, seen through a matte in the shape of opera glasses. The next shot depicts the vicomte and his friend in a loge—he still has his glasses directed at the stage. Attracted by the presentation of the uncanny, just as the sisters had intended, he gets up when the show concludes and, with a meaningful smile, says good-bye to his friend so that he can seek to satisfy his aroused desire behind the stage. There he seems to find immediately that for which he was looking: the strangely enchanting ladies cross his path. He gazes after them and, already confident of victory, follows them. At this point the film becomes an accomplice of the audience that is in front of the screen; they can take delight in how blindly Don Juan walks directly into a trap. As a parody of his exit a "hen," followed by a "rooster," walks by—the next "number" is preparing for its performance.

The following scene takes place at the sisters' apartment. Violetta, the blond and more tender of the two, was not untouched by the vicomte's charms; Edith cautions her and reminds her of their sister's tragedy [*Drama*]. Violetta continues to gaze about dreamily, though. Will male scopophilia be victorious over this masquerade by women? The bold vicomte sneaks around the sisters' house, opens a window shutter, and cuts a hole in the curtains in order to sneak an intimate peek at the sisters—a peek the camera has already taken. The male voyeurism of film production is reflected in this scene. However, in gazing at the stage of life, the protagonist suffers a shock for which the theater had prepared him only in playful fashion. The vicomte recognizes that these are the strong sisters of the woman for whose death he is responsible. Obviously, even this shock turns into fascination, because shortly thereafter we see him as he follows the dark-veiled sisters, who leave the house, and he slips a ticket to Violetta. She responds with a long gaze over her shoulder.

The following scene belongs entirely to the camera's loving gaze; this gaze, however, has assumed the countergaze of woman. We observe the intimate sphere of the sisters, watch them sleep, and become aware that we are voyeurs. Half of Violetta's face is blocked from sight, since the shot is taken through the bars of the bed frame; the face of the sleeping Edith is reflected in a round mirror next to her sister's bed. This arrangement constitutes an endearing, tender scene but not an erotically charged one; rather, it reveals the sisterly relationship in its self-reflexivity. Scopophilia cannot attach to the object because it is answered by an autonomous vitality.

The film, from its parodic commentary on the way in which possessive scopophilia is shocked by means of staging to its sublation in a camera gaze that is sympathetically withdrawn, conveys that the self-confidence of male voyeurism is a delusion. The repetition of a masquerade by the women removes any last doubts; more powerfully than before, the masquerade is now no longer restricted to the stage but occurs in the life of the protagonist. Instead of embracing the desired, compliant love object, Violetta, in the rooms of his castle, the vicomte finds himself confronted with the strong Edith, who,

with a fierce gesture, rips the mourning veil from her face when he tries to touch her. Words would not have been necessary to convey the meaning of her action, but the intertitle ensures that she is able to master speech vis-à-vis the speechless man: "You shall not make the other one unhappy as well."

The masquerade is thus identified as a deceitful maneuver that was undertaken in the interests of sisterly solidarity, and as such it finds visual explication in the following sequence. In the garden Edith, forced to escape after her spectacular performance, exchanges clothes with Violetta, who had been waiting there for her. Reciprocity of roles is characteristic of a relationship of solidarity: now Violetta stands in for Edith and draws the attention of the persecutor to herself; the actress deploys her talents as a performer during the flight, vaulting over walls, maintaining her balance as she walks across rooftops, and climbing on the scaffolding of a construction site. At the same time, Edith prepares a final shock for the vicomte through a second unexpected appearance. He believes that she is fleeing from his servants when suddenly the velvet curtains of the door part and Edith appears, standing erect like a goddess of revenge. The intentionally dramatic effect of her appearance makes him stiff with shock this time. In panic he retreats, and with a chandelier in his hand he falls backward through a trapdoor into the basement. As a servant holds Edith back with a gun, a shot is suddenly fired, and the suspense is heightened a final time.

In the final scene, Violetta and Edith stand together next to the overwhelmed vicomte; he lies on a divan and, tormented, can only beg for mercy. Stern and unmoved, the two women look down upon him. In the final shot, and leaving the fallen hero of the film behind, they step through the portiere

with their heads held high and facing the camera, their faces turned toward the audience; they hug each other demonstratively and wistfully raise their eyes to the sky in memory of the victims of/in drama [*Dramenopfer*] for whom their intervention came too late.

The treatment of the female gaze on the screen by Franz Hofer—the advocate of women's social emancipation in the cinema—may seem exceptional in retrospect. Yet whether it is true that the films presented here established the aesthetic "denominator" of a specific genre, that of the sensational film— similar to the way Asta Nielsen defined social drama—can be verified today only with great difficulty. What can be shown, however, is that Hofer's work maintains a specific relationship—both aesthetic and social—to emancipatory impulses that manifest themselves in other genres. Hofer not only took up these impulses but clearly also inspired the further development of film during wartime. A key film for this development is Hofer's *Christmas Bells*, while this development found its protagonist in Emerich Hanus.

Two films by Emerich Hanus—who, as I noted, worked as an actor for Hofer—are preserved. Even as late as the period in which the UFA was founded, his films point toward a possible alternative to both state-supported entertainment cinema and Weimar auteur cinema.[2] These films are *The Atonement* [*Die Sühne*, 1917] and *A Fatal Oath* [*Ein verhängnisvoller Schwur*, presumably also 1917]. Both films insist on the "Other"—which, for the dominant society, was represented by cinema—as that which is stamped by the other sex rather than, as in the case of the auteur film, defining it as a stand-in for the unconscious of society. Emerich Hanus further develops the theme of the female gaze that seems threatening in its power; however, he does so in a form that, as in the case of social dramas, establishes a proximity to the social everyday life of female spectators. Both films deal with men who become blind over the course of a love relationship with an emancipated woman but who regain their sight through the care of a woman and medical intervention, respectively. The daily routine at which these films hint exhibits elements of modern culture beyond the ambience of the modern—also, and particularly, with respect to the relationship between the sexes. Among these elements are youth movement–inspired ways of dealing with the other sex; the economic independence and self-realization of a woman in a job such as painter or eye doctor; and the "comradely marriage." In 1917 these films at least attempted to capture the experience of male powerlessness and the "male" strength of women for a future peacetime in which the narrow-minded approach of the Wilhelminian public to the equality of the sexes no longer exists.

Chapter Eight

Crime and Love
in Prewar Drama,
1913–1914

The constitution of the detective film as a genre of its own was not a reaction to the specific interests of female audiences. However, it still broke with the taboo against female gaze at man, a taboo that the social drama had only opposed. Such a transgression, however, did not leave the genre untouched, as *The Wanted Letter* [*Der Steckbrief*] shows. While one consequence of the destabilization of the genre and the male position therein is drawn by Hofer, another presents itself in the combination of the forms of the detective film with those of social drama. The function of such combinations is ambivalent. On the one hand, they strengthen the position of female spectators, since they entitle—by explicitly including the audiences of love and marriage dramas—not just the women in the film but also those before the screen to an autonomous gaze at man. On the other hand, though, when, by means of elements of social drama, the "detective-like" aspect in the female gaze becomes repressed and tied to forms of representation of love and marriage, these combinations are then also, and conversely, in the service of a renewed stabilization of the position of the spectator.

The genre mixtures reflect the mixing of the sexes in cinema; as a consequence, they bear with them a deconstruction of taboos, but at the same time they also decisively encourage a "preconstruction" of the films' impact that maintains taboos. The combination of detective film and social drama paved the way for a conjunction of the recognition of the female spectator in the cinematic public sphere with the development of film production, within which the male authority of the drama saved itself by means of an identification with the subject of the new technology.

The mixed forms of criminal and love dramas can be divided into those that emphasize the professional, independent woman and those that deal primarily with rivalries between men. The first kind seems to address women's interest in self-perception, while the second kind addresses their interest in seeing the other sex. As the genres mix, the viewing interests of women are disassembled. Deprived of their possibility for autonomous interaction, the genres can be more easily linked to a male interest in the female image and in self-representation. The extent to which the genres at least partially account for women's interest in emancipation depends on the way in which they are combined.

The Professional Woman:
A Story at the Intersection of Genres

The plots of both *Czernowska* [*Die Czernowska*] and *The Fan Painter* [*Die Fächermalerin*, both 1913] break the taboo against professional occupations for women. From the outset, though, this does not constitute a radical break because these films thematize employment in the context of the family: the female protagonists are a governess and a home worker, respectively. Moreover, in both cases, over the course of the narrative of the film, the visually convincing image of the "new woman" is revoked. The forms of detective film and social drama transform from being manifestations of different approaches with reality and the social experience of the audience into elements of a strategy to confine the threatening visual appearance of the autonomous woman such that it becomes subordinate to the male story.

Czernowska is characterized in the opening credits as "a drama drawn from Russian life." The heroine is a strong, slender woman in a dark, simple, but elegantly cut dress with a light-colored collar; her hair is parted in the middle but pinned up on the sides in a snappy way. In the first scene she sits at a desk; there is a piano on her left side, a bookcase stands in the back, and beside the window there are three photographs of a dancer in different poses. She knits her brow, then begins to write. She could be one of those Russian women who were among the first female students in Germany and Switzerland before World War I.

The intertitle, though, presents her as a simple governess who is writing a letter to her lover, a crook. She suggests that they exploit the erotic weakness of her employer, a count, in order to get to his fortune. The plan is put into action, but at the last minute the murder of the count is prevented by a loyal

servant, and the criminal couple are arrested by the police. Since the film is not very "Russian" (the shooting location seems to have been the German Baltic Sea coast), it evokes the thought that she might be a Russian student and/or "anarchic" émigré. Emancipation of women and class struggle merge in the impression that one gathers from this governess, who attempts to rise above her social class by "criminal" means.

From the start the correlation between love and crime motifs established by the narrative might evoke the prejudice that, in cases in which a woman's love is "easy," crime is nearby (and vice versa)—and perhaps the correlation also sought to confirm the belief that assassinations are the result not of political rationality but of selfish passion. However, in the first part of the film the appeal of the protagonist is not yet much affected by all this. Devoid of any questionable "demonic" elements, her attractive, sober, and powerful appearance can convey a type of woman who refuses to be inscribed in traditional roles. This governess does not take her job to be a substitute

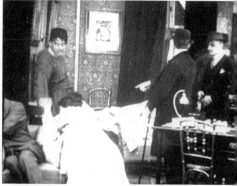

for motherhood—in order to meet their emotional needs the children turn not to her but to the old servant. Nor does she play the role of obedient love object for her employer; rather, she plays with the count's fantasies of projection. Women in the audience take especial pleasure when she pretends to be the "innocent girl" as he tries to conquer her; as he kisses her on the nape of her neck, she withdraws with all the signs of being a passive, chaste woman—which, as the audience knows, she is not. Because of her intelligence she is able to reverse roles: even as the count believes that he is seducing the governess, she is seducing him. Her self-conscious approach to sexuality emancipates the governess from the status of implicit servitude.

Czernowska was directed by Charles Decroix, who also made *The Reason of the Heart* [*Die Vernunft des Herzens*] in 1910, a film that sympathetically depicted a woman cheating on her husband. With the introduction of the theme of marriage in the later film, though, a decline of female autonomy begins once again. In the first part the detective film element enabled the spectator to participate in the way that the woman played with the patriarch; following this, the film, through the marriage, puts an end to the superior gaze of the woman. When the criminal couple attempt to do away with the newly married count during his honeymoon, they are observed by a detective, who turns out to be the loyal servant of the count. This suited audiences committed to traditional morality as well as male audiences who had been disquieted by the seductive power of "Czernowska." Now they can enjoy her disempowerment. In the final scene the proud woman, wearing her negligee and in distress, falls at the feet of the count, and the police, without pity, pick her up and lead her away.

Like *Czernowska, The Fan Painter* also acts out a social drama against the background of a crime story. The former film, however, took a relatively simple approach in its depiction of these two elements; it consisted of basically two parts: one in which social drama takes up a motif from detective film (the woman who has the power of the gaze) and another in which the detective story in return adopts the patriarchal element of social drama. *The Fan Painter* is a formally ambitious film with respect to its use of effects that employ light and shadows, double exposure tricks, and montage. Its extensive use of crosscutting, remarkable for a German film of this period, may be attributed to no small extent to the American influence of the New Century production company.[1] However, the crosscutting is above all the form of the mediation between the crime and the love story.

The specific visual attraction of this film is to be found in its depiction of a fan painter at work in her home. In a simple living room that is furnished with a bed, a closet, an armchair for the mother, and a round table and chairs, the worker sits at a small desk. This long shot is followed by a close-up so that the audience gets a good view of the protagonist's work. The camera is positioned behind her back so that the gaze of the camera is directed at the fan that lies across the inclined surface of the desk and at the palette in the painter's hand. The shot lasts long enough for us to be able to study the painter, who is bent over her work; as well as her short, wavy hair, which leaves her neck free; the braided border along the neckline of her dress; the buttons that secure her dress in the back; and the folds of the cloth that run across her hunched back. Subsequently, the film returns to a long shot and shows how the fan painter interrupts her work in order to give a glass of water to her mother and to caress her.

The attraction that is constituted in this sequence through a depiction of the woman's work situation is heightened even further in what follows as the film integrates an erotic story. A young man who is interested in the young woman enters the room, kisses the mother's hand, greets the daughter, pulls up a chair, and sits down next to the painter. His hat and coat have been left on the bed in the background. He takes her hand and presses it to his heart; she stands up and turns away; an intertitle verbalizes her rejection of his love. He stands up as well but does not let go of her hand. Thus they stand, amidst her everyday life, but this is not stylized into a clichéd expression of a "moment of love"; the prop department even thought of providing the worker with a handkerchief in her waistband.

Just as in other social dramas, erotic suspense is intensified by an object, in this case, a fan. However, in contrast to films such as *Pearls Mean Tears* and *By a Hair's Breadth,* the fetish in this film is "unfolded," so to speak; it reveals its fetish character. A fan, carelessly picked by the young man, betrays the woman's desire for love, which she had invested in the fan: "The fan reveals her love." She used the fan as a screen for her dream of love; it is a film within a film. In close-up we see, along with the young man, that his and her heads, turning toward one another, are painted on the fan, surrounded by roses. He shows his discovery to the painter of this image. In the dreamlike unified gaze of the protagonists, the two faces on the fan, smiling, incline toward one another for a moment until they are almost touching. But then the trick sequence is aborted, "reality" again enters the picture, and the young man leaves in haste.

This sequence in the middle of the film focuses its attention on the fan painter, especially on the gaze of loving desire directed at the man to which

she gave expression in her painting. A representative for the (male) audience, the young man enters the living room in order to make an explicit declaration of love to this attractive figure in her workplace. The form of female self-perception in the image of the working woman is not destroyed by this entrance. Even though she reciprocates his feelings, the heroine does not want to exchange her place at the painting desk with one in the kitchen, as a wife. This insistence on autonomy, however, has its basis in an earlier story of criminality, which in this case as well produces feminine autonomy only to bring about its downfall in the end.

The film began with an impressive courtroom scene, but this time it is not a woman who is the object of the verdict but a man, a husband and father who has been accused of treason [*Landesverrat*]. A long shot shows us a phalanx of judges on the left, the state attorney in the middle, a crowd of spectators in the background on the left, and the accused, hunched over and unrepentant, in the foreground at the gate. The daughter is asked to come forward as a witness; she positions herself directly in front of the accused so that she is now in the middle of the frame; the attorney recedes into the background. Rather than confining herself to the role of witness, the daughter becomes the advocate of society, of the fatherland, against her father. She succeeds where the phalanx of men failed and brings her father to make a confession. In a gripping scene—which the camera captures in a medium shot—she throws herself, pleading, on his chest, and he hugs her and kisses her on her forehead. A long shot depicts him making his confession in front of the gathered public.

If one recalls the beginnings of the social drama in *Cruel Marriage,* the roles are now reversed; even though the frame of the courtroom is similar, there are significant changes. The image of the patriarch on the wall is missing; rather than a woman defending herself, now the patriarch has to defend himself in front of the judges, while his daughter represents the public sphere, which demands a confession from the isolated man. The court sentences the father to prison and releases the daughter into her own social life.

From the outset, though, the intertitles wish to make clear that this should not be understood in an emancipatory sense, and so they emphasize the compassion of the daughter: "Mother and I will atone along with you and live our lives in deep mourning." As a consequence the film is much more a reflection on the connection between the working bourgeois woman and the impoverishment of the middle classes than an attempt, on the part of women, to become emancipated. On a deeper level, though, the film could be read as a return of the archaic fantasies of patricide on the part of the "sons," fantasies within which the daughters are now included as well, and they play an exonerating role. Modern woman becomes responsible for the fulfillment of the fantasy (i.e., the lawful deposing of the patriarch), but at the same time she is made responsible for the father's salvation (which restores peace of mind)—though it turns out that this is a salvation less of his physical life than of his metaphysics.

The images of the woman and her autonomous life and work initially push the detective story completely into the background. The detective story only regains its validity by disrupting the scenes of her social life and by inter-rupting these with shots that show the father in prison. Along with a distinct lighting that connects the different settings, the montage is more than an external conjunction of separate locales: it represents the internal connection with the father, which prevents the female protagonist from living out the happiness in her independent life that she dreams of experiencing with the man of her choice. The light that falls through the prison bars onto the father's face corresponds to the beautiful semblance that adorns the painter's fan; the father gazes upward longingly, touches the prison bars with his hand—then turns around and calls a guard, who brings him paper and pencil. He writes to his wife and daughter.

Subsequently, we see that Fred Beverley also writes Kitty to announce his visit. The montage that mediates between the hero of the detective film and the female protagonist of the social drama wavers between, on the one hand, adopting the standpoint of the woman, that is, her interest in combining the old emotional tie with her new love, and, on the other hand, enforcing the *one* story that preceded the start of the film, the story in which the father-daughter relationship was still intact. In one scene crosscutting turns into an internal montage, transforming the image of the working woman into a depiction of the drama of her soul, which pits the emotional tie to her father against her love for the man whom she has chosen. Her lover visits her, and, with her mother, the pair sit at the table; suddenly, the part of the background of the room in which the bed and the closet were standing metamorphoses into the walls of the prison, and the father appears, looking up longingly toward the barred window. When the scene in the background has attained the same optical presence as the foreground, Kitty suddenly jumps up, to the bewilderment of the other two: it was her projection we saw. "Is something wrong?" Fred asks. In that moment the father's image disappears, the daughter covers her face with her hands, and her lover tries in vain to calm her. Finally, she leans against her mother.

Shortly thereafter, though, the mother dies, and Fred again proposes to Kitty; at the same time, the father is released from prison. After an employment of parallel montage and the superimposition of two stories, the film now returns to the unity of the story. Via the detour of a retreat from the world into a monastery, the criminal again becomes a father, and the fan painter, through a suicide attempt, once again becomes a daughter. From the hands of her father, now elevated into a clergyman, the born-again daughter is transferred to the hands of the husband. Femininity shifts from a "natural" fact into a "metasocial" fact.

The ending, which depicts the heroine in her new, now male-determined social position of marriage and motherhood, implies the negation not only of her own self-determined social existence but also of the reality of her mental conflict. This conflict is reduced to the paranoid idea that the guilt of the father rendered the position of "wife" impossible for her. But modern society, represented by Fred Beverley, does not hold against the woman the "sins of the fathers"—sins that force her into employment—as though these created an ineradicable stigma.

By being mediated, the forms of the social drama and the detective film dissolve in favor of the presentation of the unity of the story. In the end, melodrama comes to their aid: it represses in the mind of the female spectator the conjunction of self-perception, which occurs when confronted with the fan painter, and a detective-like gaze at psychic conflicts. The melodramatic ending calms the fears that the new mass medium, representative of a democracy such as the United States, must have evoked: it shows how, thanks to an internalization of patriarchy and its transformation into second nature, woman comes to constitute a placeholder for patriarchy amidst modern democracy.

Male Rivalry: Between the Domination
of the Female Gaze and Aesthetic Emancipation

Czernowska and *The Fan Painter* offered a social drama set against a criminal background. In *On a Lonely Island* [*Auf einsamer Insel,* 1913], *And the Light Went Out* [*Und das Licht erlosch,* 1914], and *High Voltage* [*Hochspannung,* 1913] the relationship is exactly the opposite: the detective story is in the foreground, while aspects of social drama bind themselves to this. With respect to their content, then, these films do not focus on the story of the woman but rather on a story of rivalry between men. The disappearance of the heroine as the center of the screen in favor of a presentation of competing men withdraws the object from the spectators, though it does not withdraw the gaze from women in the audience. Rather, in place of the female protagonist this gaze—as the female gaze of the detective film that has been displaced to a position in front of the screen—becomes the point of reference for male rivalry.

Although the female gaze is allowed to relate to the male sex, the latter at the same time determines the former. Against the background of social drama, the competing men represent class oppositions or generational conflict. In the context of the detective film they engage in the contradiction between tradition and modernity or between the archaic and modernity. In every case a decision is made in favor of the lower class, the sons, and modernity—and thereby a decision that is not in the interests of the emancipation of woman. In contrast with the detective films, woman is excluded from bringing about a "happy solution," and the unity of drama is restored. The return to the world of social drama, the return of the hero to the woman who waits lovingly for him, thus means at the same time the return of the son, of modernity, of the little man, into a framework that is defined by the invisible presence of the archaic Oedipus.

On the other hand, though, there is also in this case a difference between the visual register of the film and its dramatic construction. With respect to the film's visual register, the opposition between tradition and modernity—an opposition over which, in the register of the narrative, the protagonists must still fight—has been decided from the outset, and decided differently: the technical medium, the attraction of cinema, has left behind the literary drama and the theater. As a consequence, these films oscillate between the new gaze—which they indifferently (in a double sense) offer to women—and relapse into old forms of authority, through which the influence of female spectators on the style of the film is again eliminated.

The film *On a Lonely Island*—produced by Eiko and directed by and starring Joseph Delmont—attempts to insist on the claim to emancipation of the new medium by concentrating exclusively on visual style, against which the drama of the narrative becomes negligible. However, precisely by doing so the film puts the artist in a position of authority vis-à-vis the experiences of the audience. Aesthetic emancipation begins to disassociate itself from social emancipation.

Extraordinary beauty unfolds through the unrestricted work of the camera; the setting seems like it was made for the camera, and every moment of the story seems to have been designed for it as well. The film was shot on the Dutch island of Marken, and many scenes document life in a fishing village, the departure of the boats, the hay harvest by the dyke, the sociability of a Dutch country parlor, and wedding customs.

The film tells the story of Pieter Boes, who is poor, and Sutje de Jong, the daughter of a wealthy fisherman. They love each other, but Sutje's father supports the marriage suit of Dirk de Vaat, who is also rich. In order to achieve his goal, rich Dirk tries to get rid of poor Pieter by abandoning the sleeping man on a boat without any sails. Dirk marries Sutje, but a few years later Pieter returns and protects Sutje and her child from Dirk, who is always drunk and violent. One day, while he is drunk, Dirk sets fire to his ship. Pieter saves him, but Sutje's husband subsequently dies as a result of the accident. In the end, poor Pieter is able to sit at the table in Sutje's parents' home after all, and the lovers take each other by the hand.

The calm, consistently stable camera turns these shots into tableaux: a landscape with dykes; ocean scenery; a Dutch interior. Long shots preponderate, and they are only interrupted with medium long shots in order to capture equally picturesque scenes, such as landscapes, lovers, people waiting at the beach, and similar motifs. The orientation toward landscape and genre painting is obvious. In addition to being reminiscent of the "Dutch masters," the images are close to the paintings of Liebermann and Leibl and their realist and (with respect to the treatment of light) impressionist approach to art, which turned against the fusty and florid Gründerzeit aesthetic. It is as though the film wanted to show how it could even surpass painting in this respect. The wooden planks of the piers breathe the warmth of the sun's rays, and the couple sitting on the bridge make palpable the happiness of intimacy.

The film announces that human beings, after having been imprisoned in the armory of history, are now returned to the outside world, to the present, to light and air, to the vitalizing elements. The technical medium of reproduction outdoes painting by (re)turning even the moments of artistry itself to the external world, to nature: it reflects itself in the filmic material, while the cameraman simply points the lens and chooses the setting. Thus, for example, the attraction of a scene at a dyke clearly emerges from an oscillation between impressions of painting and reality: filmed in a long shot, the dyke arches diagonally across the image, and protruding above its ridge are the masts of ships and the rooftops of houses that stand behind it, protected by it. In the middle ground groups of people harvesting hay are scattered across the slope of the dyke. A canal stretches along the foreground. As if the gaze of the camera itself would be drawn into the image, a boat moves from the bottom edge of the frame into the tranquil shot.

Insofar as the film makes use of its ability to record the flow of reality, it concentrates entirely on mobility in serenity: the tremulous rays of the sun, their reflection on the surface of the water, the gentle breeze that bends the grass and draws the sails taut. The film ignores the possibility of demonstrating the dynamism of a mobile camera by technological means in favor of an interest in unmastered but "human" nature. In contrast with the unrest of the narrative, the shots of nature radiate reconciliation [*Aufgehobenheit*], which eventually only remains to be confirmed by the narrative: the injustice that

obtains between rich and poor as well as destructive hatred, jealousy, and possessiveness are adjusted by the elements. The ocean returns the abandoned man to life; the fire removes the "bad" husband from the path of the lovers.

With so much nature arching equally over the passions of humans, whether men or women, the question of the historical repression of woman falls by the wayside. The desire for aesthetic emancipation from literary narrative tradition—which expresses itself in the painterly style of the film, in photographic beauty—is at the same time an abstraction from the difference between the sexes, which was at least addressed at the start of narrative cinema. Aesthetic emancipation aims to absolve technology from its fixation on the mastery of nature, on the semblance of reconciled nature. Yet in addressing this fixation, it neglects the expression of human inner nature, of sexually specific mastery. The form of visual attraction does not reveal a secret complicity with the love story of the woman; rather, it is a secret complicity with the man in love and, moreover, with the author as producer. The latter

ultimately puts his own cinematic interests, which are never neutral, above those of the audience and thus above those of women.

With respect to its visual style, the final part of the film displays three peculiarities, each of which, in its own way, is less a matter of its orientation toward painting than of the authority of the narrator and the male gaze behind the camera. The first peculiarity is a striking combination of montage and camera movement that depicts Pieter's return from the sea or, more precisely, his path toward the village. A narrator, who has camera and montage at his disposal, recalls, once again, the return of "Odysseus": he leaves the ship and makes his way toward the houses, in front of which children play and women hang up clothes, and the camera, along with him, moves past the buildings. The second shot could have been the first glance of the man who returns home at his former—and still—beloved: through the beams and struts of a wooden staircase that stands in the foreground, the camera focuses on the house on the other side, though it can only get the lower half of the house into the frame because of the tight angle. A woman steps into the doorway, her feet in wooden shoes, and all that is visible are her unclothed lower legs, her skirt, and her hands, which she uses to support herself on the wall for a moment. The wooden struts and their shadows enframe and dominate the image; it is marked by the gaze of the man at the woman's body, reflected by the gaze of the camera in an optically attractive play of light and shadow. The shot is remarkable not only because of this aspect of voyeurism but also because its ability to capture details makes it stand out from the usual long and medium long shots; it depicts the fragmentation of the body rather than harmony with nature.

The third peculiar form of visualization is close to the old cinema of attractions: the mise-en-scène of the fire on Dirk's ship is reminiscent of the popular depictions of fires, with a lot of smoke and red tinting. In this context too the camera associates itself with Pieter's gaze; it is with him as he looks out the window and sees people running toward the harbor. During the showdown, at the climax of the rivalry between the men, the film remembers once again the old methods of appealing to human passions and scopophilia. However, by reflecting upon them, the film simultaneously separates "pure show/pure seeing" [*reine Schau*], which is male and technologically identified, from the pleasure [*Lust*] that an audience, however gendered, might have.[2]

And the Light Went Out, in turn, emphasizes its connection to the cinema of attractions. The film tells the story of Werle, a shipowner; his patriarchal exercise of power, which leads to an attempt to murder his rival; and his death during his attempt to cover up the crime. Out of jealousy he sends his employee Gerd Lind to India; he also forces his own ward, Inge Sörensen, to marry him instead of Lind. When Lind returns, years later, the patriarch bribes two sailors to help him overwhelm the lighthouse guard and turn off the lighthouse signal. Lind's ship runs aground, but he is saved. Werle forbids him to enter his house. When he is caught one night talking with Inge, Lind allows himself to be arrested as a thief in order to avoid compromising his beloved.

The criminal nearly seems to prevail. But then his "fate" catches up with him: he perishes as the result of his own criminal actions, so to speak. He returns to the scene of the crime in order to destroy his written confession, which is buried there. It was supposed to bind his accomplices, but it also makes it possible for him to be blackmailed. As he digs, a lamp that tips over causes a fire from which he is not able to escape. Inge is free and finally gets a chance to redeem Lind's sacrifice and clear him of the suspicion of having committed a crime.

Beyond this dramatic story the photographic style of the film finds its focus in an "attraction": the shot of a lighthouse with a rotating light at its top. In social dramas the female narrative perspective entered into a coalition with elements of the cinema of attractions against dramatic form. The style of *And the Light Went Out* ties itself to this coalition, but it conveys the attraction through drama rather than through the female narrative perspective within the latter, and only by means of this mediation does the style of the film link itself to a female gaze amidst the male scopophiliacs in the cinema. The lighthouse is simultaneously an attraction and a suspense-producing object or fetish. Linked to the criminal patriarch, it conveys the patriarchal element of the drama for the scopophilic eye. When the narrative hints that it might turn away from depicting a just fate for Werle, this corresponds to a form of desire in sensation [*Sensationslust*] that is more interested in the attractions of the crime story than in "justice." However, the latter wins out in the end, and Lind will fulfill the role of the good husband and employer.

In the beginning and at the end the gaze of the female spectator is still represented by that of the female protagonist; in the main part of the story, though, the latter recedes into the background in favor of the story of male rivalry. The female spectator thus takes up the gaze of the heroine and sees *instead* of her.[3] In the first scene Gerd Lind and Inge Sörensen sit opposite one another; he draws her portrait, and she flirts with him across the canvas. Then Werle, the shipowner and patriarch, enters this love story that is just beginning, and he brings to bear a power that finally turns openly to crime. Werle arrogates to himself patriarchal power in both his employment relation-

ship with Lind and his role as custodian of the young woman (a role that he takes on shortly after this scene). However, violence directed against the woman occurs through a repression of her gaze: he not only knows how to prevent her from seeing and objecting to what he is doing; he also prevents her from seeing her lover's letters.

The woman in front of the screen sees these things in place of Inge, but at the same time the spectator is distanced from the events. She only becomes involved in the events on the screen as a visual attraction that arouses her scopophilia. While Lind's departure was already hidden from the perception of the female protagonist, the camera—and the eye of the female spectator—accompanies the young man up to the gangplank, follows him onto the ship, and captures the dark silhouette of the heavyhearted man who is departing, seen against the lighter background of the sea. Fishing boats sit in the water, and in the distance a steamer passes by; the sparkle on the waves has an especially comforting effect. Mimetically, the camera clings to the farewell gaze of the painterly eye.

In the following scene the camera-eye is directed, in detective-like fashion, at the activities of Werle, the shipowner. When the letter that announces Lind's return arrives, Werle leaves the house wearing a dark coat, his collar pulled up, his face hidden underneath his hat, and he enters a dark pub. Entirely "Other" than a respectable citizen, he conspires there with two dark figures. The camera follows the three men through narrow streets to the harbor and then, in a swaying boat, out to the lighthouse. The camera observes as the criminals enter the lighthouse, climb up the stairs, and overwhelm the guard, and it captures the moment when the searchlight goes out.

With both love and penetrating analysis, the camera relates the gaze of the female spectator to man; the differences between the two are prescribed by the dramatic narrative. However, visual attractions and tinting awaken an unplanned, "improper" scopophilia. The tinting changes from night blue, used in the scene of the power-crazed shipowner's walk in the dark, to yellow, during the scene in which the crime is planned, and to red, during the scene in which the plan is executed, as the guard is overwhelmed. The red is taken up in the following sequence, which tells the counterstory, namely, how Lind's ship approaches the harbor. Lind stands at the railing, as in the farewell scene. This time, however, the camera does not remain with his musing gaze at the sea but wanders down into the depths of the body of the ship, creating metonymic images of what it might look like deep inside the man who returns home. The shots of the firemen with naked upper bodies, stoking the blaze of the fire, are drenched in red.

In the figure of the lighthouse masculinity presides over the entire main part of the film (i.e., the crime story) as sensual attraction and as a social achievement; this is accomplished through technical detail, with which the

light-sensitive film material in turn is able to play. There is hardly a shot that does not include the lighthouse: the rotating searchlight shines through the window of Werle's office as well as into the seamen's pub; it is small and distant yet clearly visible in the dark because of the bright, moving light at its tip. The lighthouse is omnipresent and dominates the place like the patriarch Werle. The lives of the seamen are dependent upon it, as are the lives of travelers and the life of Gerd Lind.

Lind's return might also mean a return to social drama and to the judgment [*Urteil*] of the patriarch. However, the element of the cinema of attractions, which maintains the desire for sensation, a deep scopophilia that is beyond both loving and destructive forms of sympathy for this man, is more effective. The execution of Werle's "sentence" [*Urteilsvollstreckung*] presents a climax of attraction with the play of light and color in the red-tinted shot of the lighthouse fire. Both the satisfaction that we take in the way that the criminal employer and husband meets his end and our hope that love will

be realized merge in this view of the burning lighthouse; at the same time, though, our emotions urge us in vain to be done with the fetish that arouses scopophilia yet also binds us by means of spectacle. In the final scene the tower shines through the window as before. The union of the lovers occurs under its sign.

It is the sign of the phallus. However, the lighthouse represents more than a symbol. As the material bearer of the sign, it constitutes, in its literal oscillation, a mirror for the entire film, whose facets it reflects. The lighthouse is a technical achievement and an intriguing accessory of the criminal. In this respect it constitutes an element of the detective film aspect; it is also the suspense-producing object of social marriage drama; and it is a means of decision and a judge in the drama of male rivalry. As real attraction it offers more than a substitute for female scopophilia, which is denied. However, through its phallic connotations—which it also derives from its function in the competition between the men—it simultaneously defines desire, again objectifying it. This attraction distances the gazes of the male and female spectators from the structures of the power struggle and its solution—yet doesn't it simultaneously arrest this gaze by building a myth around "technical potency" by means of the cinema of attractions?

High Voltage, a Messter production, does not entirely belong to the mixed-genre films, since it is missing the detective film element proper. However, male rivalry still plays a central role. In addition, *High Voltage*, as a film that dispenses with the "extravagance" of aesthetic stylization, is an example of the successful "enthronement" of the son, of modernity in place of the father and tradition, as legitimate successor—so successful, in fact, that the destruction of the patriarch is unnecessary. This success also implies that the subject of the new medium takes over the position of the literary narrator and succeeds him.

High Voltage has the virtue of providing an almost undramatic, narratively and photographically precise depiction of social circumstances, of the differences and barriers between the milieus of the grand and petit bourgeois. The crime itself is merely implied as a possibility, though one that no longer has a chance in this world, which is already and finally liberally organized and enlightened. The optimism of this film relates it to the detective film, with which it also shares a cinematographic enthusiasm for urban ambience and sites of technology, in this case, a power plant. However, the detective, who is obsolete in this bright, clean, bourgeois world, has resigned in favor of the upwardly mobile petit bourgeois citizen, who pursues his career as engineer in the midst of industrialization. "Democratization," advancing in this way in the realm of employment, leaves much to be desired in the private sphere. Yet it is not the power relation between the sexes that motivates the film but rather the fact that the love between the engineer, with his petit bourgeois background, and the power plant owner's daughter meets with the resistance of class barriers.

While in this film, just as in *On a Lonely Island*, the father's prohibition sits next to his proper rival's desire for possession, this does not lead to a criminal conspiracy. His untimely prohibition is not associated with the arrogance of power but rather with an outdated social interest. The fall of the patriarch is thus depicted as a cathartic event that fosters a renewal of social consciousness. Crime is replaced by accident. During a hike in the mountains the ground under the feet of the factory owner becomes unstable; he falls and finally hangs helplessly over an abyss. The technologically adept young man

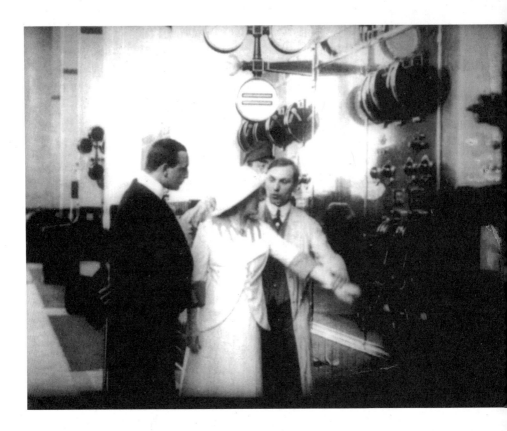

literally takes the rescue into his own hands by cutting up his rubberized coat into strips and winding them around his hands in order to be able to rappel down to the fallen man by means of the high-voltage cable. The daughter, a modern woman, does not remain passive but runs to the power plant in order to switch off the current. She had listened well to the instructions that the engineer once had given to the new employee, his rival, at the switchboard.

Apparently, all dramatic contradictions and oppositions are resolved, and the judgment [*Urteil*] has no power over the protagonists, including the heroine. Power has shifted to the narrator, though, who holds all the threads in his hand and who allows a "resolving event" [*lösendes Ereignis*] to occur at the right moment. A semblance of freedom is inherent in the film because the omnipotent narrator hides behind the camera, behind cinematic realism [*Abbildrealismus*]. It seems as though we are looking with the camera at a social world, whereas in fact the camera shots depict concepts of reality created by the narrator—hence the well-ordered, straightforward nature of

all the parts of this film, which is ignorant of breaks, daring shot composi-
tions, or changes in speed.

The young engineer is the representative of the narrator in the film. He
pursues his social advancement through his modern occupation, but he also
has, besides his technical interest—so to speak—a "poetic" need that he
expresses with his love for the daughter of the factory owner. His second need
serves his advancement no less than the first. Since the young hero is first
and foremost a representative of the narrator and only subsequently a bearer
of dramatic action, the dramatic conflict between him and the patriarch is
reduced from an expression of a social conflict (in which the emancipation
of the woman would play a role) to an Oedipal conflict inherent in the narrative. In this latter conflict the woman plays a part only as an object.

High Voltage reflects the Oedipal constitution of the male object-relation.
The beginning of the film depicts the home of the engineer, a friendly, petit
bourgeois living room in which he sits at the table with his mother. No paternal presence disturbs this idyll. The following scenes of his relationship with
his beloved are set outside in a park landscape. Then we see the office of the
patriarch, who is negotiating the marriage of his daughter with a business
partner. These three scenes outline the psychic constellation: the tie to the
mother, the "natural" inclination toward the young woman, and the social
claim on the sexual relationship represented by the father. The following
scenes show how the object choice of the young man is still played out on
the basis of his happy relationship with his mother—a happiness that is suddenly interrupted when the father, seeking to strengthen his economic power
by means of a son-in-law, no longer favors the petit bourgeois "mama's boy."
The hero loses his social position. In the moment of paternal intervention,
which involves a violent separation from the mother, the love relationship
transforms into fantasy-projection [*Wunsch-Projektion*]. Only after the son
has (re)installed the father within existence (i.e., the rescue) does he receive
from him the reality, as possession, of his earlier projection. His fantasy of
marrying the daughter is fulfilled.

In the center of the film, there is a sequence that gives expression to this
projective relationship of the hero (as a representative of the narrator) and thus
can be taken as paradigmatic for the appearance of woman in future narrative
cinema. It is a matter of a film within the film that reflects the becoming-pro-
jection of woman. After he has left his mother and his beloved, the hero leans
thoughtfully against a tree in the solitude of a mountain region. A countershot

depicts the object of his thoughts, the young woman. She sleeps at home in her room, which is decorated in a cozy way with flowered wallpaper, ruffled curtains, and a bed with a carved wooden frame. In her arms she holds the now-dried bouquet of flowers that her lover had once given her; she caresses it in her sleep. While in *The Shadow of the Sea* the bouquet of flowers was an object that constituted a narrative motif as both an expression of desire and a representative of the story, in this case it is no longer anything but a fetish. This bouquet stands at the intersection of a visualization of spatially distant reality—a visualization that film is able to provide—and the projection of male desires onto this reality—into which narrative cinema can develop. Against the background of the flowered wallpaper a film appears through double exposure: the couple walk out of the flowered wallpaper toward the spectator; as they reach the foreground they stop and kiss each other. The apparition disappears, but along with it the bouquet of flowers in the arms of the sleeping woman disappears as well. Even the bouquet already seems to have been a "projection": the woman's dream is part of the man's projection.

This scene, which emphasizes the man's projective relationship with the woman, leads into the decisive reencounter with the father, an event that also brings some "drama" into a film that has been narrating its story fairly smoothly so far. Supported by the attraction of realistic outdoor shots, the acrobatic achievements of the camera create suspense, which is heightened by the crosscutting between the savior on the high-voltage cable, the father hanging over the abyss, and the daughter on her way to the power plant so that she can switch off the current. However, these material and formal effects only work on the basis of the audience's prior knowledge of the dangerous "high voltage" in the cable. The audience was informed of this when the engineer conducted a tour of the plant for the business partner's son, who was supposed to marry into this business. He explained the functions of the switchboard to his rival and the woman who accompanied him. Only the woman will make use of what she learned. This undramatically staged scene eventually takes on a suspense-producing function because of this information rather than because it brings together the rivals and the object of their conflict within the sober, technical atmosphere of the plant during an equally sober lesson about technical details.

The actual drama of *High Voltage* is situated less on the surface of the action but more beneath it in a psychological dynamic that might be constructed through cinematic means but that springs from the mind of the narrator and produces narratively a corresponding effect in the mind of the spectator. In

this drama of the soul the patriarch constitutes not an actual opponent but rather—as representative of social reality—a fixed point toward which the young hero needs to orient himself: at this fixed point his social existence will either fail or prove itself. At the turning point of events the engineer loses his position; however, in the deeper level of the film this is not because he wants to marry the daughter of the factory owner but rather because he first needs to succeed in separating himself from his mother before his social "love choice" can be realized. *A Mother's Love* calmed the fears of the petit bourgeois woman about losing her socially advancing son to society; *High Voltage* no longer grants her any expression but only proves the son right. While the film began with an affectionately arranged scene at home with the mother, it ends in a grand bourgeois salon, where the son's engagement is celebrated as a happy ending and the mother merely attends.

The fact that the mother in the film and the happiness of the lovers are subordinate to the son's desire to advance socially represents the subordination of the interest of female audiences to the social and economic interest of film in advancement. A sequence from the first part of the film confirms that the gaze of women in cinema is defined by the sight [*Anblick*] of man and that the exposure [*Preisgabe*] of man is sublated by this definition. This sequence depicts how the photographic medium connects the women, mother and lover, by means of their gaze at the man and by means of their thought of the child: the lover visits the mother, and both are united in viewing a photo album. The gaze of the camera is caught by a page that features a photo of a boy in the center, while on the side, hardly visible in the cinematic frame, one can see part of the portrait of a woman. The young woman takes the picture of little Hans with her as a present. On her way back she again becomes engrossed by the photograph and is suddenly surprised by the actual object of her affection. Just in time she is able to hide from the gaze of the man what she has been holding in her hand. He is not supposed to see that she "sees" him. Though early cinema developed, under the veil of darkness, a female gaze that suddenly gazed back from the bright screen, in subsequent years a cinema of narrative film develops that banishes the female gaze into the invisibility of the dark movie theater, where—in the sense of a fading-out [*Ausblendung*] of social reality—this gaze itself becomes blind.

Afterword

This book is dedicated to a lost cinema. When it was written this book sought to stand up for this cinema by means of both text and image, and this intention is still valid today. The reproduction of film stills in the book, which was particularly important to me, was intended to direct the reader's attention to these forgotten films; the stills were intended to create a first appearance, a temptation for future rescreenings. Since 1990 the films have indeed been shown at many festivals and in movie theaters, though still by no means often enough.[1] The text, for its part, wanted to establish in our time an initial context for the films, one that would make it possible to revive the glamour and importance of these films in the eyes of contemporary spectators. With my background in feminist film critique it seemed to me back then that I had discovered women's history there in the catacombs of the archives and in the light of the editing table projector, and I immersed myself in this history, in a cinema in which female audiences played a constitutive part. It was especially important for me to show how in this cinema, in the formation of a public film sphere, an unheard-of change in the relationship between the sexes played itself out. Yet I also wanted to show how the aesthetic of these early films developed through a conflict between emancipation and reaction. I was able to observe this film-immanent antagonism through the magnifying glass of the contradiction between the development of the films and the journalistic reaction of the period.

In the German original the book is comprised of two parts. The first part deals with the films; the second, with contemporary writings about cinema. In terms of my goal of presenting my reception of the films, both parts belong together. For in the defensive or interventionist attitudes of movie reformers, the intelligentsia, and literary writers, I found, precisely in their negation, the confirmation of women's influence, of women's emancipation, which I had discovered in the thematic and formal position of the films. Thus, the appearance of women's stories in these films was answered by a journalistic battle against cinema as a social space in which the sexes met in the dark. In similar fashion the educated bourgeoisie countered the filmic reflection and relativization of drama (which had as its basis the connection between female narrative perspective and elements of a cinema of attractions) by attempting, through all available means, to subjugate the feature film to a dramatic form. When, around 1913, a number of literary writers turned their attention to the modern aspects of the new medium, they focused on its technicity, blinding themselves to the freedom of the female gaze (the threatening and saving qualities of which were brought into play especially by detective films and sensational films). And finally, even as in these films a cinema in which male and female audiences could communicate on the basis of their differences seemed to be forming, we can at the same time see the beginning of a valorization of cinema as a place for scopophilia—which further emphasized sexuality even while ignoring the differences between the sexes.

In the eighties, viewing these early films constituted a radical experience. It triggered in me the need not only to talk and write about this other cinema but also to bring its historically unfulfilled importance to bear on social and cultural critique, not least film studies and film theory. Reading film publications from that period amplified this need in its own way: the initial journalistic, literary, and theoretical debate about the cinema bore all the marks of repression and ignorance about that medium through which the other sex had entered the public sphere.[2] In my eyes these texts laid the foundation for the indifference or naïveté of later film theory and film studies vis-à-vis women in the cinema—an attitude that came under attack only in the context of the women's movement in the seventies. The lived experience and perception of these early films seemed to me to be a unique opportunity to make up for something, namely, to bring the female spectator who had been repressed and ignored by film theory to bear on the development of this theory, to let her get a word in.

Over the course of the eighties, as I was working on *The Uncanny Gaze*, "early cinema" was rediscovered in many places: at the silent film festivals of Pordenone and Bologna, at the seminars of the Nederlands Filmmuseum, in film archives and their movie theaters, and at universities. Over the course of the following years these discoveries initiated coalitions of film restorers, archivists, and researchers in organizations and projects such as Domitor (the society for the study of early cinema) and Archimedia (a European educational project that sought to encourage all realms of work relevant to the exhibition and further study of film history). Meanwhile, isolated studies of early cinema in the eighties have coalesced into their own research area within film studies, and it now presents itself as such in a number of publications. Common to these publications is the fact that they are dedicated not just to a piece of film history but rather to cinema in general in all its facets, including social, economic, and aesthetic aspects. In my case as well my strong desire finally to make public that which showed itself in early films only to be repressed in early film journalism during the years that followed transformed a revision of theories of film into a theory of cinema.[3]

By dividing itself into a discussion of the films, on the one hand, and contemporary publications, on the other, *The Uncanny Gaze* expressed an antagonism between the manifestation of women in movement in one case and their repression or denial in the other. Yet there is another conflict at work behind this first one, namely, that between the new phenomenon of the cinema, which accommodated the classes and the sexes, and the old structures of a literary public sphere. Prior to World War I these positions presented themselves as relatively distinct: attempts to "bourgeoisify" the cinema were isolated and relatively unsuccessful; texts such as those of Dadaist Walter Serner, which sided with the cinema and its unbourgeois potential, were equally isolated. However, when one is looking for a theory of cinema in the face of a history of film during which the power of the producers drastically restricted the possibilities of filmmakers, what becomes especially important are those singular voices of the literary public sphere that indirectly testify to a passionate experience of the cinema and to sexual agitation. Serner's short text "Cinema and Scopophilia," written shortly before World War I broke out, seems to contain something that, in reality, was lost shortly afterward. The confrontation between a feminist position and theoretical history written by men was in the foreground when I wrote *The Uncanny Gaze*. Today, though this confrontation is still not resolved, it is for me mixed with something touching: I find myself touched by the bliss of a theory that involuntarily registers a part of that which was, in practice, repressed and destroyed.

It was my project at the time to create, in the present of film audiences, a place for the early cinema that had been lost. My book was supposed to be a medium for this project. Today it might also "make present" something else, something that was still present when the book was written but was even then already beginning to dwindle: a cinema movement initially formed in the seventies by female critics, theoreticians, filmmakers, and spectators. *The Uncanny Gaze* is now as much a documentation of early German cinema as it is a document of the feminist—and, above all, independent—cinema of the seventies and early eighties, and it should be read with an eye to both contexts.

That said, I would like to conclude by mentioning a few instances in which, in the meantime, my understanding and treatment of early cinema have changed. These changes are due in part to my subsequent experience of film and in part to theoretical work that has appeared in the meantime and that has rendered problematic some of my earlier terminology.[4]

The Uncanny Gaze outlines a history of film only up to 1914. World War I seemed to constitute a decisive caesura, a point when emancipatory movements in general, including cinema, came to a standstill. A cinema that differed from that which counted as "German"—from Expressionist film to UFA melodrama, from "Caligari to Hitler"—came to an end. Yet further research on trade journals from the war years as well as discoveries in film archives have since made me realize that the history of a "cinematographic making-public of the other sex" continued between 1914 and 1918.[5] Attempts to prohibit cinema, for example, were again rekindled and were directed especially against women, who had "stayed home." And Franz Hofer, for example, continued to work in film, providing a space within which actresses could affect audiences with their performances. In the face of the war, though, this space lost its character as a new public sphere and instead became a subterranean place for recollection, intimate bodily sensations, and imaginings. Finally, Emerich Hanus made films during the latter war years that reemerged from this underground in order to address the blindness of men.

However, in the countermovement that worked against the development of Wilhelminian cinema and toward the foundation of both the UFA and the alienation of film production from female audiences, the actress Asta Nielsen stands out. In *The Uncanny Gaze* I had no interest in again emphasizing Nielsen's historically determined exceptionality in film. On the contrary: I wanted to move away from the celebration of a star and reestablish her work in the more general context of new possibilities that had opened up through the conjunction of actresses and female audiences. However, in considering film-historical developments after 1914, Nielsen's exceptional character becomes important:

not only did she leave the realm of traditional culture as cinema expanded, but from the outset she was aware of both new possibilities and the risk inherent in her position. This awareness enabled her to avoid surrendering when she was confronted with changes in film production. In 1914 she lost her work context in Wilhelminian cinema, but already by 1916 she had returned to Berlin and began to carry on elements of early cinema's narrative films under altered social, political, and film-political conditions. In my eyes Nielsen allows for a perspective on film history that makes visible a countermovement that lies below the surface that is constituted by the perception of producers, directors, and cameramen. Within this countermovement it is actresses as well as actors who make films, films understood not as works but rather as processes that, in the final analysis, occur within the audience.[6]

Two terms appear again and again in *The Uncanny Gaze,* and they served to connect feminist theory of the seventies and early eighties with the then current discussion of early cinema. On the one hand, there is the concept of the gaze, and on the other, the concept of a *cinema of attractions.* Both terms have lost their theoretical charge. Clearly, film debates and analyses are no longer propelled by the male and the female gaze. Extensive use of the concept of a cinema of attractions, on the other hand, has led to an inflation of the term and thus a loss of its initial power. On a descriptive level, however, both terms still hit the mark: the mise-en-scène of women's gazes as well as the elements of fairground, vaudeville, and circus are undeniable in these films, as is the formation in the films of a coalition between women and an unbourgeois milieu. Yet both the term *cinema of attractions* and its success have actually hindered any attempt to take up and further this coalition through scholarship and theory.

This has happened for two reasons. On the one hand, the notion of attraction was introduced in order to distinguish an "Other" cinema of the early period from narrative film, which latter appeared to be a precursor of Hollywood. I am not certain that scholars really succeeded in restricting this view to a "cinéma du premier temps" and in validating a return to early narrative film as a "cinéma de la seconde époque" in its own right.[7] On the other hand, the use of the term *attraction* had a (film-)political implication—the reference to the Soviet montage of attractions—that made it difficult to transfer the term to a different political agenda, such as feminism.

The question of the female gaze, which occupied feminist film critique and psychoanalytical film theory in the seventies and early eighties, was—as is widely known—ignited by a political reflection on Hollywood cinema. A dominating gaze was found to be inscribed in Hollywood films, a gaze that belonged to the male individual, both his presence behind the camera and his representation in the film. This discovery provoked inquiry into the female gaze of the audience and provoked as well the suspicion that these films repressed and eliminated the female gaze. Yet the effect of these films, that which takes place in the movie theater between film and audience, is not the formation of the gaze. In the cinema the gaze at the screen becomes a means through which film can evoke memories, sensations, and fantasies that overcome the subject of the gaze and abolish his or her power of distanciation. The critique had evoked precisely the same effect on the unconscious as well. Yet this effect cannot be countered by renewed control but by recognizing the audiences' potential for sensation, fantasy, desire, dream, and recollection. With respect to these abilities, an analysis of the strategies of the gaze as they were developed by the dominant cinema becomes less important than an attention to all those instances in films that reveal the involuntary and the ungraspable by means of light, color, and movement. Early narrative film, with its rarely logically coherent narrative, determined more by lucky chance than by systematic planning, has made this especially evident. Film reception by an audience begins with embodied perception rather than a targeting gaze and proceeds on the basis of something that, if it cannot find expression in social life, seeks to realize itself in perception.

Thus, cinema moves us to speak about play and perception, imagination and utopia.

Notes

Foreword

1. The question of gender in the cinema reform movement and the beginnings of German film aesthetic and film theory are elaborated in greater detail in the book's second part, which is not included in this edition. See also Schlüpmann's afterword.

2. See Schlüpmann, *Abendröthe*, chap. 1.

3. Schlüpmann, *Öffentliche Intimität*, esp. 90–119.

4. Schlüpmann, *Ungeheure Einbildungskraft*, 7.

5. Both retrospectives were cocurated by Karola Gramann under the auspices of Kinothek Asta Nielsen.

6. See, for example, Schlüpmann's important essay "Celluloid & Co."

7. Mulvey, *Death 24x a Second*, 29.

8. Kracauer, *Theory of Film*, 218.

Introduction

1. At this point there is no recent comprehensive study on the development of cinema in Germany. Zglinicki's *Der Weg des Films* is still of interest because of the abundance of its materials. However, the book lacks the film-historical and analytical thoroughness of Sadoul, *Histoire générale du cinéma I*.

2. On the details of film production and distribution, see Bächlin, *Film als Ware*.

3. The substantial catalog by Lamprecht, *Deutsche Stummfilme 1903–1931*, provides an overview of German silent film production. Yet it is by no means complete, especially in the case of the first years.

4. Zglinicki refers to statistics about the percentage of German productions on the German market. According to him, shortly before 1914 Germany's share was 15 percent; France's, 30 percent; the United States', 25 percent; Italy's, 20 percent; and the rest was provided by Denmark and England (*Der Weg des Films*, 359).

5. According to Fraenkel, the number of film companies quadrupled between 1910 and 1914 from 24 to 104 (*Unsterblicher Film*, 183). If one follows Lamprecht's

index—which is problematic with respect to its comprehensiveness—the rise in production occurs in 1911, from 33 films indexed in 1910 to 179 films in 1911.

6. All dates according to Zglinicki, *Der Weg des Films.*

7. The last ten years [1979–89] have brought with them an enormous increase in research on early cinema (i.e., cinema before World War I). The initiating event was the FIAF conference in Brighton in 1978, during which international archives presented for the first time an enormous amount of film material from this period. Since then there has been a call to make up for decades of ignorance, uninterest, a lack of tradition, and the formulation of prejudices. Concerning film tradition, we are in many cases too late: only a fraction of the immense film production of the first two decades has been preserved at all; even these films are far from being completely inventoried and secured (i.e., they are still threatened by physical decay). See Francis, *Cinema 1900–1906,* which contains an analytical filmography that was curated primarily by André Gaudreault.

8. See Sloan, *The Loud Silents.*

9. *Gründerzeit,* or Founding Epoch, refers to the first decades that followed the foundation of the Prussia-led German empire in 1871.—Trans.

10. On the state-supporting role of the UFA, see Barkhausen, *Filmpropaganda für Deutschland.*

11. May, *Screening out the Past,* 46.

12. The phrase is in English in the original.—Trans.

13. "Since 1880, approximately," Rosenberg wrote in 1928, "the back of the German bourgeoisie had been broken politically." On the lack of successful democratization before World War I, he wrote: "The demand for a parliamentary system in Germany meant in reality the transference of power from the Prussian aristocracy to the German middle class rather than from the Emperor to the Reichstag" (Rosenberg, *Imperial Germany,* 42; *Die Entstehung der deutschen Republik,* 45).

14. Ringer, *The Decline,* 7; *Die Gelehrten,* 17.

15. "It argues that the state derives its legitimacy not from divine right, for that would stress the prince's whim, nor from the interests of the subjects, for that would suggest a voting procedure, but exclusively from its services to the intellectual and spiritual life of the nation. It clearly follows that government must give material aid to the cultural and educational program of the elite and that it must do so without demanding an immediate practical return" (Ringer, *The Decline,* 11; *Die Gelehrten,* 20).

16. Ringer, *The Decline,* 123–24; *Die Gelehrten,* 116.

17. Rosenberg established a direct link between the missing political will of the proletariat and the deficits of a political education that the proletariat could only receive, directly or indirectly, from the bourgeoisie, as the example of England shows: "Among the German middle class no such tradition existed. . . . At school, in the army, and in the factory, the German workman only learnt to write and to read, the technique of his employment, discipline, and organization. He never achieved a political cosmogony. He had no conception of how the political, economic, and

social revolution for which he longed could be accomplished, and no knowledge of which road would lead him out of his present distresses to a better future. Nor, although in some respects it accomplished much, was the educational activity of the Social Democrat Party able to fill in these gaps" (*Imperial Germany,* 45–46; *Die Entstehung der deutschen Republik,* 48).

18. This expansion is also represented by a new role for women, that is, that of *Kulturpflege,* the safeguarding and promotion of culture. This was not just the production of ideology; it also implied changes in the everyday life of women, as Hausen explains: "Until the turn of the twentieth century, esteem for an education that enables more than superficial conversation, and esteem for a willingness to respond to the needs of husband and children, moved more and more into the foreground" (Hausen, " . . . eine Ulme," 94). Hausen also connects the increase in the age at which women became married to an increase in efforts to obtain an education.

19. It is this aspect especially that Kaes emphasizes in his introduction to *Kino-Debatte,* 12.

20. Meyhöfer, *Das Motiv des Schauspielers,* 37.

21. See the work of Gunning, especially "The Cinema of Attraction"; and Gaudreault, especially *Du littéraire au filmique.*

22. See, for example, Musser, "The Nickelodeon Era Begins," 6.

23. Geitner quotes this sentence from Paul, *Levana oder Erziehlehre,* 234 (see *Schauspielerinnen,* 274).

24. Laermann, "Die riskante Person," 133.

25. In *Die Ordnung der Geschlechter* Honegger points out how the definition of womanhood was withdrawn from public discussion and self-thematization by female authors and became "scientized." The "science of the woman" [*Wissenschaft vom Weibe*] is part of anthropology (which was aspiring to be a universal science at the time) before it was established as "gynecology" in the nineteenth century.

26. Meyhöfer, *Das Motiv des Schauspielers,* 277: "Near the end of the nineteenth century, the liberal bourgeoisie had to come to terms with both its elimination from parliaments and the fading of its ideals of freedom and individuality. For the liberal bourgeoisie, the theater becomes a bulwark against bad reality and the sense that one lacks a future."

27. In "Early Silent Cinema" Hansen had already pointed toward the specific relationship of early German cinema to female audiences. On the role of women in American movie audiences of the early period, especially among immigrants, see also Hansen, *Babel and Babylon.*

28. Compare Altenloh, *Zur Soziologie des Kino,* 91: "Unless one is dealing with a small intellectual elite, basically the same holds true for women of the upper classes as for the young shop girls [*Handlungsgehilfinnen*] that have been discussed in detail here; except that the former, insofar they are not also restricted in their spare time by some kind of job, go to the movies even more frequently."

29. Compare Lamprecht's silent film index in *Deutsche Stummfilme 1903–1931.* The term *drama* is also used in many different combinations: *Drama aus dem Leben*

(drama taken from life), *Kriegsdrama* (war drama), *Sensationsdrama* (sensational drama), *realistisches Drama* (realist drama), and so on.

30. On Danish moral drama, see my essay "Im Gegensinn der Worte."

31. Altenloh, *Zur Soziologie des Kino*, 12: "Nordic films, especially those from Denmark, have added a fundamentally new 'tone' [*Note*] to film dramaturgy: this is, as I already noted, essentially social 'drama.' And even though they have only competed on the film market for a few years, this kind of film seems to have taken the prize."

32. Altenloh, *Zur Soziologie des Kino*, 58.

33. My understanding of drama in film is influenced by Teresa de Lauretis's discussion of narration in film. Her concept of the Oedipal narrative subject proceeds from the assumption that the constitution of the narrator precedes the emergence of classical drama. The mythical origin of the narrative subject disappears in the textual structure of the drama, while the hero himself seems "free" from this mythical origin and appears as an agent who is the "origin" of the story. In drama psychoanalysis first became able to perceive "Oedipus." See Lauretis, "Desire in Narrative," 112.

34. Geitner, *Schauspielerinnen*, 272.

35. In her autobiography Asta Nielsen describes the minimal instructions she received from directors and scripts: "Literally standing on bare ground, I grew from what was demanded of me. My imagination [*Phantasie*] had to create poetically for me. For, often enough, my scene was only minimally sketched. I can remember a certain manuscript that said: The child dies. Asta's main scene" (*Die schweigende Muse*, 140).

36. Laermann hints at the contradictions that are produced by the emergence of the actress; Geitner stresses how, in order to solve these contradictions, an acting theory of sensibility is developed: "The conception of sensible-natural expressivity tries to master the problem of performance art in its own way: the actress becomes someone who senses, who presents her nature. When, for example, Friedrich Theophilus Thilo, in his epistolary novel from 1780–82, presents his protagonist Emilie Sommer as actress, then neither the public nor the performativity that is asked of the actress onstage is able to harm Emilie's *nature*. . . . Thilo's novel creates in the figure of Emilie, in complete contrast to Diderot's Paradox of the Actor, the paradoxical performance of an actress who does not act" (*Schauspielerinnen*, 270).

37. See, among others, Kellen, *Die Not*, from 1902; among more recent texts see Giesing, *Ibsens Nora*; Möhrmann, "Die Herren zahlen."

38. On the case of Lindau and Schabelsky see Giesing, *Ibsens Nora*, 289ff.; Mehring, *Der Fall Lindau*.

39. The bracketed phrase appears in the original.—Trans.

40. Szondi, *Theory of the Modern Drama*, 51–52; *Theorie des modernen Dramas*, 85.

41. Through her concept of the "primitive narrator" Mayne has already outlined a cinematic narrative subject that is not necessarily an omnipotent male subject ("Der primitive Erzähler"). I use the term *narrative perspective* in order to emphasize the

importance of a female standpoint in early narrative film. This female standpoint is neither a function of the male standpoint nor an already successful form of female subjectivity in contrast to male subjectivity.

42. For a summary of the second part of *The Uncanny Gaze* see the author's afterword.—Trans.

43. Altenberg, "Das Kino," 63–64.

Chapter 1: The Heart of Reason

1. *The Deployment of the Sentry* was shot in 1896; the other two films were shot by Guido Seeber around 1898.

2. Presumably shot by the brothers Skladanowsky around 1896.

3. *Annabelle's Butterfly Dance* and *Annabelle's Serpentine Dance* were made by the Edison Manufacturing Company.

4. Zglinicki, *Der Weg des Films,* 269.

5. Moreck, *Sittengeschichte des Kinos,* 170.

6. See Wierling, *Mädchen für alles.* Concerning the "working hours" of maids, she says: "Maids rented themselves out as a person, which included their entire man-power. As a consequence, they had to accept, for example, being hired as a nurse at very low wages, but then being employed as a 'girl for everything' [*Mädchen für alles*] in the household. . . . However, renting the complete manpower of maids had an even greater impact on the expansion of the period during which her services were to be available. . . . According to a study commissioned by the alliance of German women's clubs [Bund deutscher Frauenvereine] and conducted within several cities, most maids ended their workday around nine o'clock at night—which, since their workday began between six and seven o'clock in the morning, results in a daily working period of 14 to 15 hours" (88–89).

7. Adorno and Horkheimer, *Dialectic of Enlightenment,* 139; *Dialektik der Aufklärung,* 165.

8. *Biedermann* refers to a typical representative of the Biedermeier period (ca. 1815–48). This term, coined after the period itself, is often used in a derogatory way to refer to the rise of a depoliticized "petty" bourgeoisie.—Trans.

9. The article is reprinted in Greve, Fehle, and Westhoff, *Hätte ich das Kino!* 24.

10. Decroix, [no title].

Chapter 2: The Femininity of Men

1. On the two latter films see Gunning, "The Cinema of Attraction."

2. The available copy at the SDK has the title *Aus eines Mannes Mädchenjahren* [*On a Man's Maiden Years*], which, however, presumably has a later date. In an extensive 1916 review of the film in Berlin that unquestionably refers to the film under discussion here, the film is entitled *Aus eines Mannes Mädchenzeit* [*On a Man's Maidenhood*] (see *Der Kinematograph,* no. 517 [1916]: 22).

3. So far, the participation in cinema of the homosexual movement—which, especially before World War I, became an undeniable public force—is only known for the

period after the war. *Different from the Others* [*Anders als die Andern*], a film made in 1919 by Richard Oswald, counts as the first "gay film" (about this film see Theis, "Anders als die Andern"). There seems to be no information about the relationship of the homosexual subculture in the German empire to cinema. At any rate, Theis and Sternweiler's essay on the leisure-time activities of homosexuals contains no references to this ("Alltag im Kaiserreich").

Chapter 3: Reaction in the Melodrama

1. See Gledhill, *Home Is Where the Heart Is,* 5–42; on nonfilmic and filmic forms of melodrama, see especially the excellent introductory essay by Gledhill, "The Melodramatic Field." In addition, for the Anglo-Saxon discussion see Brooks, *The Melodramatic Imagination,* which provides a fundamentally different evaluation of melodrama than is suggested by the German tradition.

2. In 1908 (no. 65) *Der Kinematograph* published an article entitled "Wie singende Bilder (Tonbilder) entstehen" ["How Singing Pictures (Sound Pictures) Are Made"]. The author had attended recordings at Messter's studio. Aside from its discovery of how many of the company's productions were sound pictures at that time, the text contains another interesting remark: "Over the course of a year, the company spends thousands on payments for the performers. . . . The performances are delightful, but they . . . [can] also make one feel melancholy, in those cases in which the artists have died, and now one seems to see and hear them alive before oneself."

3. Altenloh, *Zur Soziologie des Kino,* 57.

4. See the text collage "Henny Porten. Vom primitiven Lichtspiel zur Filmkunst."

5. Altenloh, *Zur Soziologie des Kino,* 79.

6. See Häfker, *Kino und Kunst.*

7. On the film's censorship, see the remark in Corinna Müller's filmography in Belach, *Henny Porten,* 178: "In the publication of the censorship decisions by the Berlin Police Commission from August 5, 1911, the film with the title *Ein Streik und seine Folgen* [*A Strike and Its Consequences*] is listed under the rubric 'Completely Forbidden.' Censorship remarks: 'Strike, the cutting of a cable, the operation on a child' (Birett, *Verzeichnis,* 15). In a publication from August 16, 1911, the abolition of the prohibition is announced; an extract: 'The picture is now only forbidden for children. Strike, cutting of the cable, and the operation on the child have been cut out' (Birett, *Verzeichnis,* 16). When it was submitted for a final time under the title *Tragedy of a Strike,* the scene 'Cutting of a Cable' was again included in the film (Birett, *Verzeichnis,* 20). The film was released, though proscribed for children."

Chapter 4: Excursus

1. On Henny Porten see Belach, *Henny Porten.* A discussion of this star's fatally German character is absent from this publication. The only analytical essay included in the book, Knut Hickethier's "Mütterliche Venus und leidendes Weib," simply rounds off the carefully compiled but familiar image of Porten. Even though the essay addresses her "national physiognomy," it takes an altogether concilia-

tory path. Hickethier's attempt to locate a solution in Alexander Kluge's notion of "female productive force" is aggravating, since it bypasses not only the feminist discussion in the 1970s of Kluge's theory but also insights into the behavior of women and the women's movement during World War I. Following a quote from Porten's autobiography in which she comments upon the tasks of women during the war, Hickethier writes: "Yet that which, with respect to her terminology, seems to coalesce seamlessly into the German-national physiognomy, remains fragile. When Henny Porten wrote these sentences, women, during World War I, had just begun to take over tasks that had been previously reserved only for men, and thus, women also gained a new independence. Don't these sentences show something of that 'superior mode of production' [*überlegene Produktionsweise*] which Alexander Kluge addresses, which woman has at her command as soon as she is able to grasp society in its entirety? In Porten-like fashion, Kluge likes to explain the superiority of this mode of production with the example of the mother-child relationship" (161).

2. Hickethier, "Mütterliche Venus und leidendes Weib," 7.

3. See Honegger and Heinz, *Listen der Ohnmacht*.

4. On film adaptations of *Vulture Wally*, see Berg-Ganschow, "Der Widerspenstigen Zähmung."

5. *The Mountain Is Calling* [*Der Berg ruft*, 1937] is a famous UFA melodrama (a *Heimat* film and mountain film) directed by and starring Luis Trenker.—Trans.

Chapter 5: Contradictions of Social Drama

1. Literally, "arbor" or "gazebo." *Die Gartenlaube* was the first mass-produced magazine in Germany. From its first issue in 1853 to the turn of the century, it developed from an entertaining and educational political journal to a conservative bourgeois "family paper" that focused on sentimental entertainment, and it increasingly shifted its focus from text to images. The magazine was widely read (2–5 million readers) and was popular especially for its serial novels. It was taken over by Alfred Hugenberg's media empire in 1916 and continued until 1944 as *Die neue Gartenlaube*.—Trans.

2. Rennert, "Victor Hugo und der Kino," 130ff.

3. See Stöcker, "Aus dem Leben einer Prostituierten" and "Aus den Aufzeichnungen einer Prostituierten."

4. Here, as throughout the book, "numbers" is used in the sense of "vaudeville numbers."—Trans.

5. See "Berliner Plauderei," *Der Kinematograph*, no. 87 (August 26, 1908).

6. I was able to watch a copy of this film, in addition to a number of other pornographic films from the Wilhelminian era, at the Deutsche Filmmuseum. "Saturn" is the production company in most cases; aside from that, only titles are known (but whether these stem from this period is not always clear): *The Unfaithful Woman* [*Das ungetreue Weib*], *The Angler* [*Der Angler*], *The Girls' Chamber* [*Die Mädchenkammer*], *At the Photographer* [*Beim Fotograf*], *On the Bank of the Pond* [*Am Ufer des Teiches*], *Shower* [*Dusche*], *A Nice Hotel* [*Ein feines Hotel*].

7. The quote is from Kant, *Philosophical Correspondence*, 235–36.—Trans.

8. See my contribution *"Der Gang in die Nacht"* in Jung and Schatzberg's publication of the contributions to an international conference in Luxemburg in 1989, *Filmkultur zur Zeit der Weimarer Republik.*

9. On the emergence and importance of monopoly film distribution, see Müller, "Emergence of the Feature Film." [See also Müller's book-length study from 1994, *Frühe deutsche Kinematographie.*—Trans.]

10. The extent of Gad's support for Nielsen emerges from her autobiography; see, for example, *Die schweigende Muse,* 132: "From my first success [after *The Abyss* (*Afgrunden*)] I gained confidence, and I was likewise reassured by the fact that Urban Gad was engaged to write and direct both films. Thus we received a certain right of codetermination and had, in any case, many opportunities to influence scenes."

11. *B. Z. am Mittag,* October 22, 1928, reprinted in Seydel and Hagedorff, *Asta Nielsen.*

12. From contemporary reviews one can infer that at least in one copy of *Sins of the Fathers* the problem of alcoholism took up more space. In this preserved copy alcoholism plays a rather subordinate role; it is part of the milieu from which the protagonist originates. It becomes clear in these reviews that there were scenes that are missing in the preserved copy. Then again, it is a question to what extent the gaze of the critic focused on the social problem of alcoholism and overlooked other, less "proletariat"-specific problems.

13. The quote by Taine is missing from the theater play by Lindau upon which the script is based; see Lindau, *Der Andere.* Hippolyte Taine (1828–93) might not have been a psychoanalyst, but he was a scientific novelist influenced by Comte, for whom the psychological interpretation of stories was of special importance. The auteur film did not engage in an open relationship with psychoanalysis, which was, like cinema, fighting for bourgeois recognition at that time; rather, it invoked psychology within the framework of established science. Some of Freud's disciples, by contrast, received cinema with far more interest (cf., e.g., Andreas Salomé, "Kino," 67). Rank began his extensive essay "Der Doppelgänger" with a description of Hanns Heinz Ewers's film *The Student of Prague.*

14. This transformation in the relationship between the sexes and the relationship to the "dark side" of bourgeois life that the film establishes escapes Kracauer as he writes, with respect to the ending of the film: "Hallers regains his health and gets married: the prototype of a citizen immune to all psychological disturbances" (*From Caligari to Hitler,* 34; *Von Caligari zu Hitler,* 40).

15. Accordingly, Adorno and Horkheimer see in film as mass culture merely this "prescription": "When a film presents us with a glamour girl, it may officially approve or disapprove of her, she may be glorified as a successful heroine or punished as a vamp. Yet as a written character the glamour girl announces something quite different from the psychological speech banners draped around her grinning mouth, namely the injunction to be similar to her. The new context into which these preprepared images enter as so many letters is always that of the command" ("The Schema of Mass Culture," 81; "Das Schema der Massenkultur").

16. See Szondi, *Theory of the Modern Drama.* Szondi describes how modern drama tries to rescue its classical form in many ways—in Naturalism and *Jugendstil*—before it finds a way to modified forms in Expressionist drama, in epic theater, and so on. Erwin Piscator's Political Revue constitutes one of these "attempts at a solution," since it incorporates film into theater: "The epic nature of the motion picture, which is grounded in the opposing spaces of the camera and its object, in the subjectively codetermined representation of objectivity as objectivity, allowed Piscator to add to the stage action those things that escaped dramatic actualization—the alienated reification of 'the social, the political and the economic'" (Szondi, *Theory of the Modern Drama,* 68). What this quote indicates about the extension of theater through its inclusion of film is true, of course, to a much greater degree for film in general, for then there is the possibility of abolishing the crisis of drama in the theater through the form of film drama. This possibility has barely been developed—not least because of commercial circumstances, which hardly allowed for such aesthetic development.

17. The year that marks the beginnings of the auteur film, 1912, was also a decisive year in the competition between stage and screen. On July 18, 1912, an assembly of the stage writers' association [Bühnenschriftstellerverband] demanded a general boycott by all stage artists and dramatists. However, the film producers, who had been dealing with the cultural-bourgeois battle against cinema for years and thus had developed strategies of assimilation, were stronger. In the summer and fall of that same year contracts were made with authors such as Gerhard Hauptmann, Hermann Sudermann, and Arthur Schnitzler. In November 1912 a cartel agreement with the stage writers' association was established. When *The Other* premiered on February 1, 1913, the industry celebrated it as the result of a victory in its fight with the stage. The interest of the entire cultural-bourgeois feuilleton in this event demonstrates, in striking fashion, its success.

18. The German word *Aufklärung* is used here and in all other cases in a threefold sense. As the term for "enlightenment" it connotes a philosophical position and historical period. However, it also suggests, in a visual sense, light and clarity. Finally, one can speak of the *Aufklärung* or "illumination," literally, "clearing up," of a crime.—Trans.

Chapter 6: Perspective "from Below" or Perspective "from Outside"

1. *Leo the Ancillary Waiter,* a film that I did not analyze further in the chapter on comedy, presents an example of a lumpen proletarian comedy hero; apparently, this Bolten-Baeckers production is just one of a whole series of "Leo" films. So far I have only been able to locate a few other titles: *Leo, the Widow's Friend* [*Leo der Witwenfreund*], *Leo on His Honeymoon* [*Leo auf Hochzeitsreise*], *Leo as Reporter* [*Leo als Reporter*]. It is unclear, however, if any of these films have been preserved.

2. In the case of German cinema we have no knowledge of any female director among the auteur directors; it was really only the New German Film that gave female directors a chance. In contrast, the first female Swedish director, Anna Hofmann-

Udgren, must be counted among the "auteur directors." She directed film adaptations of Strindberg such as *The Father* [*Der Vater*, 1912].

3. As much as the detective novel is tied to England, the detective film combines multiple influences, for example, that of the French *cinéroman*.

4. See Kracauer, *Von Caligari zu Hitler*, 25.

5. See, for example, Stöcker, "Zur Emanzipation des Mannes."

6. See Bucher, "Harry Piel," in *Screen Series*. On Joseph Delmont, see Kahlenberg, "*Der geheimnisvolle Klub* and *Auf einsamer Insel*."

7. See Fred Gehler on Harry Piel in Dahlke and Karl, *Deutsche Spielfilme*, 302ff.

8. The spelling of the names follows the Dutch copy.

9. *The Suicide Club* is the title of a collection of three related short stories that revolve around a secret club. The stories first appeared in the *London Magazine* in 1878 and had already been adapted in a short film of the same title by D. W. Griffith in 1909.—Trans.

10. All information according to Lamprecht, *Deutsche Stummfilme 1903–1931*.

11. Cf. Greve, Fehle, and Westhoff, *Hätte ich das Kino!* 85, 253; this compilation reprinted the program notes for two films of the Hofer-Film-GmbH from 1921.

Chapter 7: Uncanniness of the Female Gaze

1. On this group of female French cineasts see Des Femmes de Musidora, *Paroles . . . elles tournent!*

2. Both of these films are at the archive of the Nederlands Filmmuseum, Amsterdam. Only *The Atonement* is indexed in Lamprecht, *Deutsche Stummfilme 1903–1931*; the dating of *A Fatal Oath* is therefore only provisional.

Chapter 8: Crime and Love in Prewar Drama, 1913–1914

1. For American film, crosscutting can be traced back to 1908, when it appeared in the Biograph film *Her First Adventure*. After that, D. W. Griffith especially developed this technique further. See Salt, "The Early Development of Film Form," 287.

2. In a way that is difficult to render in English, Schlüpmann is playing here with *Schaulust*, the compound German word for "scopophilia."—Trans.

3. That is, rather than with her.—Trans.

Afterword

1. The first public rescreening took place in 1990 in Italy at the film festival Il Giornate del Cinema Muto under the title *Prima di Caligari*.

2. See note 5 on the meaning of *Veröffentlichung* in this context.

3. My outlines of a theory of the cinema can be found in the following publications: *Abendröthe der Subjektphilosophie*, *Öffentliche Intimität*, and *Ungeheure Einbildungskraft*.

4. Film studies' turn away from the dominance of semiotics and psychoanalysis has made room for—amongst other things—a (re)discovery of the film-theoretical writings of Siegfried Kracauer, Walter Benjamin, and the so-called Frankfurt School.

See Miriam Hansen, "Room-for-Play: Benjamin's Gamble with Cinema," *October 109* (Summer 2004): 3–45; "Introduction," Siegfried Kracauer, *Theory of Film: The Redemption of Physical Reality* (Princeton N.J.: Princeton University Press, 1997): vii–xlv; and *The Other Frankfurt School: Kracauer, Benjamin, Adorno on Cinema, Mass Culture, and Modernity* (Berkeley: University of California Press, forthcoming). See also Nia Perivolaropoulou, "Le travail de la mémoire dans Theory of Film de Siegfried Kracauer," *Protée* (Chicoutimi, Québec), vol. 23, no. 1 (Spring 2004): 39–48; "Du flâneur au spectateur: modernité, grande ville et cinéma chez Siegfried Kracauer," Stéphane Füzességy et Philippe Simay (eds.), *Simmel, Benjamin, Kracauer : la ville en état de choc* (Paris: Editions de l'éclat, 2008): 125–48; and "Les Jacques Offenbach de Siegfried Kracauer: Biographie, histoire et cinéma," Philippe Despoix, Peter Schöttler und Nia Perivolaropoulou (eds.), *Siegfried Kracauer, penseur de l'histoire* (Paris: Ed. de la Maison des sciences de l'homme, 2006): 165–86.

5. "The Cinematographic Making-Public of the Other Sex" ["Die kinematographische Ver-öffentlichung des anderen Geschlechts"] is the title of the first part of the book that comprised the discussion of German films from 1895 to 1914, that is, the part that is translated here. "Ver-öffentlichung" in this context refers both to the fact that in the cinema, women gained a new visibility (i.e., were "made public") and to the fact that by means of this visibility and the space the movie theater provided, women were entering the bourgeois public sphere (*Öffentlichkeit*).—Trans.

6. A comprehensive book on Asta Nielsen entitled *Sprache der Liebe: Asta Nielsen, ihre Filme, ihr Kino 1910–1933* [*Language of Love: Asta Nielsen, Her Films, Her Cinema 1910–1933*], edited by Karola Gramann, Eric de Kuyper, Sabine Nessel, Heide Schlüpmann, and Michael Wedel, is forthcoming from the Filmarchiv Austria.

7. See Kuyper, "Le cinéma de la seconde époque."

Bibliography

Early Writings on Cinema

MAGAZINES

Die Bildspielkunst, Berlin (test issue August 15, 1913)
Bild und Film, M. Gladbach (first issue March 1912)
Deutsche Kinorundschau, Berlin (first published 1914)
Erste Internationale Film-Zeitung, Berlin (first published 1907)
Erste internationale Kinematographen-Zeitung, Hamburg (first published 1914)
Film-Kunst. Illustrierte Wochenschrift für moderne Kinematographie, Berlin (1913)
Das Filmrecht. Juristische Beilage der Erste Internationale Film-Zeitung (first published 1913)
Die Film-Welt, Berlin (continuation of *Erste Internationale Film-Zeitung* from October 1919 on)
Der Kinematograph, Düsseldorf (first issue January 6, 1907)
Kunst im Kino, Berlin (first published 1912)
Lichtbild-Bühne, Berlin (first published 1908)
Das Lichtbild-Theater, Berlin (first published 1909)
Die Lichtbildkunst in Schule, Wissenschaft und Volksleben, Storkow (Mark); with inserts: *Die Lichtbildschule und Volk und Film* (first published 1912)
Lichtspiel-Zeitung, Berlin (first published 1912)
Union-Theater-Zeitung, Berlin (first published 1910)
Welt im Film, Zürich (first issue November 5, 1913)

TEXT COLLECTIONS

Güttinger, Fritz, ed. *Kein Tag ohne Kino. Schriftsteller über den Stummfilm.* Frankfurt am Main, 1984.
Kaes, Anton, ed. *Kino-Debatte. Texte zum Verhältnis von Literatur und Film 1909–1929.* Tübingen, 1978. Kaes's introduction translated as "The Debate about Cinema: Charting a Controversy (1909–1929)." *New German Critique* 40 (Winter 1987): 7–33.

ARTICLES AND MONOGRAPHS

Altenberg, Peter. "Das Kino." *Wiener Allg. Zeitung,* April 1912.

Altenloh, Emilie. *Zur Soziologie des Kino.* Jena: Diederichs, 1914.

Andreas Salomé, Lou. "Kino." In *In der Schule bei Freud. Tagebuch eines Jahres 1912/13.* Munich: Kindler, 1965.

Auer, Fritz. "Das Zeitalter des Films. Eine Kino-Umfrage." *Der Kinematograph,* no. 379 (April 12, 1911).

Decroix, Charles. [No title.] In "Kunst und Literatur im Kino." Special issue, *Die Lichtbild-Bühne* 23, no. 5 (1913).

Häfker, Hermann. *Kino und Kunst.* Mönchengladbach: Volksvereins-Verlag, 1913.

Kellen, Tony. *Die Not unserer Schauspielerinnen. Studie über die wirtschaftliche Lage und die moralische Stellung der Bühnenkünstlerinnen.* Leipzig: O. Wiegand, 1902.

Lindau, Paul. *Der Andere. Schauspiel in vier Aufzügen.* Leipzig: Reclam, 1906.

Lukács, Georg. "Gedanken zu einer Ästhetik des Kinos." *Frankfurter Zeitung,* September 10, 1913; an earlier, shorter version was published on April 16, 1911, in *Pester Lloyd.*

Mehring, Franz. *Der Fall Lindau.* Berlin: Brachvogel und Ranft, 1890.

Moreck, Curt. *Sittengeschichte des Kinos.* Dresden: Paul Aretz, 1926.

Paul, Jean. *Levana oder Erziehlehre.* In *Sämtliche Werke. Historisch-Kritische Ausgabe.* Vol. 12. Ed. Eduard Berend. Weimar, 1937. [*Levana, or: The Doctrine of Education.* Boston: Ticknor and Fields, 1863.]

Porten, Henny. *Wie ich wurde. Selbstbiographie.* Berlin: Volkskraft-Verlag, 1919.

Rank, Otto. "Der Doppelgänger." *Imago,* no. 3 (1914).

Rennert, Malwine. "Victor Hugo und der Kino. Französische und deutsche Filmkunst." *Bild und Film* 2 (1912–13): 129–31.

Serner, Walter. "Kino und Schaulust." *Die Schaubühne* 9, nos. 34–35 (August 28, 1913): 807–11.

Simmel, Georg. *Philosophische Kultur.* Leipzig: W. Klinkhardt, 1911.

Stöcker, Helene, ed. "Aus dem Leben einer Prostituierten." *Die neue Generation,* no. 1 (1914).

———. "Aus den Aufzeichnungen einer Prostituierten." Parts 2–4. *Die neue Generation,* nos. 3, 5, 7 (1914).

———. "Zur Emanzipation des Mannes." In *Die Liebe und die Frauen.* Minden in Westfalen: J. C. C. Bruns' Verlag, 1906.

Turszinsky, Walter. "Kinodramen und Kinomimen." *Die Schaubühne* 4 (1910): 989–92.

Reference Books and Film Histories

Birett, Herbert. *Verzeichnis der in Deutschland gelaufenen Filme. Entscheidungen der Filmzensur 1911–1920.* Berlin: Saur, 1980.

Bock, Hans Michael, ed. *Cinegraph. Lexikon zum deutschsprachigen Film.* Munich: Edition Text + Kritik, 1984.

Bucher, Felix. *Screen Series: Germany.* London: Zwemmer, 1970.

Dahlke, Günther, and Karl Günther, eds. *Deutsche Spielfilme von den Anfängen bis 1933. Ein Filmführer.* Berlin: Henschelverlag, 1988.

Diederichs, H. H. *Anfänge deutscher Filmkritic.* Stuttgart: R. Fischer and U. Wiedleroither, 1986.

Deutsches Institut für Filmkunde und Stiftung Deutsche Kinemathek. *Verleihkatalog.* Frankfurt am Main, 1986.

Fraenkel, Heinrich. *Unsterblicher Film. Die große Chronik. Von der Laterna Magica zum Tonfilm.* Munich: Kindler, 1956.

Gregor, Ulrich, and Enno Patalas. *Geschichte des Films 1895–1939 I.* Rheinbek bei Hamburg: Rowohlt, 1976.

Lamprecht, Gerhard. *Deutsche Stummfilme 1903–1931.* 9 vols. and an index. Berlin: Deutsche Kinemathek, 1967–70.

Sadoul, Georges. *Histoire générale du cinéma I (1832–1909): L'invention du cinéma.* Paris: Éditions Denoël, 1946.

———. *Histoire générale du cinéma II (1897–1909): Les pionnières du cinéma 1897–1909.* Paris: Éditions Denoël, 1947.

Toeplitz, Jerzy. *Geschichte des Films I (1895–1928).* Berlin: Henschelverlag, 1972.

SECONDARY LITERATURE

Adorno, Theodor W. "Das Schema der Massenkultur" (Anhang zur *Dialektik der Aufklärung*). In *Schriften 3.* Frankfurt am Main: Suhrkamp, 1970. 299–35. ["The Schema of Mass Culture." In *The Culture Industry: Selected Essays on Mass Culture.* Ed. J. M. Bernstein. London: Routledge, 1991. 53–84.]

Adorno, Theodor W., and Max Horkheimer. *Dialektik der Aufklärung. Philosophische Fragmente.* Amsterdam: Querido, 1947. [1944; *Dialectic of Enlightenment.* New York: Continuum, 1988.]

Bächlin, Peter. *Film als Ware.* Basel: Burg-Verlag, 1947.

Balázs, Béla. *Der sichtbare Mensch oder die Kultur des Films* (1924). In *Schriften zum Film.* Vol. 1. Munich: Akad. Kiadó, 1982.

Barkhausen, Hans. *Filmpropaganda für Deutschland im Ersten und Zweiten Weltkrieg.* Hildesheim: Olms, 1982.

Belach, Helga, ed. *Henny Porten. Der erste deutsche Filmstar 1890–1960. Mit Beiträgen von Hans Feld, Knuth Hickethier, Corinna Müller, Helmut Regel und autobiografischen Texten von Henny Porten.* Berlin: Haude und Spener, 1986.

Berg-Gantschow, Uta. "Der Widerspenstigen Zähmung." *Frauen und Film* 35 (October 1983): 24–28.

Brooks, Peter. *The Melodramatic Imagination: Balzac, Henry James, Melodrama and the Mode of Excess.* New Haven: Yale University Press, 1976.

Des Femmes de Musidora. *Paroles . . . elles tournent!* Paris: Des Femmes, 1976.

Fell, John L. *Film before Griffith.* Berkeley: University of California Press, 1983.

Francis, David, ed. *Cinema 1900–1906: An Analytical Study.* Brussels: FIAF Publications, 1982.

Frevert, Ute, ed. *Bürgerinnen und Bürger. Geschlechterverhältnisse im 19. Jahrhundert.* Göttingen: Vandenhoeck und Ruprecht, 1988.

Gaudreault, André. *Du littéraire au filmique. Système du récit.* Paris: Méridiens Klincksieck, 1988.

Geitner, Ursula, ed. *Schauspielerinnen. Der theatralische Eintritt der Frau in die Moderne*. Bielefeld: Haux, 1988.

Gerhard, Ute. *Verhältnisse und Verhinderungen. Frauenarbeit, Familie und Rechte der Frauen im 19. Jahrhundert. Mit Dokumenten*. Frankfurt am Main: Suhrkamp, 1978.

Giesing, Michaela. *Ibsens Nora und die wahre Emanzipation der Frau. Zum Frauenbild im Wilhelminischen Theater*. Frankfurt: Peter Lang, 1984.

Gledhill, Christine. "The Melodramatic Field: An Investigation." In *Home Is Where the Heart Is: Studies in Melodrama and the Woman's Film*. Ed. Christine Gledhill. London: BFI Publications, 1987. 5–39.

Greve, Ludwig, Margot Fehle, and Heidi Westhoff, eds. *Hätte ich das Kino! Ausstellungskatalog des Schiller-Nationalmuseums Marbach*. Munich: Kösel, 1976.

Gunning, Tom. "The Cinema of Attraction: Early Film, Its Spectator and the Avant-Garde." *Wide Angle* 18, nos. 3–4 (1986): 63–70.

Habermas, Jürgen. *Strukturwandel der Öffentlichkeit. Untersuchungen zu einer Kategorie der bürgerlichen Gesellschaft*. Neuwied, 1962. [*The Structural Transformation of the Public Sphere: An Inquiry into a Category of Bourgeois Society*. Cambridge, Mass.: MIT Press, 1989.]

Hansen, Miriam. *Babel and Babylon: Spectatorship in American Silent Film*. Cambridge, Mass.: Harvard University Press, 1991.

———. "Early Silent Cinema: Whose Public Sphere?" *New German Critique,* no. 29 (Spring–Summer 1983): 147–84.

———. "Introduction." *Siegfried Kracauer, theory of Film: The Redemption of Physical Reality*. Princeton, N.J.: Princeton University Press, 1997. vii–xiv.

———. "Room-for-Play: Benjamin's Gamble with Cinema." *October 109* (Summer 2004): 3–45.

Hausen, Karin. ". . . eine Ulme für den schwankenden Efeu. Ehepaare im deutschen Bildungsbürgertum." In *Bürgerinnen und Bürger. Geschlechterverhältnisse im 19. Jahrhundert*. Ed. Ute Frevert. Göttingen: Vandenhoeck und Ruprecht, 1988. 85–117.

Hickethier, Knut. "Mütterliche Venus und leidendes Weib." In *Henny Porten. Der erste deutsche Filmstar 1890–1960*. Ed. Helga Belach. Berlin: Haude und Spener, 1986.

Honegger, Claudia. *Die Ordnung der Geschlechter. Die Wissenschaft vom Menschen und das Weib*. Frankfurt am Main: Europäische Verlagsanstalt, 1984.

Honegger, Claudia, and Bettina Heintz, eds. *Listen der Ohnmacht. Zur Soziologie weiblicher Widerstandsformen*. Frankfurt am Main: Europäische Verlagsanstalt, 1984.

Kahlenberg, Friedrich P. "*Der geheimnisvolle Klub* and *Auf einsamer Insel*. Two German Feature Films Made by Eiko-Film in 1913." In *Before Caligari: German Cinema, 1895–1920*. Ed. Paolo Cherchi Usai and Lorenzo Codelli. Pordenone: Edizioni Biblioteca dell'Immagine, 1990. 326–37.

Kant, Immanuel. *Philosophical Correspondence, 1759–99*. Trans. Arnulf Zweig. Chicago: University of Chicago Press, 1967.

Kracauer, Siegfried. *Theory of Film*. 1960; Princeton, N.J.: Princeton University Press, 1997.

————. *Von Caligari zu Hitler. Eine psychologische Geschichte des deutschen Films.* Frankfurt am Main: Suhrkamp, 1979. [*From Caligari to Hitler: A Psychological History of the German Film.* Princeton, N.J.: Princeton University Press, 1947.]

Kuyper, Eric de. "Le cinéma de la seconde époque." *Revue Cinémathèque,* nos. 1–2 (May–November 1992).

Laermann, Klaus. "Die riskante Person in der moralischen Anstalt. Zur Darstellung der Schauspielerin in deutschen Theaterzeitschriften des späten 18. Jahrhunderts." In *Die Schauspielerin. Zur Kulturgeschichte der weiblichen Bühnenkunst.* Ed. Renate Möhrmann. Frankfurt am Main: Insel Verlag, 1989.

Lauretis, Teresa de. "Desire in Narrative." In *Alice Doesn't: Feminism, Semiotics, Cinema.* Bloomington: Indiana University Press, 1984.

May, Lary. *Screening out the Past: The Birth of Mass Culture and the Motion Picture Industry.* Chicago: University of Chicago Press, 1983.

Mayne, Judith. "Der primitive Erzähler." *Frauen und Film* 41 (December 1986): 4–16.

Messter, Oskar. *Mein Weg mit dem Film.* Berlin-Schöneberg: M. Hesse, 1936.

Meyhöfer, Annette. *Das Motiv des Schauspielers in der Literatur der Jahrhundertwende.* Cologne: Böhlau, 1989.

Möhrmann, Malte. "Die Herren zahlen die Kostüme. Mädchen vom Theater am Rande der Prostitution." In *Die Schauspielerin. Zur Kulturgeschichte der weiblichen Bühnenkunst.* Ed. Renate Möhrmann. Frankfurt am Main: Insel Verlag, 1989.

Möhrmann, Renate, ed. *Die Schauspielerin. Zur Kulturgeschichte der weiblichen Bühnenkunst.* Frankfurt am Main: Insel Verlag, 1989.

Müller, Corinna. "Emergence of the Feature Film in Germany between 1910 and 1911." In *Before Caligari: German Cinema, 1895–1920.* Ed. Paolo Cherchi Usai and Lorenzo Codelli. Pordenone: Edizioni Biblioteca dell'Immagine, 1990. 94–113.

————. *Frühe deutsche Kinematographie: Formale, wirtschaftliche und kulturelle Entwicklungen 1907–1912.* Stuttgart: Metzler, 1994.

Mulvey, Laura. *Death 24x a Second: Stillness and the Moving Image.* London: Reaction Books, 2006.

————. "Visual Pleasure and Narrative Cinema." *Screen* 16, no. 3 (1975): 6–18. [German translation by Karola Gramann published in Gislind Nabakowski et al., eds. *Frauen in der Kunst.* Vol. 1. Frankfurt am Main: Suhrkamp, 1980.]

Musser, Charles. "The Nickelodeon Era Begins: Establishing the Framework for Hollywood's Mode of Representation." *Framework* (Autumn 1983): 4–11.

Negt, Oskar, and Alexander Kluge. *Öffentlichkeit und Erfahrung. Zur Organisationsanalyse von bürgerlicher und proletarischer Öffentlichkeit.* Frankfurt am Main: Suhrkamp, 1972. [*Public Sphere and Experience: Toward an Analysis of the Bourgeois and Proletarian Public Sphere.* Foreword by Miriam Hansen, trans. Peter Labanyi, Jamie Daniel, and Assenka Oksiloff. Minneapolis: University of Minnesota Press, 1993.]

Nielsen, Asta. *Die schweigende Muse.* Munich: Heyne, 1977. [Originally published in Danish as *Den tiende Muse.* Copenhagen: Gyldendalske Boghandel, 1945–46.]

Perivolaropoulou, Nia. "Le travail de la mémoire dans Theory of Film de Siegfried Kracauer," *Protée* (Chicoutimi, Québec), vol. 23, no. 1 (Spring 2004): 39–48.

———. "Du flâneur au spectateur: modernité, grande ville et cinéma chez Siegfried Kracauer." In *Simmel, Benjamin, Kracauer: la ville en état de choc*. Ed. Stéphane Füzesséry et Philippe Simay. Paris: Editions de l'éclat, 2008. 125–48.

———. "Les Jacques Offenbach de Siegfried Kracauer: Biographie, histoire et cinéma." In *Siegfried Kracauer, penseur de l'histoire*. Ed. Philippe Despoix, Peter Schöttler und Nia Perivolaropoulou. Paris: Ed. de la Maison des sciences de l'homme, 2006. 165–86.

Ringer, Fritz K. *Die Gelehrten. Der Niedergang der deutschen Mandarine 1890–1933*. Munich: Deutscher Taschenbuch-Verlag, 1987. [1969; *The Decline of the German Mandarins: The German Academic Community, 1890–1933*. Hanover: University Press of New England, 1990.]

Rosenberg, Arthur. *Die Entstehung der deutschen Republik*. Berlin: Rowohlt Verlag, 1928. [*Imperial Germany: The Birth of the German Republic, 1871–1918*. New York: Oxford University Press, 1970.]

Salt, Barry. "The Early Development of Film Form." In *Film before Griffith*. Ed. John L. Fell. Berkeley: University of California Press, 1983.

Schlüpmann, Heide. *Abendröthe der Subjektphilosophie: Eine Ästhetik des Kinos*. Basel: Stroemfeld Verlag, 1998.

———. "Celluloid & Co.: Filmwissenschaft als Kinowissenschaft." *Frauen und Film* 65 (September 2006): 39–77.

———. "*Der Gang in die Nacht*. Das Motiv des Blinden und der Diskurs des Sehens im Weimarer Nachkriegsfilm." In *Filmkultur zur Zeit der Weimarer Republik. Beiträge zu einer internationalen Konferenz vom 15. bis 18. Juni 1989 in Luxemburg*. Ed. Uli Jung and Walter Schatzberg. Munich: K. G. Saur, 1992. 38–53.

———. "Henny Porten. Vom primitiven Lichtspiel zur Filmkunst." *Frauen und Film* 26 (December 1980): 8–12.

———. "Im Gegensinn der Worte. Die Pioniere des skandinavischen Kinos 1896–1986." *Frauen und Film* 41 (December 1986): 17–31.

———. *Öffentliche Intimität: Die Theorie im Kino*. Basel: Stroemfeld Verlag, 2002.

———. *Ungeheure Einbildungskraft: Die dunkle Moralität des Kinos*. Basel: Stroemfeld Verlag, 2007.

Seydel, Renate, and Allan Hagedorff, eds. *Asta Nielsen. Ihr Leben in Fotodokumenten, Selbstzeugnissen und zeitgenössischen Betrachtungen*. Berlin: Henschelverlag, 1981.

Sloan, Kay. *The Loud Silents: Origins of the Social Problem Film*. Urbana: University of Illinois Press, 1988.

Szondi, Peter. *Theorie des modernen Dramas*. Frankfurt am Main: Suhrkamp, 1963. [*Theory of the Modern Drama*. Minneapolis: University of Minnesota Press, 1987.]

Theis, Wolfgang. "Anders als die Andern. Geschichte eines Filmskandals." In *Eldorado. Homosexuelle Frauen und Männer in Berlin 1850–1950. Geschichte, Alltag, Kultur*. Berlin: Frölich und Kaufmann, 1984.

Theis, Wolfgang, and Andreas Sternweiler. "Alltag im Kaiserreich und in der Weimarer

Republik." In *Eldorado. Homosexuelle Frauen und Männer in Berlin 1850–1950. Geschichte, Alltag, Kultur.* Berlin: Frölich und Kaufmann, 1984.

Vondung, Klaus. "Zur Lage der Gebildeten in der wilhelminischen Zeit." In *Das wilhelminische Bildungsbürgertum. Zur Sozialgeschichte seiner Ideen.* Ed. Klaus Vondung. Göttingen: Vandenhoeck und Ruprecht, 1976.

Wierling, Dorothee. *Mädchen für alles. Arbeitsalltag und Lebensgeschichte städtischer Dienstmädchen um die Jahrhundertwende.* Bonn: J. H. W. Dietz, 1987.

Zglinicki, Friedrich von. *Der Weg des Films.* Berlin: Rembrandt, 1956; repr. Hildesheim: Olms, 1979.

Filmography

The year indicates the year of production.

Pm	=	premiere	M	=	music
P	=	production	A	=	actors
D	=	direction	OS	=	outdoor shots
S	=	script	C	=	censorship
Ca	=	camera	Co	=	currently [spring 1990]
Se	=	stage sets			available copy

1.I.F.Ztg.	=	*Erste Internationale Film-Zeitung*
Ki	=	*Der Kinematograph* (Düsseldorf)
FiWe	=	*Die Film-Welt*
F	=	*Der Film* (Berlin)
LBB	=	*Lichtbild-Bühne* (Berlin)
LBT	=	*Das Lichtbild-Theater* (Berlin)
B u. F	=	*Bild und Film* (M. Gladbach)
LBK	=	*Die Lichtbildkunst in Schule,*
		Wissenschaft und Volksleben (Storkow)

The information is based upon the following sources: the indexes of the Bundesarchiv (BA), the Stiftung Deutsche Kinemathek (SDK), the Staatliches Filmarchiv der DDR; Gerhard Lamprecht, *Deutsche Stummfilme;* Herbert Birett, ed., *Verzeichnis in Deutschland gelaufener Filme;* Hans Michael Bock, ed., *Cinegraph;* Deutsches Institut für Filmkunde und Stiftung Deutsche Kinemathek, *Verleihkatalog;* Helga Belach, ed., *Henny Porten;* Asta Nielsen, *Die schweigende Muse;* and the film magazines listed above.

The films marked with an asterisk (*) are not explicitly mentioned in the text, but they belong to the material to which the text relates.

Die Abenteuer eines Journalisten [*The Adventures of a Journalist*]
1914, 3 acts, P: Kinoskop-Film, D: Harry Piel, A: Ludwig Trautmann.
C: 7/10/1914, Berlin, forbidden for children [*für Kinder verboten*]; 1914, Munich,
contested scenes: 1. A criminal plants a bomb (in close-up) 2. The presentation of the man who has been killed by the explosion.
Co: Bundesarchiv, magazine no. 13834, 922 m, tinted.

Alexandra—Die Rache ist mein [*Alexandra—Revenge Is Mine*]
1914, Pm: 1/22/1915, 1,282 m, 4 acts, P: Messter-Film GmbH (Berlin), D: Curt A.
Starck, S: based upon the play by Richard Voß (1886), A: Henny Porten, Fritz
Fehér, Henny Steinmann, Ernst Reschke, Max Maximilian.
C: Berlin, forbidden for children and teenagers [*Jugendverbot*].

Der Andere [The Other]
1912–13, Pm: 1/21/1913, Berlin, P: Vitascope GmbH (Berlin), D: Max Mack, S:
Paul Lindau, Ca: Hermann Böttger, A: Albert Bassermann, Emerich Hanus, Nelly
Ridon, Hanni Weisse, Leon Rosemann, Otto Collot, C. Lengling, Paul Passarge.
C: Munich, contested scene: The presentation of the pair dance in the pub Zur
lahmen Ente in act 1.
Co: SDK, 1,392 m.
The press for this film is documented in H. H. Diederichs, *Anfänge deutscher
Filmkritik,* 55–63; another overview by the contemporary press can be found in
1.I.F.Ztg., no. 10 (1913): 57ff.

Auf einsamer Insel [*On a Lonely Island*]
1913, Pm: 12/5/1913, 3 acts, P: Eiko-Film GmbH (Berlin), D: Joseph Delmont, A:
Mia Cordes, Fred Sauer, Joseph Delmont, OS: the island of Marken in Holland.
C: 9/1913, Berlin, forbidden for children.
Co: BA, magazine no. 10051, 487 m, tinted.
Ki, no. 356 (1913), no. 360 (1913).

Aus eines Mannes Mädchenzeit [*On a Man's Maidenhood*]
1912, 3 acts, P: Messters Projektion GmbH (Berlin), A: Wilhelm Bendow, Manny
Ziener, Rudolf Senius, Olga Engl, Siegfried Dessauer.
C: 1913, forbidden for children (acts 1 and 2).
Co: SDK, 475 m.
Ki, no. 517 (1916): 22.

Die Czernowska [*Czernowska*] (after 1915: *Die Rolle der Erzieherin* [*The Role of the
Governess*])
1913, Pm: 4/18/1913, 2 acts, 972 m, P: Charles Decroix-Film der Monopolfilm-
Vertriebs-GmbH Hanewacker und Scheler, D and S: Charles Decroix, A: Bernd
Aldor, Käte Wittenberg, Wolfgang Neff.

C: 4/10/1913, Berlin, forbidden for children (acts 1–3); Munich: forbidden.
Co: BA, magazine no. 10748, 519 m, tinted.
1.I.F.Ztg., no. 14 (4/5/1913): 22–23, no. 15 (4/12/1913): 22–23, no. 19
(5/10/1913): 50, no. 50 (9/27/1913): 25.

Der Desperado von Panama* [*The Desperado from Panama*]
1914, P: Deutsche Bioskop, D: Joseph Delmont, Ca: Karl Hasselmann, A: Joseph
Delmont, Alesso, Stauber.
Filmed on location at the Panama Canal.
Co: Nederlands Filmmuseum, fragment, tinted.

[Nonfiction films from around 1898]
D and P: Guido Seeber.
Lokomotivtransport der sächsischen Maschinenfabrik durch die Straßen von Chem-
nitz am 28.6.1898 [*The Transport of a Locomotive of the Saxonian Machine Factory*
through the Streets of Chemnitz on June 28, 1898]; *König Albert von Sachsen passi-*
ert die Interimsbrücke zum Wettin-Bundesschießen in Döbeln [*King Albert of Saxony*
Passes the Interim Bridge to the Wettin Federation Shooting in Döbeln]; *König Albert*
von Sachsen wird in Chemnitz empfangen [*The Reception of King Albert of Saxony in*
Chemnitz]; *Chemnitzer Feuerwehr Ausfahrt* [The Fire Brigade of Chemnitz at Work];
Sächsischer Schützenzug I (in Chemnitz am 31.5.98) [*Saxonian Rifle Club Parade* (in
Chemnitz on May 31, 1898)]; *Sächsischer Schützenzug II (in Leisnig am 26.6.98)*
[*Saxonian Rifle Club Parade* (in Leisnig on June 26, 1898)]; *Ausfahrt der sächsis-*
chen Chinakrieger [*Departure for China of the Saxonian Warriors*].
Co: SDK.

Don Juan heiratet [*Don Juan Marries*] (later titled: *Der Herzensknicker* [*The Heart-*
breaker])
1909, Pm: 4/1909, 281 m, P: Duskes Kinematographen- und Film-Fabriken GmbH
(Berlin), D and S: Heinrich Bolten-Baeckers, Ca: Charles Paulus, Se: Kurt Dürnhofer, A: Joseph Giampietro, Klara Kollendt.
C: 4/26/1909, Berlin.
Co: BA, magazine no. 10124, 263 m, tinted; SDK.

Das Ende vom Liede* [*The End of the Song*]
1914–15, 1,021 m, Pm: 2/19/1915, P: Messter-Film GmbH (Berlin), D: Rudolf
Biebrach, S: Henny Porten, based on a text by Richard Voss, Se: Henny Porten
(design), A: Henny Porten, Ludwig Trautmann, Rudolf Biebrach, Hermann Seldeneck, Paul Conradi, Ethel Scharon.
C: 1915, Berlin, forbidden for children and teenagers (Belach); 1914, Berlin,
forbidden for children (Birett).
Co: BA, magazine no. 10880, b/w.
FiWe, no. 44 (11/8/1919); *F*, no. 26 (1920): 42.

*Engelein** [*Little Angel*]
1913, Pm: 1/3/1914, 1,617 m, P: PAGU (Projektions AG Union, Frankfurt a.m.),
  D and S: Urban Gad, Ca: Axel Graatkjaer, Karl Freund, Se: Fritz Seyffert, A: Asta
  Nielsen, Alfred Kühn, Max Landa, Fred Immler, Hanns Kräly, Adele Reuter-Eich-
  berg, Martin Wolff, Erner Hübsch.
C: 12/13/1913, Berlin.
Co: Münchener Stadtmuseum.

Es wäre so schön gewesen [*It Would Have Been So Nice*]
1910, Pm: 9/24/1910, 275 m, P: Vitascope GmbH (Berlin), A: Arnold Rieck.
Co: SDK, 275 m.
1.I.F.Ztg., no. 10 (3/8/1913): 110.

Die Fächermalerin [*The Fan Painter*]
1913, Pm: 5/16/1913, 829 m, P: New Century Film Co. (Berlin), D and S: Rudolf
  Meinert, A: Arthur Wellin (Deutsches Schauspielhaus Berlin), Frau Adalbert,
  Claire Praetz (New Yorker Theater), Herr Fischer (Pabst Theater).
C: Berlin, forbidden for children (acts 1–3).
Co: SDK, 16 mm: 316.7 m.
1.I.F.Ztg., no. 18 (5/3/1913): 103, no. 38 (9/20/1913): 146.

Der Film von der Königin Luise, I. Abteilung [*The Film of Queen Luise,* part 1]
Pm: 1/24/1913, 701 m, part 2: *Aus Preussens schwerer Zeit* [*On Prussia's Hard
  Times*], Pm: 2/21/1913, 3 acts, part 3: *Die Königin des Schmerzens* [*The Queen
  of Pain*], Pm: 3/21/1913, 2 acts; 1912–13, P: Deutsche Mutoskop- und Biograph-GmbH (Berlin), D: Franz Porten, Ca: Werner Brandes, A: Hansi Arnstädt,
  Walter Steinbeck, Hanni Reinwald, Otto Reinwald, Louis Ralph.
Co: BA, magazine no. 10173, 655 m, b/w.
1.I.F.Ztg., no. 5 (2/1/1913): 83, no. 14 (4/5/1913): 4ff.; *Ki*, no. 305 (1912), no.
  309 (1912); LBT 4, no. 44 (1912).

[Films from 1896]
D and P: Max Skladanowsky.
Berlin Alexanderplatz, Unter den Linden, Alarm bei der Berliner Feuerwehr [*Alarm
at the Berlin Fire Department*]; *Einfahrt des Eisenbahnzuges in Berlin-Schönholz*
[*Arrival of a Train in Berlin-Schönholz*]; *Die Wache zieht auf* [*The Deployment of
the Sentry*]; *Eine lustige Gesellschaft vor dem Tivoli in Stockholm* [*A Gay Party in
Front of the Tivoli in Stockholm*]; *Komische Begegnung im Tiergarten zu Stockholm*
[*Funny Encounter at the Stockholm Zoo*]
Co: SDK, 150 m.

*Eine Fliegenjagd oder die Rache der Frau Schulze** [*Fly Hunting; or, The Revenge of Mrs. Schulze*]
around 1906, P: Max Skladanowsky (P.f.A.-Film), D: Eugen Skladanowsky, A: Eugen Skladanowsky, Frida Cotrelli (formerly at Circus Renz).
C: 1913, Berlin, forbidden for children.
Co: BA, magazine no. 108927, 174 m, b/w.

Fräulein Piccolo [*Miss Piccolo*]
1914–15, 1,017 m, P: Luna-Film GmbH (Berlin), D and S: Franz Hofer, Ca: Gotthard Wolf, Se: Fritz Kraencke, A: Dorrit Weixler, Franz Schwaiger, Alice Hechy, Max Lehmann, Helene Voß, Martin Wolff, Karl Harbacher, Ernst Lubitsch.
C: 1915, Berlin, forbidden for children; 1918, forbidden for the duration of the war, now forbidden for children.
Co: SDK, 747 m.
All reviews occurred only after the war: *FiWe,* no. 9 (3/1/1919): 28; *LBB,* no. 48 (11/30/1918): 15, no. 14 (1/25/1919): 36ff.; *DF,* no. 50 (12/14/1918): 34, 35 (illustration), no. 51 (12/21/1918): 6 (illustration), no. 1 (1/4/1919): 10 (illustration), no. 6 (2/8/1919): 28; *Ki,* no. 572 (1917): 30.

*Der fremde Vogel** [*The Foreign Bird*]
1911, Pm: 11/3/1911, 974 m, P: Deutsche Bioskop for PAGU, D and S: Urban Gad, Ca: Guido Seeber, A: Asta Nielsen, Hans Mierendorff, Eugenie Werner, Louis Ralph, Carl Clewing, Maria Karsten.
Co: SDK, 906 m.

*Das gefährliche Alter** [*The Dangerous Age*]
1911, Pm: 4/15/1911, 760 m, 2 acts, P: Messters Projektion GmbH (Berlin), D: Adolf Gärtner, Ca: Carl Froelich, A: Elise Waldmann, Poldi Müller, Erich Kaiser-Titz, the tenor Novotny, Hermann Seldeneck, Robert Garrison. According to Lamprecht, this film is not based on Karin Michaelis's novel.
Co: BA, magazine no. 14246, 654 m, tinted.

Das Geheimnis des Chateau Richmond (2. Bild der *Miss Nobody-Detektivserie*) [*The Mystery of the Château Richmond* (part 2 of the Miss Nobody Detective Series)]
1913, Pm: 4/1913, P: Carl Werner (Berlin), D: Willy Zeyn, Ca: Georg Paezel, Se: Kurt Dürnhöfer, A: Senta Eichstaedt, Fred Selva-Goebel, Walter Göbel (Schauspielhaus), Hermann Seldeneck.
Co: SDK.

Der geheimnisvolle Klub [*The Mysterious Club*]
1913, 3 acts, 828 m, P: Eiko-Film GmbH (Berlin), D: Joseph Delmont, A: Joseph Delmont, Fred Sauer, Ilse Bois.

C: 10/1913, Berlin, forbidden for children; 1913, Munich, partially forbidden;
8/4/1915, forbidden for the duration of the war.
Co: BA, magazine no. 10214, 827 m, tinted.
Ki, no. 358 (1913): 62.

*Die geheimnisvolle Streichholzdose** [*The Mysterious Matchbox*]
1909–10, 98 m, P: Deutsche Bioskop GmbH, D: Guido Seeber, S and Ca: Guido
Seeber.
C: 2/28/1910, Berlin, forbidden for children and teenagers.
Co: BA, magazine no. 10215, 88 m, tinted.

Grausame Ehe [*Cruel Marriage*]
ca. 1910.
Co: BA, magazine no. 10237, 171 m, b/w.

Der Hauptmann von Köpenick [*The Captain from Koepenick*]
1906, Pm: 1906, 218 m, P: Mechanische Werkstätten für Kinoapparatebau
Buderus, D: Carl Buderus, Carl Sonnemann, A: Carl Sonnemann, the company's
mechanics: Adolf Peck, Georg Bock, Fritz Keil, Harry Heimers, Emil Wernicke,
Ernst Lewecke, the carpenter Ortmann, and a hairstylist from the theater.
Co: BA, magazine no. 10258, 150 m, b/w.

Der Hauptmann begnadigt [*The Captain Is Granted Amnesty*]
1908, 105 m, 1 act, P: Internationale Kinematographen- und Lichteffekten GmbH
and others, Ca: Karl Jaensch, Franz Maletzko.
C: 8/21/1908, Berlin, forbidden.
Co: SDK.

Heimgefunden: Von Stufe zu Stufe. Lebensbeichte einer Probiermamsell [*The Way
Home: Step by Step. A Model's Life-Confession*]
ca. 1910, produced in Berlin.
Co: BA, magazine no. 14918, 371 m, b/w ("The main title was added later, as a
parody"); SDK.
LBT, no. 4 (1912).

*Eine Herzenseroberung (Bild aus dem Leben)** [*A Conquest of the Heart (Picture
Taken from Life)*]
1911, Pm: 4/29/1911, ca. 177 m, P: Pharos-Film der Deutschen Mutoskop- und
Biograph-GmbH (Berlin).
Co: Nederlands Filmmuseum, tinted.

Hochspannung [*High Voltage*]
1913, Pm: 9/1913, 850 m, P: Messters Projektions GmbH (Berlin), A: Gottfried
Krause (Stadttheater Bern).

C: 1913, Berlin, forbidden for children; Munich, partially forbidden.
Co: BA, magazine no. 10280, 506 m, tinted.
1.I.F.Ztg., no. 35 (8/20/1913): 29 (illustration).

Das humoristische Album* [*The Humorous Album*]
3 scenes: "Der neue Schaukelstuhl" ["The New Rocking Chair"], "Der hohle Zahn"
    ["The Hollow Tooth"], "Der neue Hut" ["The New Hat"].
1911, 165 m, P: Deutsche Mutoskop- und Biograph-GmbH (Berlin).
Co: BA, magazine no. 10289, 133 m, b/w.
Ki, no. 242 (1911).

Hurra! Einquartierung! [*Hooray! Accommodations!*]
1913, Pm: 8/1913, 2 acts, 550 m, P: Luna-Film-Industrie (Berlin), D and S: Franz
    Hofer, A: Manny Ziener, Franz Schwaiger, Dorrit Wexler, Rudolf del Zopp, Karl
    Harbacher.
C: 7/2/1913, Berlin, forbidden for children.
Co: BA, magazine no. 13987, 471 m, tinted.
1.I.F.Ztg., no. 19 (5/10/1913): 86, no. 29 (7/19/1913): 23, no. 30 (7/26/1913):
    69 (illustration), no. 31 (8/2/1913): 120 (illustration), no. 33 (8/16/1913):
    89; *B u. F* 4, no. 1 (1914–15): 28.

Ich will keine Stiefmutter [*I Do Not Want a Stepmother*]
ca. 1910, 188 m, P: Deutsche Bioskop GmbH (Berlin).
Co: BA, magazine no. 13992, 176 m, tinted.

Ilse's Verlobung* [*Ilse's Engagement*]
1914, Pm: 1/15/1915, 1 act, 384 m, P: Eiko-Film GmbH (Berlin), D: Gustav
    Trautschold.
C: 8/12/1914, Berlin, forbidden for children.
Co: BA, magazine no. 13993, 385 m, tinted.
Ki, no. 419 (1915): 26.

Im Glück vergessen [*Forgotten because of Happiness*]
1911, 658 m, P: Messters Projektions GmbH (Berlin), D: Adolf Gärtner, S: Luise
    del Zopp, Ca: Willy Gaebel, A: Henny Porten, Friedrich Zelnik, Rudolf del Zopp,
    Stefanie Hantzsch, Karl Fentz.
C: Berlin, forbidden for children; contested scenes: suicide scene, death scene;
    Munich, forbidden in act 1: the fall from the bridge.

Die Jagd nach der Hundertpfundnote oder Die Reise um die Welt (Nobody-Serie)
[*The Chase for the One-Hundred-Pound Bill; or, The Trip around the World* (Nobody
Series)]
1913, 2,021 m, P: Karl Werner (Berlin), D: Willy Zeyn, Ca: Georg Paezel, Se: Kurt

Dürnhofer, A: Senta Eichstädt, Hansi Dege, Fred Selva-Goebel, Josef Coenen, Adele Reuter-Eichberg, Ernst Körner, Karl Harbacher, Cowboy-Jenkins.
C: 8/1/1913, Berlin, acts 1 and 4 forbidden for children; Munich, contested scenes: act 1: all gambling scenes at the roulette table; act 4: 1. the Chinese robbing the European, 2. the fistfight on occasion of the arrest of the Chinese; act 5: the raid on the farm, the close-up of the female detective in chains; act 6: the scene at the roulette table.
Co: BA, magazine no. 10313, 1,377 m, b/w.
1.I.F.Ztg., no. 27 (7/5/1913): 100ff., 112 (illustration), no. 35 (8/30/1913): 123.

*Japanisches Opfer** [*Japanese Sacrifice*]
1910, 2 acts, 257 m, P: Messters Projektion GmbH (Berlin), A: Friedrich Zelnik, Lupu Pick, Max Mack, Albert Steinrück.
Co: BA, magazine no. 10722, 237 m, b/w.

*Jugendstürme (Ein Offiziersroman)** [*Turbulences of Youth (An Officer's Novella)*]
1912, Pm: 11/2/1912, 3 acts, P: Duskes GmbH (Berlin), D and S: Fritz Bernhardt, Ca: Eugen Illés, A: Alfred Braun, Fräulein Alma, Herwart Retslag, Herr Feist, Paul Moleska, Willi Marrée.
Co: Staatliches Filmarchiv der DDR, b/w.
LBT 4, no. 39 (1912).

Karl Valentin's Hochzeit [*Karl Valentin's Wedding*]
1912–13, A: Karl Valentin, Georg Rückert.
Co: BA, magazine no. 10333, 192 m, b/w.

*Kasper-Lotte** [*Punch's Judy*]
1913, Pm: 3/7/1913, 255 m, P: Deutsche Bioskop GmbH (Berlin), D: Emil Albes, S: Luise Heilborn-Körbitz, A: Hilde and Lotte Müller.
C: 2/1/1913, Berlin.
Co: Nederlands Filmmuseum.

*Die Kinder des Majors** [*The Children of the Major*]
1914, 3 acts, P: Eiko-Film GmbH (Berlin).
C: 2/21/1914, Berlin, forbidden for children, Eiko changes the title: *A Novella from a Little Garrison;* 1916, Munich, forbidden for the duration of the war.
Co: BA, magazine no. 15553, 793 m, tinted.

*Künstlerliebe** [*An Artist's Love*]
1911, 270 m, P: Messters Projektion GmbH (Berlin), D: Adolf Gärtner, A: Henny Porten, Robert Garrison.

*Der Kuss des Fürsten** [*The Prince's Kiss*]
1912, P: Messters Projektion GmbH (Berlin), R: Curt A. Stark, A: Henny Porten.
Co: BA, magazine no. 10975, tinted.

*Die Landstraße** [*The Country Road*]
1913, Pm: 9/17/1913, P: Deutsche Mutoskop- und Biograph-GmbH (Berlin), D:
    Paul von Woringen, S: Paul Lindau, A: Carl Goetz, Rudolf Klein-Rhoden, Paul
    Bildt.
Co: Staatliches Filmarchiv der DDR.
1.I.F.Ztg., no. 36 (9/6/1913): 21ff. (illustrations).

Leo der Aushilfskellner [*Leo the Ancillary Waiter*]
1912, 280 m, P: Éclair/Bolten-Baeckers, D: Pierre Velber, A: Leo Peukert, Jacques
    de Ferandy.
(Titles of other installments in the series: *Leo der Witwenfreund* [*Leo, the Widow's
    Friend*], *Leo auf Hochzeitsreise* [*Leo on His Honeymoon*], *Leo als Reporter* [*Leo as
    Reporter*].)
Co: SDK.
1.I.F.Ztg., no. 7 (2/15/1913): 20, no. 8 (2/22/1913): 108; *LBK*, no. 23 (1913):
    79.

*Madeleine**
1912, 3 acts, 936 m, P: Deutsche Bioskop GmbH (Berlin), D: Emil Albes, Ca: Karl
    Hasselmann, A: Ilse Oeser, Ludwig Trautmann, Hugo Flink, Emil Albes.
C: 8/13/1912, Berlin, forbidden for children; contested scenes: a German betray-
    ing a German officer, the German officer's escape; 1914, Berlin, change of title:
    Der Überfall auf Schloss Boncourt [*The Attack on the Castle Boncourt*].
Co: BA, magazine no. 14955, 499 m, tinted.
1.I.F.Ztg., no. 18 (5/4/1912): 41ff. (illustrations), 44, no. 19 (5/11/1912): 1 (il-
    lustration); *Ki,* no. 280 (5/8/1912), no. 282 (5/22/1912), no. 284 (6/5/1912);
    B u. F 2, no. 3 (1912–13): 73ff.

Der Mann im Keller (Stuart Webbs–Serie) [*The Man in the Basement* (Stuart Webbs
Series)]
1914, P: Continental-Kunstfilm GmbH (Berlin), D: Hoe May, S: Ernst Reicher, Ca:
    Max Faßbender, A: Ernst Reicher, Max Landa, Olga Engl, Alice Hechy, Eduard
    Rothauser, Josef Schelepa.
C: 1914, Munich, partially forbidden; 1916, Berlin, forbidden for the duration of
    the war.
Co: SDK, 1,206 m, tinted.
LBB, no. 10 (3/8/1919): 66ff.; *Ki,* no. 382 (1914).

*Medea**
1910, Pm: 1/14/1911, 224 m, P: Messters Projektion GmbH (Berlin), D: Rudolf
Lorenz, S: based on the drama by Franz Grillparzer, A: Bernard Wenkhaus, Dora
von Warberg, von Bischoff, Frau Höcker-Berens.
Co: BA, magazine no. 10420, 232 m, tinted.

Meißner Porzellan [*Meissen Porcelain*]
1906 (BA: 1907), 77 m, P: Messters Projektion GmbH (Berlin), D: Franz Porten,
Ca: Carl Froelich, M: Salon-Gavotte by Carl Alfredy, text: Leo Herzberg, A and
singing: Rosa Porten, Henny Porten.
C: 1/16/1909, Berlin.
Co: BA, 74 m/81 m, b/w.

*Mericke aus Neuruppin kommt nach Berlin** [*Mericke from Neuruppin Visits Berlin*]
1911, P: Messters Projektions GmbH (Berlin), D: Adolf Gärtner, A: Gerhard Dammann.
Co: SDK, 40 m, b/w.

*Eine moderne Jungfrau von Orleans** [*A Modern Joan of Arc*]
1914, P and D: Skladanowsky.
C: Berlin, forbidden for children.
Co: Deutsches Institut für Filmkunde, b/w.

Der Müller und sein Kind [*The Miller and His Child*]
1911, 690 m, P: Messters Projektion GmbH (Berlin), D: Adolf Gärtner, S: based on
the folk drama by Ernst Raupach, Ca: Willy Gaebel, Se: Kurt Dürnhöfer, A: Henny
Porten, Friedrich Zelnik, Robert Garrison.
C: 1912, Munich, forbidden; 1913, Munich, act 1 approved, act 2 forbidden.
Co: SDK, b/w.

Mutterliebe [*A Mother's Love*]
1909, 159 m, P: Duskes Kinematographen- und Film-Fabriken GmbH (Berlin),
Ca: Charles Paulus, A: Heinerle from the Berliner Theater des Westens (Curt
Bois).
LBT, no. 27 (7/4/1912).
C: 10/18/1909.
Co: SDK, 156 m, b/w.

*Pauline**
1914, Pm: 3/27/1914, 3 acts, P: Vitascope GmbH (Berlin) (consolidated with
PAGU), D: Henri Etiévant, Se: Hermann Warm, A: Gertrud Arnold, Fred Sauer,
Alice Scheel-Hechy, Einar Linden.
Co: BA, magazine no. 14971, 992 m, tinted.

Perlen bedeuten Tränen [*Pearls Mean Tears*]
1911, 1 act, 302 m, P: Messters Projektion GmbH (Berlin), D: Adolf Gärtner, A:
Henny Porten, Hugo Flink, Curt A. Stark.
C: 1911, Berlin; 1913, Munich, forbidden; 1915, Berlin, forbidden for children.
Co: BA, magazine no. 14972, 235 m, partially tinted; SDK.

*Prosit Neujahr!** [*Happy New Year!*]
1909–10, D and S: Guido Seeber.
Co: SDK.

Das Recht aufs Dasein [*The Right to Existence*]
1913, 3 acts, ca. 1,000 m, P: Eiko-Film GmbH (Berlin), D: Joseph Delmont, A:
Joseph Delmont, Fred Sauer.
C: 4/1913, Berlin, forbidden for children.
Co: BA, magazine no. 14242, 867 m, tinted; SDK.
1.I.F.Ztg., 1913 (illustration); *Ki*, 5/25/1913.

*Richard Wagner**
1913, Pm: 5/31/1913, 2,055 m, P: Messters Projektion GmbH (Berlin), D and S:
William Wauer, D and Ca: Carl Froelich, M: Giuseppe Becce, A: Giuseppe Becce,
Olga Engl, Manny Ziener, Miriam Horwitz, Ernst Reicher, Max Maximilian, Wil-
liam Wauer.
Co: SDK.

Der Rosenkavalier [*The Cavalier of the Rose*]
1911, P: Messter-Film (Berlin).
Co: magazine no. 10495, 118 m, tinted.
LBT, no. 32 (1911); *Ki,* no. 239 (1911).

*Ruths Spielzeug** [*Ruth's Toy*]
ca. 1914, danced by Else and Sophie Zimmermann.
Co: BA, magazine no. 15522, 83 m, tinted.

Der Schatten des Meeres [*The Shadow of the Sea*]
1912, Pm: 12/7/1912, 2 acts (ca. 38 mins.), P: Messters Projektion GmbH (Berlin), D: Curt A. Stark, S: based on the East Frisian legend "Der Gonger," Ca: Carl
Froelich, A: Henny Porten, Curt A. Stark, Lizzy Krüger, Frau Retzlag.
C: 10/23/1912, forbidden for children.
Co: BA, magazine no. 10504, 596 m, b/w; SDK.
1.I.F.Ztg., no. 45 (9/22/1912): 7 (illustration); *LBT,* no. 46 (11/14/1912), no. 50
(12/12/1912).

Die Schlangentänzerin [*The Snake Dancer*]
1909, P: PAGU, Ca: Karl Hasselmann.
(First film by the PAGU, shot on the rooftop of the company's office building in
   Frankfurt a.M., Kaiserstraße 64, against black velvet drapery.)
Co: SDK.

Schriftsteller. Merkels mimische Darstellungen* [*Poets. Merkel's Mimic Performances*]
ca. 1910, P: Duskes Kinematographen- und Filmfabriken GmbH (Berlin).
Co: BA, magazine no. 10514, 130 m, b/w.

Schuldig* [*Guilty*]
1913, Pm: 1/9/1914, 1,679 m, P: Messters-Film GmbH (Berlin), D: Hans Ober-
   länder, S: based on Richard Voss, Ca: Carl Froelich, A: Eduard von Winterstein,
   Harry Liedtke, Henny Porten, Erich Kaiser-Titz, Jacob Tiedtke, Martha Anger-
   stein, Leopoldine Konstantin, Toni Imperkoven, Adolf Edgar Licho.
Co: Staatliches Filmarchiv der DDR.

Der Schuss um Mitternacht* [*The Gunshot at Midnight*]
1914, Pm: 3/20/1914, 3 acts, 890 m, P: Vitascope GmbH (Berlin; consolidated
   with PAGU), D: Walter Schmidthässler, A: Hanni Weisse, Ernst A. Becker, Hermann Seldeneck, Thea Sandten.
C: 3/4/1914, forbidden for children; 1914, Munich, forbidden.
Co: BA, magazine no. 10966, 657 m, tinted.

Die schwarze Kugel [*The Black Ball*] or *Die geheimnisvollen Schwestern* [*The Mysterious Sisters*]
1913, Pm: 10/26/1913, 3 acts, P: Luna-Film-Industry (Berlin), D: Franz Hofer, A:
   Mia Cordes, Manny Ziener, Paul Meffert, Ernst Pittschau.
C: 10/1913, Berlin, forbidden for children; 1913, Munich, forbidden.
Co: BA, magazine no. 14974, 457 m, tinted; Nederlands Filmmuseum. (This copy
   includes a reel that explains the title *The Black Bullet:* the sisters paint black
   one of the balls they use for juggling onstage. The sister who will hold the
   black ball in her hands at the end of the performance will take revenge on the
   man.)
1.I.F.Ztg., no. 32 (8/9/1913): 20; *Ki,* no. 586 (1918): 33.

Das schwarze Los* [*The Black Lottery Ticket*]
1913, 1,415 m, P: Deutsche Bioskop GmbH (Berlin), D: John Gottowt, S: Adolf
   Paul, Ca: Karl Hasselmann, A: Alexander Moissi, Paul Biensfeldt, Emil Albes, Jo-
   hanna Terwin, Heinrich Lux, John Gottowt, OS: at Lake Lugano and Lake Como.
C: 8/21/1913, Berlin, forbidden for children.
Co: magazine no. 10520, 1,041 m, tinted; SDK.

Die schwarze Natter [*The Black Viper*]
1913, Pm: 5/2/1913, 3 acts, P: Luna-Film-Industrie (Berlin), D and S: Franz
  Hofer, A: Ludwig Trautmann, Margarete Hübler, Mirjam Harwitz, Herr Seldeneck,
  Herr Hanus.
C: 4/1913, Berlin, forbidden for children; Munich, forbidden.
Co: BA, magazine no. 15109, 703 m, tinted.
1.I.F.Ztg., no. 11 (3/15/1913): 87, no. 12 (3/22/1913): 140, no. 14 (4/5/1913):
  19ff.

*S1**
1913, Pm: 11/14/1913, 1,258 m, P: PAGU, D and S: Urban Gad, A: Asta Nielsen,
  Siegwart Gruder, Charly Berger, Paul Meffert, Herr Sachs, Mary Scheller, Frau
  Lumbye.
C: 11/3/1913, Berlin, forbidden for children and teenagers.
Co: Staatliches Filmarchiv der DDR; Münchener Stadtmuseum.

Der Sieg des Hosenrocks [*The Victory of the Pant Skirt*]
1911, Pm: 9/2/1911, 160 m, P: Vitascope GmbH (Berlin), D: Max Obal, Ca: Guido
  Seeber, A: Max Obal, Lena Voss.
Co: SDK.

*The Silent Signal** (distributed under the English title)
1914, copy production Messter (manufacturing no. 9302, also producer?).
Co: BA, magazine no. 10863, 240 m, tinted.

Der Steckbrief [*The Wanted Poster*]
1913, Pm: 10/31/1913, 3 acts, P: Luna-Film-Industrie (Berlin), D: Franz Hofer, A:
  Maria Forescu, Paul Meffert.
C: 10/1913, Berlin, forbidden for children.
Co: BA, magazine no. 16249, 808 m, tinted.
1.I.F.Ztg., no. 36 (9/6/1913): 19.

*Stille Nacht—heilige Nacht** [*Silent Night—Holy Night*]
1909, P: Deutsche Bioskop GmbH (Berlin).
Co: SDK.

Die Sünden der Väter [*The Sins of the Fathers*]
1912–13, Pm: 2/28/1913, 911 m, P: Deutsche Bioskop for PAGU, D and S: Urban
  Gad, Ca: Guido Seeber, A: Asta Nielsen, Hermann Seldeneck, Miss Stoike, Fritz
  Weidenmann, Max Wogritsch, Emil Albes.
C: 1/28/1913, Berlin, forbidden for children; 1918, was forbidden for the duration
  of the war.
Co: SDK, 16 mm, 184.7 m, b/w.

1.*I.F.Ztg.*, no. 10 (3/8/1913): 40; *LBB*, no. 1 (1/4/1919): 55; *F*, no. 19 (5/10/1919): 29.

Die Suffragette* [*The Suffragette*]
1913, Pm: 11/14/1913, 1,258 m, P: PAGU, D and S: Urban Gad, A: Asta Nielsen, Siegwart Gruder, Charly Berger, Paul Meffert, Herr Sachs, Mary Scheller, Frau Lumbye, Max Landa.
C: 9/2/1913, Berlin.
Co: BA, magazine no. 15005, 275 m, b/w; SDK.

Die Sumpfblume* [*The Marsh Marigold*]
1913, Pm: 9/2/1913, 4 acts, 1,259 m, P: Treumann-Larsen-Film-Vertriebs-GmbH (Berlin), D: Rudolf del Zopp, A: Wanda Treumann, Viggo Larsen, Richard Liebsny.
Co: Nederlands Filmmuseum, tinted.

Tanz der Salomé [*Salomé's Dance*]
1906 (1902?), P: Messters Projektion GmbH (Berlin), D: Oskar Messter, A: Adorée Villany. A Biophon Sound Picture.
Co: BA, magazine no. 16233, 79 m, b/w; SDK.
Walter Panofsky (*Die Geburt des Films* [Würzburg: Triltsch, 1940]) mentions a 1902 Salomé film by Messter.

Theodor Körner (Von der Wiege bis zu seinem Heldentod) [*Theodor Körner (From the Cradle to His Heroic Death)*]
1912, Pm: 8/31/1912, 1,300 m, P: Deutsche Mutoskop- und Biograph-GmbH (Berlin), D: Franz Porten, Gerhard Dammann, Ca: Werner Brandes, A: Friedrich Fehér, Hermann Seldeneck, Thea Sandten; the costumes of the hunters from Lützow come from the arsenal of the Berliner Zeughaus.
Co: BA, magazine no. 10567, 716 m, b/w.
LBT 4, nos. 30 and 33 (1912).

Tilly Bébé. Die berühmte Löwenbändigerin [*Tilly Bébé. The Famous Lion Tamer*]
1908, 220 m, P: Deutsche Bioskop, Ca: Ernst Schüssler.
Co: SDK.

Tragödie eines Streiks [*Tragedy of a Strike*]
1911, 355 m, P: Messters Projektion GmbH (Berlin), D: Adolf Gärtner, Ca: Carl Froelich, A: Henny Porten, Robert Garrison, Lotte Müller.
C: 8/16/1911, Berlin, forbidden for children

Die Tragödin Sarah Bernhardt als Hamlet (in der berühmten Duell-Szene mit Laertes)
[*Tragic Actress Sarah Bernhardt as Hamlet (In the Famous Duel Scene with Laertes)*]
Co: SDK.

Um Haaresbreite.—Trugschlüsse eines Indizienbeweises [*By a Hair's Breadth.—Wrong Conclusions on the Basis of Circumstantial Evidence*]
1912, 2 acts, ca. 663 m, P: Messters Projektion GmbH (Berlin), D: Curt A. Stark, Ca: Carl Froelich, A: Henny Porten, Lotte Müller, Ernst Pittschau.
C: 8/28/1912, Berlin, forbidden for children.
Co: BA, magazine no. 10376, 562 m, b/w.
1.I.F.Ztg., no. 5 (2/1/1913): 83.

Und das Licht erlosch [*And the Light Went Out*]
1914, P: Imperator-Film CombH, D: Fritz Bernhardt, A: Eduard Rothauser, Beatrice Altenhofer, Edm. Breitenbach, Fritz Forberg, Reinh. Flügel.
C: 3/13/1914, Berlin, forbidden for children; contested scene: act 2, the scene of Werle bribing the two boatmen, from the point when Werle takes the money out of his wallet and hands it to the shipmen, to the point when he gets up and leaves the bar; 1914, Munich: like Berlin, and in addition the scene in act 4 where during a brawl in a shipmen's pub a shipman is beaten down to the ground.
Co: BA, magazine no. 1552, 861 m, tinted.

Vater dein Kind ruft! [*Father, Your Child Is Calling!*] (alternative title: *Im Karneval* [*During Carnival*])
ca. 1909.
Co: SDK, 117 m.

Eine venetianische Nacht* [*A Venetian Night*]
1913, Pm: 4/16/1914, P: PAGU, D: Max Reinhardt, S: Karl Vollmöller, Ca: Fridrich Weinmann, A: Alfred Abel, Maria Carmi, Ernst Mátray, Victor Arnold, Else Eckersberg.
Co: Staatliches Filmarchiv der DDR.
Ki, no. 382 (1914).

Die verflixten Koffer* [*The Darned Suitcases*]
1914, 415 m, P: Messter GmbH (Berlin), D: Erich Frisch, A: Margit Bergen, Rolf Lindau-Schulz.
Co: BA, magazine no. 14235, 448 m, tinted.

Vergebens [*In Vain*]
1911, Pm: 2/25/1911, 1 act, 360 m, P: Vitascope GmbH (consolidated with PAGU, Berlin), D: Walter Schmidthässler, A: Ewald Schindler.
Co: BA, 315 m, tinted.

*Ein vergnügter Wintertag im Berliner Grunewald** [*A Merry Winter's Day in Berlin's Grunewald*]
1909, 73 m, P: Messter, D: Carl Wilhelm.
C: 11/27/1909, Berlin.
Co: BA, magazine no. 1348, 89 m, b/w; SDK.

*Verkannt** [*Misjudged*]
1910, 238 m, P: Messters Projektion GmbH (Berlin), A: Henny Porten, Friedrich Zelnik, Robert Garrison.
C: 1912, Munich, forbidden.
Co: SDK.

*Verlobung auf der Alm** [*Engagement on the Pastures of the Alps*]
1908, P: Messter, D: Oskar Messter.
Co: BA, 45 m, b/w; original material hand-colored (no color copying yet).

Die Vernunft des Herzens [*Reason of the Heart*]
1910, 146 m, P: Deutsche Mutoskop- und Biograph-GmbH (Berlin), D: Charles Decroix, Ca: Karl Hasselmann, A: Carl Wilhelm.
C: 1912, Munich, forbidden.
Co: SDK.
[On Decroix's work as a director see *Die Schaubühne* 2, no. 6 (1910): 990ff.]

*Vordertreppe und Hintertreppe** [*Front Stairs and Back Stairs*]
1914–15, 1,074 m, P: PAGU, D and S: Urban Gad, Ca: Axel Graatkjaer, Karl Freund, Se: Fritz Seyffert, A: Asta Nielsen, Paul Otto, Fred Immler, Victor Arnold, Mary Scheller, Senta Eichstaedt, Alfred Kühne, Adele Reuter-Eichberg.
C: 9/3/1915, Berlin, contested scenes: act 1, the scene immediately following intertitle no. 14, in which one can see the lieutenant trying to force down Sabine, who is struggling against him; additionally, the two scenes following intertitle no. 11 that feature one-step dances; 1916, Munich, forbidden for the duration of the war.
Co: BA, magazine no. 10681, 792 m, tinted.

Wem gehört das Kind? [*To Whom Does the Child Belong?*]
1909 (?), P: Deutsche Bioskop.
C: Munich, contested scene: act 3, in which a naked little girl is depicted in close-up. [See also Moreck, *Sittengeschichte des Films,* 170.]
Co: SDK.

Wie Bauer Klaus von seiner Krankheit geheilt wurde [*How Farmer Klaus Was Healed of His Disease*]
ca. 1906.
Co: BA, magazine no. 10635, 84 m, b/w.

Wie sich das Kino rächt (initially: *Wie sich der Kientopp rächt*) [*How Cinema Takes Revenge*]
1912–13, 340 m, P: Eiko-Film GmbH (Berlin), D: Gustav Trautschold, S: based on an idea by Richard Rhodius, Ca: Hans Saalfrank, A: Gustav Trautschold, Kitty Derwall, Käthe Samst, Hanns Kräly, Fritz Kuhlbrodt.
Co: SDK, tinted.
Ki, no. 382 (1914); *LBT* 4, no. 35 (1912).

Willy's Streiche [*Willy's Pranks*] or *Klebalin klebt alles* [*Everything Sticks with Klebalin*]
1909, 123 m, P: Duskes Kinematographen- und Film-Fabrik GmbH (Berlin), D: Heinrich Bolten-Baeckers, A: Ernst Behmer, Curt Bois, Endresser, Anny Schnittenhelm, Kurt Stark, Gustav Prahl, Richard George.
Co: SDK.

Wintergartenprogramm [*Wintergarten Program*] on 11/1/1895
D and P: Max Skladanowsky.
Featured films: *Italienischer Bauerntanz* [*Italian Farmers' Dance*], *Komisches Reck* [*Funny High Bar*], *Der Jongleur* [*The Juggler*], *Das boxende Känguruh* [*The Boxing Kanguroo*], *Kamarinskaja*, *Akrobatisches Potpurri* [*Acrobatic Potpourri*], *Ringkampf* [*Ring Fight*], *Apotheose* [*Apotheosis*].

Wo ist Coletti* [*Where Is Coletti*]
1913, Pm: 4/4/1913, 1,554 m, P: Vitascope GmbH (Berlin), D: Max Mack, S: Franz von Schönthan, Ca: Hermann Böttger, Se: Hermann Warm, A: Hans Junckermann, Magda Lessing, Heinrich Peer, Anna Müller-Lincke, Hans Stock, Max Laurence, Axel Breidahl.
C: Berlin, forbidden for children.
Co: BA, magazine no. 10642, 1,564 m, b/w.
1.I.F.Ztg., no. 8 (2/22/1913): 83, no. 12 (3/22/1913): 66, 68ff. (illustration), 70ff., no. 13 (3/29/1913): 96ff. (drawings), no. 14 (4/5/1913): 30–36, 47, 49, 88ff., no. 15 (4/12/1913), 49–51, no. 30 (7/26/1913): 99; *Ki*, no. 502 (1916): 14; *LBT*, no. 14 (1913).

Zapata's Bande* [*Zapata's Gang*]
1914, Pm: 2/27/1914, 752 m, P: PAGU, D and S: Urban Gad, Ca: Axel Graatkjaer, Karl Freund, Se: Fritz Seyffert, A: Asta Nielsen, Fred Immler, Senta Eichstaedt, Adele Reuter-Eichberg, Mary Scheller, Hans Lanser-Ludolff, Carl Dibbern, Max Agerty, Ernst Körner, Erich Harden.
Co: Staatliches Filmarchiv der DDR.

Index

70–71, 78, 196. *See also* culture, German bourgeois; public sphere, German bourgeois

Brunhilde, myth of, 80

Buderus, Carl, 24

By a Hair's Breadth, 87, 98–100, *101;* conjugal sexuality in, 103; male libido in, 102; marriage in, 97, 98

Cabiria, 85

Cajus Julius Cäsar, 85

camera work: in *The Adventures of a Journalist,* 145, 167; in *The Black Ball,* 182–83; in *The Black Viper,* 181; in *The Fan Painter,* 193, 197; in *High Voltage,* 212; in *The Mysterious Club,* 152, 153–54; in *On a Lonely Island,* 199, 200, 202; in *The Right to Existence,* 133–34, 145–46; in *The Wanted Poster,* 167, 169

capitalism: private sphere under, 31; role of cinema in, 4, 147

Castle at the Hillside, The, 139

Cavalier of the Rose, The, 52, 52–53

censorship, of early German cinema, 64, 73, 226n7

Chamber Music, 164–65

Chase for the One-Hundred-Pound Bill, The, 156, 162–63, *164;* gaze in, 162

children: in early German cinema, 29–39, 40, 42; illegitimate, 71, 72, 80

Christmas Bells, 165, 187

cineasts, female French, 176, 230n1

cinema: of actualities, 66; "du premier temps," 219; the involuntary in, 220; as mass culture, 228n15; as public sphere, xiii, xv, 177, 189, 215; as social space, 216; sociopsychic functionality of, 82

cinema, American: crosscutting in, 230n1; female audiences of, 223n27; gaze in, 220; reform of, 2; social problems in, 13

cinema, German: Expressionist, ix, x, 126; Nazi use of, 4; New, 229n2

cinema, German early: adaptation to bourgeois culture, 6–7, 84, 104, 128–29, 217; aesthetics of, xiv–xv, 15–16, 19–20, 130, 131, 147, 168, 215, 217; ambivalent female images in, 127; authorship in, 18–20; as autonomous culture, 6; benefits for actresses, 16–17; bourgeois actors in, 126; bourgeoisie's relationship to, 3–4, 8, 12, 124; censorship of, 64, 73, 226n7; children in, 29–39, 40, 42; class difference in, 30–31, 35, 36; classical literature in, 84; economic importance of, 4, 6, 7; exclusion from culture, 10; family in, 29; female autonomy in, 177; female narrative perspective in, 19, 43–48; female productive power of, 112; female subjectivity in, x; festivals of, ix, 215, 216, 230n1; gender relations in, 12, 215; gender roles in, 86; genres of, x, 3, 36, 189–90, 223n29; "gentlemen's nights" in, 9, 34–35, 100, 102; historical drama in, 84–86; journalistic reaction to, 215, 216; length of, 104; male narrative perspective in, 20, 132; male rivalry in, 198–214; male sexuality in, 104; marriage in, 44–46, 87; material life in, xiii; mistresses in, 87–97; modernity in, xiii, 8, 15, 16, 20, 132; morally clean, 100; mothers in, 29, 30–31, 36–39, 40–42, 43; nonnarrative, xiv–xv, 9; oppositional elements of, 111, 122; opposition to, 2; as Other, 124, 187; petit bourgeois women in, 30–32; pre-Expressionist, ix, x; private sphere in, 14; professional women in, 190–98; proletarian audiences of, 129, 229n1; public discourse on, 21; in public sphere, xiii, xv, 177, 189, 215; reception of, 215,

220; renewed appreciation for, 217–18; representation of men in, 23–24; representation of women in, 12–18, 30–32, 36–39, 40–42, 177, 190–98; rescreenings of, 215, 216; restoration of, ix, xiv, xv, 217; role in capitalism, 4, 147; role in female self-perception, 9–10; self-consciousness of, 147, 177; self-understanding through, 11; short films, 23–28; sound accompaniment of, 65, 66, 226n2; street scenes in, 23; support for family, 4, 7; surviving examples of, 20, 23, 65, 222n7; technicity of, 130, 216; and theater, 9, 11–12; traveling, 2; women producers of, 181; women's emancipation in, 187, 216; women's fantasies in, 29; women's influence in, 216; women's interests in, 13; women's stories in, 28–48, 129; women writers on, xi, 21, 218; working women in, 193, 195; after World War I, 111, 218; during World War I, 87, 218

cinema, Italian monumental, 85

cinema, Russian pre-Revolutionary, ix

cinema, Soviet, montage of attractions in, 219

cinema of attractions, x, xiv; in *And the Light Went Out*, 203, 204, 207, 209; and auteur films, 128; bourgeois culture in, 66; in *Father, Your Child Is Calling!* 44–45; female audience of, 89, 100; and female narrative perspective, 87–97, 102, 216; humor in, 51; narrative cinema and, 219; in *On a Lonely Island*, 203; patriarchy in, 100; political implications of, 219; social drama in, 13; transition from, 2, 9

cinema reform movement, x, 84; audience reaction to, 64; bourgeoisie and, 3–4; effect on comedy, 61–62; on film drama, 12; gender in, 221n1; interventionist attitudes in, 215–16; on melodrama, 68; Nazi use of, 4; objection to

actresses, 16; resistance to cinema in, 21; *Sins of the Fathers* and, 120–21

cinematographs: low culture in, 6; military-industrial use of, 1; origins of, 1

civilization, culture and, 6. *See also* culture, German bourgeois

class differences: in early German cinema, 30–31, 35, 36; erasure of, 4

classical drama: narration in, 224n33; and social drama, 14, 66. *See also* theater

comedies, early German, 3; cross-dressing in, 57–58, 59–60; development of, 51; effect of reform movement on, 61–62; female audiences of, 58; gaze in, 59; homosexuality in, 57, 58; maids in, 58; male courtship in, 52–53; male femininity in, 51–64; marriage in, 53–55; orality in, 80; proletarian, 229n1; repetition in, 51, 54; role reversal in, 55, 57; sadomasochism in, 60–61; scopophilia in, 57; sexual fantasy in, 55–56, 58, 64; social order in, 57–58; trouser roles in, 165

Comte, Auguste, 228n13

Continental-Kunstfilm, 105

Cordes, Mia, 164

crime: in *The Adventures of a Journalist*, 143, 146; in *And the Light Went Out*, 204, 206; libidinally motivated, 176; in narrative cinema, 3; social mobility through, 191

crime films, 189–214; Anglo-Saxon origins of, 130; combination with love dramas, 189–90. *See also* detective films

Critical Theory, 231n4; Schlüpmann's engagement with, xii

crosscutting: in American cinema, 230n1; in *The Fan Painter*, 193, 197; in *High Voltage*, 212 cross-dressing, in comedies, 57–58, 59–60

Cruel Marriage, 43, *44,* 44–46, *45,* 87; dramatic form of, 66; women's perspective in, 45

culture, German bourgeois: adaptation of cinema to, 6–7, 84, 104, 128–29, 217; aesthetics of, 120; in cinema of attractions, 66; exclusion of cinema from, 10; exclusion of technology from, x, 5–6; expansion of, 223n18; in mass education movement, 7; in *The Mysterious Club,* 149; patriarchy in, 8; persons excluded from, 11–12

Czernowska, 190–92, *191–92;* female audience of, 192; marriage in, 192; social drama in, 198

Darwininan theory, 152

Davidson, Paul, 2, 110

Death-as-Ferryman motif, 108

Decroix, Charles, 49–50, 192

Delmont, Joseph: in *The Mysterious Club,* 147; in *On a Lonely Island,* 199; in *On Dying in the Woods,* 133; outsider status of, 131; in *The Right to Existence,* 134; technical sensibilities of, 147; work with Eiko Company, 176

Del Zopp, Louise, 72

Del Zopp, Rudolf, 164

Deployment of the Sentry, The, 23, 225n1

Dermott, Joseph, 135–36, 138

detective films, 12, 129–75; aesthetics of, 131; *And the Light Went Out* as, 209; enlightening gaze in, 147, 156; enlightenment in, 141, 168, 169, 170–71, 176; eroticism in, 17; female audiences of, 132; female gaze in, 131, 132–33, 155–57, 159–60, 189; female protagonists of, 130–31, 132–33, 154–75, 177; gaze in, 130, 134; gender relations in, 176–77; happy solution in, 199; heroes of, 132;

influences on, 230n3; male gaze in, 155; mass culture in, 142; modernity in, 20, 132; montage in, 132–33; as narrative cinema, 131; outdoor shots in, 167; outsider position in, 131, 133, 134, 155; patriarchy in, 192; scopophilia in, 132; self-consciousness in, 177; self-reflexivity in, 156; situation within society, 146; social drama and, 131, 132, 189, 193, 198; technology in, 131, 139–40, 145, 149, 154, 155, 176; trouser roles in, 130. *See also* crime films

Deutsche Bioskop (firm), 1, 105; Nielsen's work with, 110

Deutsche Kinematographengesellschaft (Cologne), 105

Deutsche Mutoskop- und biograph-Gesellschaft, 1, 49, 105

Dialectic of Enlightenment (Horkheimer and Adorno), xii; on housewives, 39

Diderot, Denis, Paradox of the Actor, 224n36

Dietrich, Marlene, 81

Different from the Others, 225n4

display, culture of, xiv

Doane, Mary Ann, xi

documentary films, subjects of, 23–24

Don Juan Marries, 51, 52–53, *54*

Dormitor (society for study of cinema), 217

dramatizing objects: enlightenment through, 127; in *The Other,* 127–28. *See also* fetishes, erotic

Dulac, Germaine, xiv

Duskes Company, 1

education: upward mobility through, 5; of women, 223n18. *See also* mass education movement, German

Eichstaedt, Senta, 155

Eiko Company, 176

Eisner, Lotte, 104; *The Haunted Screen,* ix

enlightenment: in detective films, 141, 147, 156, 168, 169, 170–71, 176; through dramatizing objects, 127; through gaze, 147, 150, 152, 156, 163, 176

Entr'acte, 53

eroticism: in detective films, 17; in early short films, 25–28. *See also* fetishes, erotic

Ewers, Hanns Heinz, 147

Expressionism, 229n16; in German cinema, ix, x, 126

family, German: in early cinema, 29; separation from public sphere, 11; support of cinema for, 4, 7; in Wilhelminian society, 7

Fan Painter, The, xi, 190, 193–98, *194–95;* camera's gaze in, 193; camera work of, 193, 197; crosscutting in, 193, 197; detective story in, 196, 197; erotic fetishes in, 194; female autonomy in, 195, 196; female gaze in, 194; femininity in, 197; film within a film of, 194; male audience of, 195; melodrama in, 198; montage in, 196, 197; patriarchy in, 196; social drama in, 198; trick sequences in, 194

Fatal Oath, A, 187, 220n2

Father, Your Child Is Calling! 29, 36–39, *37, 38;* cinema of attractions in, 44–45; female audience of, 37–38; gender relations in, 36; genres of, 36

femininity: in *The Black Viper,* 177; in *The Fan Painter,* 197; in melodrama, 68, 73; of men, 51–54; natural and emancipated, 168; as nonunitary, 15; transgressive, 25–28

fetishes, erotic: in *The Fan Painter,* 194; in *The Shadow of the Sea,* 212; in *Sins of the Fathers,* 116; in social drama, 102, 103, 104, 109, 113. *See also* dramatizing objects; eroticism

Feuillade, Louis, *ciné-romans* of, 176

FIAF Conference (Brighton, 1978), 222n7

film critics, women, 21, 218. *See also* film theory

film distribution, monopoly in, 110, 228n9

film drama: development of, 13; narrator in, 18. *See also* narrative cinema

Film of Queen Luise, The, 84

film production: alienation from female audiences, 218; cultural aspects of, 2; distribution and, 110; economic/technological aspects of, 2; following World War I, 111; independence from bourgeoisie, 7; international, 2; male authority in, 189; male voyeurism of, 185; in support of state, 4, 7, 222n10; by women, 181

film production companies, German, 1–2, 105; advertising by, 12; for narrative cinema, 48; number of, 221n5

film theory: antinarrative impulses in, xv; female gaze in, 219–20; feminist, xi, 22, 215, 217, 218, 219, 227n1; gender in, 221n1; psychoanalytic-semiotic, xi, 219, 230n4

First International Film Newspaper, The, 133

First Signs of Age, The, 164

folk art, and mass culture, 67

folk theater, 13, 68, 76

Forgotten because of Happiness, 65, *70,* 70–73, *71*

Francis, David, *Cinema, 1900–1906,* 222n7

Frankfort Institute for Social Research, xii, 231n4

Frauen und Film (journal), xii

Froelich, Carl, 105

Gad, Urban, 111, 112, 228n10; work with actresses, 173

Gartenlaube, Die (magazine), 84, 227n1

Gärtner, Adolf, 65, 97

gaze: in American cinema, 220; in comedies, 59; constitution of attractions, 89; in constitution of subject, xi; in detective films, 130, 134, 159; in early German cinema, 219; enlightening, 147, 150, 152, 156, 163, 176; gender-specific, 113, 134; in Nobody films, 159–60; at photography, 214; in *The Right to Existence,* 134–35, 136, 138; romanticizing, 169; in social drama, 134; state, 139; strategies of, 220. *See also* scopophilia

gaze, camera's, 97; in *The Adventures of a Journalist,* 139, 141; in *And the Light Went Out,* 206; in *The Black Ball,* 185; in *The Fan Painter,* 193; mobilization of, 131–54; in *The Mysterious Club,* 154; organization of, 116; social mobilization and, 154–55; in *The Wanted Poster,* 167, 169–74

gaze, female, xv; in *The Adventures of a Journalist,* 142; in *And the Light Went Out,* 204, 205; in *The Black Ball,* 183, 185; controlling, 171; corporeality of, xii; in detective films, 131, 132–33, 155–57, 159–60, 189; emancipation of, 177; enlightening, 163, 176; in *The Fan Painter,* 194; in film theory, 219–20; Hanus's treatment of, 187–88; in Hofer's films, 165, 187; male determination of, 198; male rivalry and, 198–214; male sex and, 105–28; on men, 115, 125, 160, 189, 214; in *The Other,* 125; power of, 173, 176; repression of, 220; in sensational films, 176, 181; in *The Shadow of the Sea,* 106–8, 109, 110; in *Sins of the Fathers,* 112, 113, 122; in social drama, 19, 125; sublimation of, 104; types of, xi–xii

gaze, male: on actresses, 16; in *The Black Ball,* 183–85; controlling, 90, 92; in detective films, 155; on early short

films, 25–28; on Eternal Feminine, 115; in Hollywood films, 220; in *On a Lonely Island,* 202; in social drama, 92, 100; voyeuristic, 89, 92, 97

Geiter, Ursula, 15, 224n36

gender difference: among audiences, 216; in film reception, 39; representation in cinema, 14

gender relations: in detective films, 176–77; in early German cinema, 12, 215; in *Father, Your Child Is Calling!* 36; mobility in, 157; power in, 130; in sensational films, 188; in *The Wanted Poster,* 170, 172–73; in Wilhelminian society, 7, 11, 22, 155

gender roles: in artistic process, 112; in early German cinema, 86; reversal of, 157, 161–62; transgressive, 165

General Cinematographic Theater Company, 2

genius, male, myth of, 112

genres: of early German cinema, x, 3, 36, 223n29; mixing of, 189–90

German reform movement: family in, 4; use of technology, 6. *See also* women's movement, German

Giornate del Cinema Muto, Il (festival), 230n1

Godard, Jean-Luc, *Histoire(s) du cinéma,* xv

Goebbels, Joseph, 4

Goethe Institute, film holdings of, ix

Gramann, Karola, 221n5

Griffith, D. W., 230n1, 230n9

Gründerzeit, 222n9; aesthetic of, 200; in film settings, 3; theater of, 11

Gunning, Tom, xiv

Habermas, Jürgen, xiii

Hansen, Miriam, "Early Silent Cinema," 223n27

Hanus, Emerich, 164; treatment of female gaze, 187–88

legitimacy, doctrine of, 5, 222n15
Leibl, Wilhelm, 200
Leo the Ancillary Waiter, 51
Lichtbild-Bühne (magazine), 163–64
Lichtbühne, Die (journal), 49
Liebermann, Max, 200
Lindau, Paul, 16, 224n38; script for *The Other,* 122, 126
Little Pink Slipper, The, 165
Lotte, 82
love dramas, combination with crime dramas, 189–90
Lukács, Georg, xii, 15
Luna-Film GmbH, 163, 164, 176

Mack, Max, 147; *The Other,* 122, *123,* 124–28
Madame X, the Woman of Confidential Advice, 165
Madeleine, 87
Madonna/whore dichotomy, 87
maids (servants): in comedies, 58; in early German cinema, 32–36, 124–25; in social drama, 126; working hours of, 225n6
marriage: in comedies, 53–55; in *Czernowska,* 192; in early German cinema, 44–46, 87; equality in, 103; German women's movement on, 103; grand bourgeois, 97; sexual pleasure in, 100, 102–3, 104; in social drama, 87, 97–104; in Wilhelminian society, 100
masculinity: in *And the Light Went Out,* 206–7; traditional and modern, 168
masquerade: in *The Black Ball,* 185, 186; in *The Mystery of the Château Richmond,* 160–61
mass culture: cinema as, 228n15; in detective films, 142; folk art and, 67
mass education movement, German, 6, 223n18; bourgeois culture in, 7
May, Mia, 105
Mayne, Judith, 224n41

Medusa, myth of, 169, 175
Meissen Porcelain, 65–66
Melcher, Gustav, "The Name in Film Art," 67
melodrama, Anglo-Saxon, 65, 226n1
melodrama, German, 65–75; bourgeois values in, 104; bourgeois women in, 70–71, 78; cinema reform movement on, 68; conservatism of, 73, 78; documentary reality in, 70, 71, 73, 76–83; in *The Fan Painter,* 198; female audiences of, 65, 67, 68, 69, 73; female stars of, 67; femininity in, 68, 73; as "folk mass," 66–67; folk theater in, 13, 68, 76; the individual in, 67; industrialization in, 74; mothers in, 74–75; music in, 66, 69, 83; and narrative cinema, 66; narrators of, 19; patriarchy in, 65, 66, 76, 77; and social drama, 104; suffering in, 68, 73, 82
Messter, Eduard, 1; filmstrips of, 23–24
Messter, Oskar, 1; melodramas of, 65
Messter-Film GmbH, 165; sound recordings at, 226n2
Miller and His Child, The, 65, 68–69, *69;* music in, 69
Miss Nobody, xi
Miss Piccolo, 61, 165
mistresses, cinematic, 87–97
modernity: of actresses, 15, 16; in *The Adventures of a Journalist,* 142; in detective films, 20, 132; in early German cinema, xiii, 8; in *High Voltage,* 209; in *The Mysterious Club,* 148, 151; in *The Mystery of the Château Richmond,* 157, 158; versus tradition, 198, 199; in *The Wanted Poster,* 166, 172
montage: in detective films, 132–33; in *The Fan Painter,* 196, 197; in Soviet cinema, 219
moral drama, Danish, 14, 224nn30–31
morality, female, magical aspects of, 38

sexual fantasy, in comedies, 55–56, 58, 64

sexuality: extramarital, 33–34, 88; marital, 100–103, 104

sexuality, female: of detective protagonists, 170–72; in *Sins of the Fathers*, 116

sexuality, male: in early cinema, 104; and female gaze, 105–28

Shadow of the Sea, The, 105, 105–10, *106;* audience gaze in, 107; documenting camera of, 108; female gaze in, 106–8, 109, 110; fetish object in, 212; ghost in, 108, 110; male body in, 109; male power in, 108; melodramatic aspects of, 108, 110; Porten in, 104

short films, early, 23–28; female transgression in, 25–28; male gaze on, 25–28; male protagonists of, 24; women audience of, 28–48

Siemens Company, 1

Simmel, Georg, 7

Sins of the Fathers, The, xi–xii, 104, 112–22, *114, 119, 121;* alcoholism in, 228n12; bourgeois aesthetics in, 120; cinema reform movement and, 120–21; erotic fetishes in, 116; female audience of, 113; female gaze in, 112, 113, 122; female narrative perspective of, 116; on Naturalism, 120; Nielsen in, xi–xii, 115, 116, 118, 122; painted images in, 113, 115, 118, 121; painter-model motif in, 113–15, 116–20; patriarchy in, 113; seduction scene of, 120; versions of, 228n12

Skladanowsky brothers, 1, 225n2; film-strips of, 23–24

Snake Dancer, The, 24, 26–28

Social Democrats, and narrative cinema, 3

social drama, 13–18; actors in, 102; in *And the Light Went Out,* 207; audience gaze in, 134; in cinema of attractions, 13; classical drama and, 14,

66; controlling gaze in, 90; detective films and, 131, 132, 189, 193, 198; documentation of reality, 17, 66, 97; dramatic forms of, 87; emancipatory implications of, 112–13; erotic appeal in, 17; erotic fetishes in, 102, 103, 104, 109, 113; female audience of, 98, 103; female gaze in, 19, 125; female narrative perspective in, 87, 97, 102, 103, 204; maids in, 126; male gaze in, 92, 100; male voyeurism in, 97, 100; marriage in, 87, 97–104; and melodrama, 104; mistresses in, 87–97; mothers in, 94; on Naturalism, 120–22; patriarchy in, 96, 103; puzzle solving in, 98–100; self-representation in, 15; theatrical drama and, 14, 17–18; topicality of, 68; women's interests in, 129

social mobility: camera's gaze and, 131–54; in gender relations, 157; in *A Mother's Love,* 214; through crime, 191; through education, 5

social problem films, American, 13

society, Wilhelminian: actresses' position in, 10–11, 16–17; *Bildung* in, x; detective films in, 146; family in, 7; gender relations in, 7, 11, 22, 155; homosexuality in, 226n4; marriage in, 100; servants in, 35; technolization of, 177; unconsciousness of, 187; women in, 21–22

Sonnemann, Carl, 24

sovereigns, documentation on film, 23

spectators. *See* audiences

"spicy" films, 89, 101; "gentlemen's nights" for, 9, 34–35, 100, 102. *See also* pornographic cinema, German

Sprache der Liebe: Asta Nielsen (Gramann et al.), 231n6

Starck, Curt A., 97, 105, 111

state, German: film production in support of, 4, 7, 222n10; gaze of, 139; social space in, 6

Stevenson, Robert Louis, *The Suicide Club*, 147, 230n9

Student of Prague, The, 122, 147

subject, constitution of, xi

subjectivity, female, x, 19–20

Sudermann, Hermann, 229n17

suffering: enjoyment of, 82–83; in melodrama, 68, 73, 82

Surrealists, "cinema hopping" of, xv

Szondi, Peter, 229n16

tachyscopes, 1

Taine, Hippolyte, 122, 124, 228n13

technology: in detective films, 131, 139–40, 145, 149, 154, 155, 176; enlightenment through, 149; exclusion from German culture, x, 5–6; male identification with, 189; reformers' use of, 6; in *The Right to Existence*, 134, 136; in Wilhelminian society, 177

theater: bourgeois audience of, 12, 223n26; in bourgeois public-sphere, 10–11; crisis of drama in, 18, 229n16; and early German cinema, 9, 11–12; eighteenth-century, 10; folk, 13, 68, 76; of *Gründerzeit*, 11; Naturalist, 18, 229n16; and social drama, 14, 17–18

Theodor Körner, 84

Thilo, Friedrich Theophilus, 224n36

Tilly Bébé: The Famous Lion Tamer, 25, 26, *26, 27,* 28

Tonbild, 65, 66

To Whom Does the Child Belong? 29, 32–36, *33, 34, 35;* class in, 35, 36

Tragedy of a Strike, 65, *72,* 73–75, *74,* 80; censorship of, 73, 226n7; conservatism of, 73

traveling cinema, 2

Treumann, Wanda, 105

trouser roles: Bernhardt's, 25; in comedies, 165; in detective films, 130

Turszinsky, Walter, 49

24 Hours in the Life of a Woman, 81, 82

unconscious: optical, 141; in *The Other,* 122, 124, 125, 126

Universum Film AG "UFA," 4, 187, 218; state-supporting role of, 222n10

Vampires, Les, 176

Vernon, Hedda, 105

Victory of the Pant Skirt, The, 56–57

Vitascope (production company), 105

Voigt, Wilhelm, 24

voyeurism, female, in audiences, 104

voyeurism, in *The Wanted Poster,* 170. *See also* gaze; scopophilia

voyeurism, male, 92; concerning actresses, 89; in film production, 185; in social drama, 97, 100

Vulture Wally, 81

Wanted Letter, The, 189

Wanted Poster, The, xi, 156, 163, *164,* 165–76, *166, 168, 170–74;* aesthetics of, 168; audience of, 170, 171, 174; camera work in, 167, 169; gaze in, 167, 169–74; gender relations in, 170, 172–73; gender roles in, 165; modernity in, *166,* 172; myth-turned-image in, 168–69, 176; nature in, 170, 173, 175; outdoor shots in, 166–67; voyeurism in, 170

Way Home: Step by Step. A Model's Life-Confession, The, 87, 90–97, *93–94, 96;* documentary elements in, 91; female narrative perspective in, 98; narrative in, 92, 93, 95; patriarchy in, 103

Wegener, Paul, 122

Weimar Republic: films of, 111, 126; sexual equality in, 79–80

Weixler, Doritt, 164

Wilhelm, Carl, 48

Willy's Pranks, 51–52

womanhood: bourgeois, 77; German, 76, 226n1; patriarchal representation of, 76; scientized, 223n25 women: aggression myths concerning, 80; as allegory, 121; autonomy of, 79, 177, 190, 192, 195, 196; in bourgeois public sphere, 10, 45, 129, 216, 231n5; directors, 229n2; education of, 223n18; effect of industrialization on, 79; emancipation of, 129, 131, 157, 187, 190, 216; feminist film theory by, xi, 22, 215, 217, 218, 219, 227n1; film critics, 21, 218; as film producers, 181; French cineasts, 176, 230n1; impoverished, 196; Madonna/whore dichotomy of, 87; male projection of, 13, 15; "male" strength of, 188; masquerade by, 185, 186; narcissistic, 127; in narrative cinema, 28–48; "new," 190; petit bourgeois, 30–32, 70–71, 78; productivity of, 79, 112, 227n1; professional, 190–98; representation in early German cinema, 12–18, 30–32, 36–39, 40–42, 177, 190–98; self-determination of, 46, 197, 198; self-perception of, 9–10, 195; sexual curiosity of, 102; as sexual objects, 87; in short films, 24–28; social problems of, 86; subjectivity of, x, 19–20; in Wilhelminian society, 21–22; wives, 97–104; working, 58, 193, 195. *See also* audiences, female; femininity; gaze, female; mothers

women's cinema movement, xii, 218

women's clubs, German, 225n6

women's movement, German: cinema and, x, 131; conservatism in, 79–80; during World War I, 227n1; on marriage, 103; Porten and, 79–82

women's movements, of 1970s, 216

World War I: in *The Adventures of a Journalist*, 139, 146–47; cinema during, 87, 218; cinema following, 111, 218; German women's movement during, 227n1

Zglinicki, Friedrich von, *Der Weg des Films*, 221n1

Ziener, Manny, 57, 164

Heide Schlüpmann is a professor of film at Johann Wolfgang Goethe-Universitat in Frankfurt, Germany, a coeditor of the journal *Frauen und Film (Women and Film)*, and the author of *Öffentliche Intimität: Die Theorie im Kino (Public Intimacy: Theory in the Cinema)* and other works.

Inga Pollmann is a doctoral student in cinema and media studies at the University of Chicago.

Miriam Hansen is Ferdinand Schevill Distinguished Service Professor in the Humanities at the University of Chicago and the author of *Babel and Babylon: Spectatorship in American Silent Film*.

Women and Film History International

A Great Big Girl Like Me: The Films of Marie Dressler
  Victoria Sturtevant

The Uncanny Gaze: The Drama of Early German Cinema
  Heide Schlüpmann

Universal Women: Filmmaking and Institutional Change
in Early Hollywood
  Mark Garrett Cooper

The University of Illinois Press
is a founding member of the
Association of American University Presses.

· ·

Composed in 9.5/14 Officina Serif STD
with Officina Serif and Sans display
by Celia Shapland
at the University of Illinois Press
Designed by Copenhaver Cumpston
Manufactured by Thomson-Shore, Inc.

University of Illinois Press
1325 South Oak Street
Champaign, IL 61820-6903
www.press.uillinois.edu